HOUGHTON MIFFLIN
Spelling and Vocabulary
Words for Readers and Writers

Shane Templeton
Senior Author

Donald R. Bear
Author

Brenda Sabey
Consultant

Sylvia Linan-Thompson
Consultant

 HOUGHTON MIFFLIN   BOSTON

Acknowledgments

Select definitions in the Spelling Dictionary are adapted and reprinted by permission from the following Houghton Mifflin Company publications:

Copyright © 2003 THE AMERICAN HERITAGE CHILDREN'S DICTIONARY

Copyright © 2003 THE AMERICAN HERITAGE STUDENT DICTIONARY

Printed in the U.S.A.

ISBN-13: 978-0-618-49194-0   ISBN-10: 0-618-49194-5

23456789-KDL-15 14 13 12 11 10 09 08 07 06

Contents

Cycle 1

Unit 1

Unit 2

Unit 3

Unit 4

Unit 5

5

Student's Handbook

Learning to Spell

1 **Look** at the word.
- What are the letters in the word?
- What does the word mean?
- Does it have more than one meaning?

airplane

2 **Say** the word.
- What are the consonant sounds?
- What are the vowel sounds?

3 **Think** about the word.
- How is each sound spelled?
- Do you see any familiar spelling patterns?
- What other words have the same spelling pattern?

4 **Write** the word.
- Think about the sounds and the letters.
- Form the letters correctly.

5 **Check** the spelling of the word.
- Does it match the spelling on your word list?
- Do you need to write the word again?

Learning Vocabulary

1) Look at the word.
- Do suffixes, prefixes, or other word parts give clues to the meaning?

2) Study the context of the word.
- Do other words around the word give you a clue to the meaning?

3) Check the dictionary.
- Practice saying the word.
- Study the meaning and the sample sentence.
- Read the context again to see how the word fits in.

4) Create a word-study notebook.
- Write the definition of each word. Write your own sample sentence.
- Make webs of vocabulary words on the same topic.
- Use your notebook when you write.

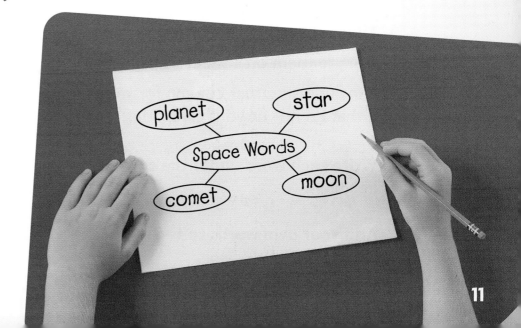

Sorting Words

What Is a Word Sort?

In a word sort, you sort words into groups. Each unit in this book begins with a word sort. Word sorts help you learn to spell, to think about words, and to read other words.

You can sort words by

- **sound** (such as long *a* or short *a*)
- **spelling pattern** (such as *ai* or *ay* for long *a*)
- **syllable pattern** (such as VCCV or VCV)
- **word parts** (such as prefixes or suffixes)
- **word meaning** (such as "types of clothing")

Making a Word Sort

You can make your own word sorts, using Spelling Words from one or more units. Here's how.

1. **Read the words.**

2. **Think of sorting categories.**
   - Write them on a sheet of paper.
   - Include an *Other* column for words that do not fit your categories.

3. **Write each word under the correct heading.**

4. **Add your own words to the sort.**

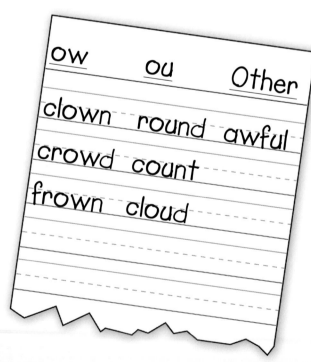

ow	ou	Other
clown	round	awful
crowd	count	
frown	cloud	

Sorting with a Partner

Write your sorting categories and your Spelling Words
on separate cards or slips of paper.

1 **Share a sort.**

- Trade category and word cards
  with a partner, and sort.

2 **Challenge each other.**

- Switch word cards.

- Figure out your partner's
  categories, and sort.

3 **Go on a word hunt.**

- Choose one or more sorting categories.

- Look for words that fit each category.

Your Word-Study Notebook

As you sort words, add to your word-study notebook.

- Add to the sorts you have begun, or make up new ones.

- Collect tricky words, such as *weigh*, or words you confuse,
  such as *hear* and *here*.

- Collect interesting vocabulary words, such as words
  about soccer, travel, weather, or music.

Thinking and Writing

When you write, use new **vocabulary** words and correct **spelling**. Here is how vocabulary and spelling fit into the steps of the **writing process**.

prewrite → draft → revise → proofread → publish

1 Prewrite

- Make a list of exact words as you brainstorm ideas and plan your work. You can use them when you draft.

- Look in your word-study notebook to find interesting words.

2 Draft

- Don't worry about spelling now. Just get your ideas down.

- If you think of an interesting word, write it. You can change it later if it does not really fit.

3 Revise

- Use exact words in place of less interesting words.

- Use a thesaurus to find just the right word.

- Check the dictionary if you do not know a word's meaning.

④ Proofread

- Check each word. Fix spelling mistakes.
- Use the strategies below, if you can't remember how to spell a word.

⑤ Publish—Share Your Writing!

- Your new vocabulary words will interest your readers.
- Your correct spelling will make your writing easy to read.

Spelling Strategies

- Say the word to yourself. What sounds do you hear?
- Picture the word in your mind. Does it match the spelling you used?
- Think of the parts of the word. Is each part spelled correctly?
- Look up the word in a dictionary.

Using a Computer Spell Checker

Know how your spell checker works.

What It Can Do

- It finds many spelling mistakes.
- It finds some mistakes with capital letters.

What It Cannot Do

- It cannot find words that should be joined.
  car pet
- It will not find a homophone that is not correct.
  Would you like to meat my friend?
- It will not catch a misspelled word that is the correct spelling of a different word.
  My big brother nose everything!

15

Weekly Spelling Tests

1 **Before the test,**
practice the words with a friend or a family member.

2 **At test time,**
get a clean sheet of paper and a pencil or a pen.

3 **Listen carefully.**
Your teacher will read each Spelling Word
and use it in a sentence.

4 **Write the word.**
Carefully form each letter so it is easy to read.

5 **When you correct your test,**
listen closely as your teacher spells each word.
Check each letter. Circle any mistakes.

6 **Look at each corrected word.**
Then close your eyes and spell
the word to yourself.

7 **Write the correct spelling.**
Write each word you
spelled wrong.

Spelling Test
1. lay
2. groan
3. (trale) trail
4. real
5. (toda) today

Standardized Tests

1 **Make sure you understand the test format.**

- Ask for help if you need it.

2 **Read each question.**

- Decide which answer choices are wrong first. Then mark the right answer.

3 **On a spelling test**

- Remember spelling patterns that you have learned.
- Think about the spelling of prefixes, suffixes, and other word parts.

4 **On a vocabulary test**

- Look for context clues.
- Try to find meaning hints in word parts such as prefixes.

Watch for test-taking tips in this book. You will find them on the pages with practice tests.

PART 1 Spelling and Phonics

Read the Spelling Words and sentences.

Basic Words

1.	crop	*crop*	Wheat is an important **crop**.
2.	plan	*plan*	We must make a new **plan**.
3.	thing	*thing*	What is this strange **thing**?
4.	smell	*smell*	I **smell** the pizza baking.
5.	shut	*shut*	Please **shut** the window.
6.	sticky	*sticky*	Glue is very **sticky**.
7.	spent	*spent*	Andy **spent** his money.
8.	lunch	*lunch*	I eat **lunch** at noon.
9.	pumpkin	*pumpkin*	We made a **pumpkin** pie.
10.	clock	*clock*	Listen to the **clock** tick.
11.	gift	*gift*	I like the **gift** you gave me.
⚠ 12.	head	*head*	The hat fell off my **head**!
⚠ 13.	friend	*friend*	Kim is my new **friend**.
⚠ 14.	front	*front*	Knock on the **front** door.

Review
15. next **16.** hug

Challenge
17. hospital **18.** fantastic

Think about the Spelling Strategy.

Each word has the short *a, e, i, o,* or *u* sound. These sounds are shown as /ă/, /ĕ/, /ĭ/, /ŏ/, or /ŭ/. These short vowel sounds are usually spelled *a, e, i, o,* or *u*.

/ă/ pl**a**n   /ĕ/ sm**e**ll   /ĭ/ th**i**ng   /ŏ/ cr**o**p   /ŭ/ sh**u**t

⚠ How are the Memory Words different?

Sort and write the words.

Write each Basic Word under its vowel sound. Write *pumpkin* under its first vowel sound.

Sort for /ă/ and /ĕ/

1. _____
2. _____
3. _____
4. _____
5. _____

Sort for /ĭ/ and /ŏ/

6. _____
7. _____
8. _____
9. _____
10. _____

Sort for /ŭ/

11. _____
12. _____
13. _____
14. _____

Phonics

Write the Basic Word that has the same beginning sound or sounds as each group of words.

15. hut, hide, _____

16. cry, crack, _____

17. spin, speak, _____

18. think, third, _____

19. cloud, clown, _____

cloud    clown    ?

Vocabulary: Word Clues

Write a Basic Word for each clue.

20. This word means "a present."

21. This is orange and has a stem.

22. You can do this with your nose.

23. This is the opposite of *open*.

24. This is the opposite of *back*.

Challenge Words

Write the Challenge Word that completes each sentence. Use your Spelling Dictionary.

25. Jordan thought of a _____ idea.

26. Many doctors and nurses work in a _____.

smell
shut
plan
thing
crop

Phonics

15. _____

16. _____

17. _____

18. _____

19. _____

Word Clues

20. _____

21. _____

22. _____

23. _____

24. _____

Challenge Words

25. _____

26. _____

At Home — With a family member, play a scramble game. Take turns scrambling the letters of a Spelling Word. The other player unscrambles them to write the word.

19

Word Meaning

_____

1. _____

2. _____

3. _____

4. _____

Dictionary

_____

5. _____

6. _____

7. _____

8. _____

9. _____

10. _____

11. _____

12. _____

🔍 Word Meaning: Lunch Words

Some words are alike in spelling and meaning.

Practice Write words from the house to complete the paragraph.

In a few more minutes, it will be ___(1)___. I am ___(2)___ with my friends today. We like to sit at the big table in the ___(3)___. It is fun to share all of our ___(4)___!

lunch
_____
lunches
lunching
lunchtime
lunchroom

Dictionary: ABC Order

Put words in ABC order by looking at the first letter of each word. Decide which of those letters comes first in the alphabet. If the first letters are the same, look at the second letter.

gift	**t**hing	**co**at
head	**cl**ock	**cr**op

Practice 5–12. Write the words from the box in ABC order.

sticky	smell	shut	hug
friend	pumpkin	next	plan

PART 3 Spelling and Writing

Proofread a Post Card

Spelling, Statements, and Questions Proofread this post card. Use proofreading marks to fix **four** spelling mistakes, **two** missing capital letters, and **two** missing end marks.

Example: will you arrive ~~nixt~~ ^{next} week?

Dear Ethan,

    I am having a great time at the farm. I spint today riding the horses. Then I helped my grandpa feed the goats It is fun to hugg the baby goats! Wait until you smell the pumpken pie my grandma makes. you will want a whole pie for yourself. when can you come for a visit

                            Your frend,

                            Todd

Proofreading Marks

¶	Indent
∧	Add
℘	Delete
≡	Capital letter
/	Small letter

Basic
crop
plan
thing
smell
shut
sticky
spent
lunch
pumpkin
clock
gift
head
friend
front

Review
next
hug

Challenge
hospital
fantastic

Write a Post Card

prewrite → draft → revise → proofread → publish

Write a post card to a friend. Tell about a place you visited.
- Tell what you saw or did.
- Use some Spelling Words, statements, and questions.
- Proofread your work.

Power Proofreading
www.eduplace.com/kids/sv/

21

✔ **Test Tip** Read all the words carefully.

Test Format Practice

Directions Find the phrase containing an underlined word that is not spelled correctly. If all the underlined words are spelled correctly, mark "All correct."

Example: money <u>spent</u> ○ bald <u>hed</u> ○ <u>shut</u> off ○ All correct ○

1. short <u>list</u> ○ funny <u>ting</u> ○ nice <u>gift</u> ○ All correct ○

2. <u>stickey</u> tape ○ <u>flat</u> tire ○ <u>mud</u> spot ○ All correct ○

3. <u>next</u> year ○ short <u>rest</u> ○ <u>frunt</u> gate ○ All correct ○

4. huge <u>pumpkin</u> ○ no <u>smell</u> ○ big <u>hug</u> ○ All correct ○

More Practice
Now write all the misspelled words correctly on a separate sheet of paper.

5. loud <u>clock</u> ○ picnic <u>lunch</u> ○ corn <u>cropp</u> ○ All correct ○

Spelling Games
www.eduplace.com/kids/sv/
Review for your test.

6. good <u>plen</u> ○ old <u>friend</u> ○ new <u>job</u> ○ All correct ○

Real-World Vocabulary

Social Studies: Planting Crops

Write the words from the box to complete the encyclopedia article about crops. Use your Spelling Dictionary.

CROPS

A crop is something that farmers plant, grow, and finally ___(1)___ for use as food for people or animals.

Plantings called *food crops* produce food for our tables. There are three types of food crops. Farmers may plant ___(2)___, such as wheat, or ___(3)___, such as apples. They might also plant a ___(4)___ crop, such as peas.

Farmers might choose to grow *fiber crops*. Fiber crops are used to make clothing and other products. One example of a fiber crop is ___(5)___.

1. _____
2. _____
3. _____
4. _____
5. _____

eWord Game
www.eduplace.com/kids/sv/

Try This CHALLENGE

What Is It? What crop did a farmer grow to bring each of these to you? Write a word from the box to answer each one.

6. breakfast cereal   8. spinach

7. T-shirt

6. _____

7. _____

8. _____

Read the Spelling Words and sentences.

Basic Words

1. spoke | *spoke* | Jo **spoke** in a loud voice.
2. mile | *mile* | The path is a **mile** long.
3. save | *save* | Do you **save** stamps?
4. excuse | *excuse* | Please **excuse** my mistake.
5. cone | *cone* | I ate an ice cream **cone**.
6. invite | *invite* | I will **invite** her to dinner.
7. cube | *cube* | This ice **cube** is melting.
8. price | *price* | The **price** of gas is high.
9. erase | *erase* | Do not **erase** the board.
10. ripe | *ripe* | Are the peaches **ripe**?
11. broke | *broke* | The glass fell and **broke**.
12. skate | *skate* | Daryl likes to **skate**.
13. life | *life* | A turtle has a long **life**.
14. done | *done* | I have **done** my homework.

Review

15. these   16. those

Challenge

17. surprise   18. decide

Sort for /ā/ and /ī/

1. ___
2. ___
3. ___
4. ___
5. ___
6. ___
7. ___
8. ___

Sort for /ō/ and /yo͞o/

9. ___
10. ___
11. ___
12. ___
13. ___

No Long Vowel Sound

14. ___

Think about the Spelling Strategy.

Most of the words have the long *a, i, o,* or *u* vowel sound. These sounds are shown as /ā/, /ī/, /ō/, or /yo͞o/. They are usually spelled vowel-consonant-*e*.

/ā/ s**a**ve   /ī/ m**i**le   /ō/ sp**o**ke   /yo͞o/ exc**u**se

❗ How is the Memory Word different?

Sort and write the words.

Write each Basic Word under its vowel sound. Write *excuse, invite,* and *erase* under the second vowel sound.

Phonics

Write the Basic Word or Words that rhyme with each word below.

15. gave   **17.** bone   **19.** pipe

16. mice   **18.** wife   **20–21.** joke

Vocabulary: Word Pairs

Write the Basic Word that completes each pair of sentences.

22. A *foot* is a *short* distance to walk.

A _____ is a *long* distance to walk.

23. You *clap* with your *hands*.

You _____ with your *legs*.

24. A *square* has *four* sides.

A _____ has *six* sides.

cube

Challenge Words

Write the Challenge Word that fits each meaning. Use your Spelling Dictionary.

25. an unexpected event   **26.** to make a choice

Phonics

15. _____

16. _____

17. _____

18. _____

19. _____

20. _____

21. _____

Word Pairs

22. _____

23. _____

24. _____

Challenge Words

25. _____

26. _____

save   mile   spoke   excuse

At Home With a family member, take turns making up silly sentences that have two Spelling Words in them.

skate

1. _____

2. _____

3. _____

cone

4. _____

5. _____

6. _____

Word Families: Rhyming Words

Practice 1–6. Help the beavers get home. Follow each path of letters to write new words that rhyme with *skate* and *cone*. Not all the letters will work.

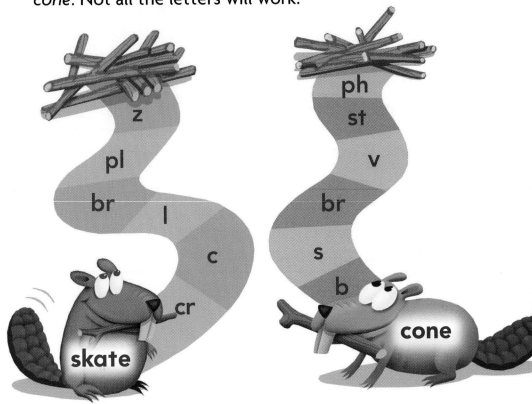

Dictionary

7. _____

8. _____

9. _____

10. _____

11. _____

12. _____

Dictionary: ABC Order

The words in a dictionary are in ABC order. To put words that begin with the same letter in ABC order, look at the second, third, or fourth letters until you find the first pair of letters that are different.

broke	**co**ne	**lif**e	**mil**e
done	**cu**be	**lik**e	**mill**ion

Practice 7–12. Write the words from the box in ABC order.

these	those	thorn
excuse	erase	invite

Proofread a Sign

Spelling, Commands, and Exclamations Proofread this sign. Use proofreading marks to fix **four** spelling mistakes, **two** missing capital letters, and **two** missing end marks.

Example: please ~~saive~~ your ticket.

 RINK RULES

Follow theze rules at all times.

1. Children pay half price.

2. You may skete all day long.

3. do not go past the orange kone

4. Return rented skates when you are dunn.

5. racing is never, never, never allowed

Proofreading Marks	
¶	Indent
∧	Add
✄	Delete
≡	Capital letter
/	Small letter

Basic
spoke
mile
save
excuse
cone
invite
cube
price
erase
ripe
broke
skate
life
done

Review
these
those

Challenge
surprise
decide

Write a Sign

prewrite → draft → revise → proofread → publish

Write a list of helpful rules for your classroom or your room at home.

- Number your list.
- Use some Spelling Words and some commands, such as *Please read all these rules.* Use some exclamations, such as *The rink will be very cold!*
- Proofread your work.

Power Proofreading
www.eduplace.com/kids/sv/

Test Tip Decide which answer choices are wrong first.

Test Format Practice

Directions Find the word that is spelled correctly and best completes the sentence.

Example: I walked one _____.

    miel   mil   mile   myle
    ◯   ◯   ◯   ◯

1. The plums are not _____ yet.
    ripp   ripe   rype   riipe
    ◯   ◯   ◯   ◯

2. You may _____ an answer if you wish.
    erase   erace   irase   erasse
    ◯   ◯   ◯   ◯

3. Where is the box for _____ crayons?
    thoze   thos   thows   those
    ◯   ◯   ◯   ◯

4. The baby _____ her new toy today.
    broak   brok   broke   browk
    ◯   ◯   ◯   ◯

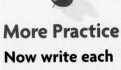

More Practice
Now write each correctly spelled word on a sheet of paper.

5. He wants to _____ the whole class to his party.
    envite   invite   invyte   invit
    ◯   ◯   ◯   ◯

6. I hope you will _____ me for stepping on your toe.
    excuze   ikscuse   excuse   excus
    ◯   ◯   ◯   ◯

Spelling Games
www.eduplace.com/kids/sv/
Review for your test.

Real-World Vocabulary

Language Arts: An Invitation

Write the words from the box to complete the invitation. Use your Spelling Dictionary.

Spelling Word Link

invite

event
honor
refreshments
attend
award

YOU ARE INVITED to a special

____(1)____ in ____(2)____ of Mrs. Clara Ramos.

She will be getting an ____(3)____ for all

her hard work at Preston School.

Some ____(4)____ will be served.

Where: Preston School Dining Hall

When: Friday, June 25, 2:00 P.M.

    Please call 555-6735 to let us

know if you can ____(5)____.

1. _____
2. _____
3. _____
4. _____
5. _____

eWord Game
www.eduplace.com/kids/sv/

Try This CHALLENGE

Yes or No? Write *yes* or *no* to answer each question.

6. Should you be pleased to receive an award?
7. Is singing a kind of refreshment?
8. Can you attend a baseball game?

6. _____
7. _____
8. _____

29

PART 1 Spelling and Phonics

Sort for /ā/

1. _____

2. _____

3. _____

4. _____

5. _____

6. _____

7. _____

8. _____

Sort for /ē/

9. _____

10. _____

11. _____

12. _____

13. _____

14. _____

Read the Spelling Words and sentences.

Basic Words

1.	lay	lay	He can **lay** the rug here.
2.	real	real	This toy animal looks **real**.
3.	trail	trail	We will follow the **trail**.
4.	sweet	sweet	The juice is very **sweet**.
5.	today	today	Sam woke up early **today**.
6.	dream	dream	What a nice **dream** I had!
7.	seem	seem	Does the room **seem** dark?
8.	always	always	The dog is **always** hungry.
9.	treat	treat	Ice cream is a great **treat**.
10.	chain	chain	A metal **chain** is strong.
11.	leave	leave	I **leave** my boots outside.
ⓘ 12.	weigh	weigh	We **weigh** fruit on a scale.
ⓘ 13.	eight	eight	Nina has **eight** goldfish.
ⓘ 14.	neighbor	neighbor	A new **neighbor** moved in.

Review

15. paint   16. please

Challenge

17. yesterday   18. explain

Think about the Spelling Strategy.

Each word has the long *a* or the long *e* sound. The long *a* sound is shown as /ā/ and can be spelled *ay* or *ai*. The long *e* sound is shown as /ē/ and can be spelled *ea* or *ee*.

/ā/ **lay**, tr**ai**l   /ē/ **rea**l, sw**ee**t

ⓘ How is the /ā/ sound spelled in the Memory Words?

Sort and write the words.

Write each Basic Word under its vowel sound. Circle the letters that spell the /ā/ or the /ē/ sound.

Phonics

Write Basic Words to answer the questions.

15. Which word begins like *drag*?

16. Which word begins like *top* and rhymes with *say*?

17–18. Which two words begin with the same two sounds you hear at the beginning of *true*?

19–20. Which two words begin like *long*?

Vocabulary: Classifying

Write the Basic Word that belongs in each group.

21. never, sometimes, _____

22. six, seven, _____

23. string, rope, _____

24. sour, salty, _____

sour

salty

?

Challenge Words

Write the Challenge Word that fits each clue. Use your Spelling Dictionary.

25. You do this to help someone understand.

26. the day before today

lay trail real sweet

At Home With a family member, make word crosses. Write a Spelling Word across a page. Take turns writing Spelling Words that cross any word you wrote.

Phonics

15. _____

16. _____

17. _____

18. _____

19. _____

20. _____

Classifying

21. _____

22. _____

23. _____

24. _____

Challenge Words

25. _____

26. _____

Word Meaning: Day Words

The words in this house are spelled alike in some ways. They are also related in meaning.

Practice Write a word from the house for each clue.

1. the time each morning when the first light appears
2. a place where children can go during the day
3. to think in a dreamy way
4. the light of the day

today
daylight
daybreak
daydream
daycare

Thesaurus: Exact Words

Pages 256–257 will tell you how to use the **Thesaurus** in this book. Use your Thesaurus to find the best words to say what you mean. The entry below shows that *actual* might be used instead of *real*.

main entry word   part of speech   definition   sample sentence

real *adj.* not artificial or made up. *Those silk flowers look **real**.*

actual really existing or happening. *The water looked cold, but the **actual** temperature was warm.*

subentry

Practice Write two words you could use in place of each of these words. Use your Thesaurus.

5–6. walk   **7–8.** blue   **9–10.** loud   **11–12.** mix

Word Meaning

1.
2.
3.
4.

Thesaurus

5.
6.
7.
8.
9.
10.
11.
12.

Proofread an Ad

Spelling and Common Nouns Proofread this ad. Use proofreading marks to fix **five** spelling mistakes and **two** common nouns that should not have a capital letter.

Example: The Ad says to visit the shop ~~todaye~~. *today*

Does your room seme dull? Do you dream about having walls the color of cotton candy? Then Gretel's House is the painte Store for you. Pleaze come in and see for yourself! Bring a Friend or a neigbor.

Our cans waigh a lot because you get a lot!

Gretel's House

Write an Ad

prewrite → draft → revise → proofread → publish

Write an ad for a store. The store can be real, or you can make it up.

- Give reasons to shop there.
- Use some Spelling Words, and make sure common nouns do not have capital letters.
- Proofread your work.

Proofreading Marks

¶	Indent
∧	Add
ℛ	Delete
≡	Capital letter
/	Small letter

Basic
lay
real
trail
sweet
today
dream
seem
always
treat
chain
leave
! weigh
! eight
! neighbor

Review
paint
please

Challenge
yesterday
explain

Power Proofreading
www.eduplace.com/kids/sv/

PART 4 Spelling Test Practice

✔ **Test Tip** Skip the hard questions. Go back to them later.

Test Format Practice

Directions Read each group of sentences. Decide if one of the underlined words is spelled wrong or if there is *No mistake*. Fill in the space for the answer you have chosen.

Example: ○ Go now, <u>please</u>.
○ Fruit is <u>swete</u>.
○ Stay on the <u>trail</u>.
○ No mistake

---

1. ○ She has <u>eighte</u> pens.
   ○ You are my <u>neighbor</u>.
   ○ I <u>spoke</u> with Kate.
   ○ No mistake

5. ○ He is <u>allways</u> nice.
   ○ I sat up <u>front</u>.
   ○ She likes to <u>skate</u>.
   ○ No mistake

2. ○ The <u>paint</u> is dry.
   ○ I <u>shut</u> the door.
   ○ It is sunny <u>todae</u>.
   ○ No mistake

6. ○ He will <u>leave</u> soon.
   ○ Did you <u>weigh</u> this?
   ○ Here is a <u>treat</u>.
   ○ No mistake

3. ○ The rose is <u>reele</u>.
   ○ Whose shoes are <u>these</u>?
   ○ We <u>invite</u> you to lunch.
   ○ No mistake

7. ○ I <u>erase</u> the marks.
   ○ The <u>chane</u> is gold.
   ○ We <u>dream</u> at night.
   ○ No mistake

4. ○ My computer <u>broke</u>.
   ○ The dogs <u>seem</u> fine.
   ○ Will you <u>save</u> that?
   ○ No mistake

8. ○ Mom ran a <u>mile</u>!
   ○ Sean is my <u>friend</u>.
   ○ I will <u>lai</u> the box here.
   ○ No mistake

More Practice Now write all the misspelled words correctly on a separate sheet of paper.

Spelling Games
www.eduplace.com/kids/sv/
Review for your test.

Real-World Vocabulary

Science: Food Chains

Write the words from the box to complete the two food chains. Start at the bottom of the chain. Use your Spelling Dictionary.

Spelling Word Link

chain

deer
worm
hawk
robin
wolf

3 _____

2 _____

1 _____

5 _____

4 _____

grass

Try This CHALLENGE

Food Chain Make another food chain like the ones on this page. Use a separate piece of paper.

eWord Game
www.eduplace.com/kids/sv/

35

Read the Spelling Words and sentences.

Basic Words

1. load — load — Can you carry this **load**?
2. open — open — The door is wide **open**.
3. told — told — My teacher **told** us a story.
4. yellow — yellow — The sun looks bright **yellow**.
5. soak — soak — I love to **soak** in my tub.
6. shadow — shadow — Look at my long **shadow**.
7. foam — foam — The water has **foam** on it.
8. follow — follow — Please **follow** the sign.
9. glow — glow — Fireflies **glow** at night.
10. sold — sold — The store **sold** newspapers.
11. window — window — Jon peeked out the **window**.
12. coach — coach — Our team has a new **coach**.
13. sew — sew — Use this needle to **sew**.
14. though — though — We jogged, **though** it rained.

Review
15. cold   16. most

Challenge
17. tomorrow   18. clothes

Think about the Spelling Strategy.

Each word has the long *o* sound. This sound is shown as /ō/. The /ō/ sound can be spelled *oa*, *o*, or *ow*.

/ō/ l**oa**d, **o**pen, yell**ow**

How are the Memory Words different?

Sort and write the words.

Write each Basic Word under its spelling of the /ō/ sound. Circle the letter or letters that spell the /ō/ sound.

Sort for *oa*
1.
2.
3.
4.

Sort for *o*
5.
6.
7.

Sort for *ow*
8.
9.
10.
11.
12.

Other Spellings
13.
14.

Phonics

Use Basic Words in these exercises.

1. Write the word that begins with a long vowel sound.
2. Write the word that rhymes with *roam*.
3. Write the word that has the /ă/ sound.
4. Write the word that ends with the same sound that you hear at the end of *week*.

Vocabulary: Making Inferences

Write the Basic Word that matches each clue.

19. A leader wants you to do this.
20. This is made of glass.
21. This is something you carry.
22. You do this to put a button back on a shirt.
23. The moon and stars do this.
24. This is another name for a teacher.

Challenge Words

Write the Challenge Word that completes each sentence. Use your Spelling Dictionary.

25. We are going away _____.
26. Have you packed all the _____ you need?

load
open
yellow

Phonics

15. _____

16. _____

17. _____

18. _____

Making Inferences

19. _____

20. _____

21. _____

22. _____

23. _____

24. _____

Challenge Words

25. _____

26. _____

At Home With a family member, take turns "finger spelling" a Spelling Word into the other's hand and guessing the word.

Word Meaning

1. _____

2. _____

3. _____

4. _____

5. _____

6. _____

7. _____

8. _____

9. _____

10. _____

11. _____

12. _____

Word Meaning: Synonyms

A **synonym** is a word that means the same or almost the same as another word.

My alarm clock **glows** in the dark.
The nightlight **shines** brightly.

Practice Write the synonym for each word on the cups. Use the words from the box. Use your Spelling Dictionary.

load	quickly	enjoy	happy
damp	tiny	filth	look
spin	final	start	correct

1. turn
2. small
3. wet
4. begin
5. fast
6. pack
7. see
8. glad
9. last
10. dirty
11. right
12. like

PART 3 Spelling and Writing

Proofread an E-mail Message

Spelling and Proper Nouns Proofread this e-mail message. Use proofreading marks to fix **six** spelling mistakes and **two** missing capital letters in the names of people or pets.

Example: My dog, fluffy, sits at the ~~windoe~~ window and watches us.

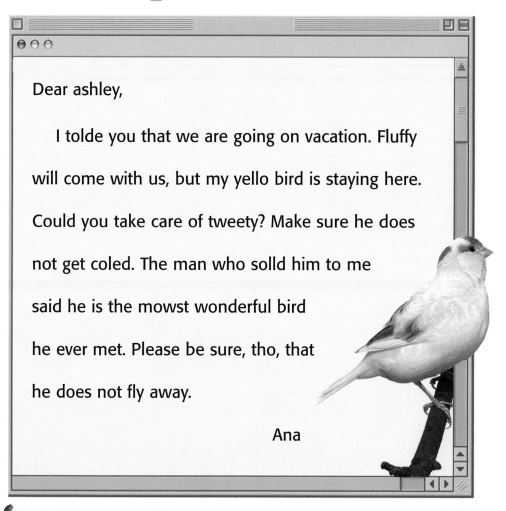

Dear ashley,

I tolde you that we are going on vacation. Fluffy will come with us, but my yello bird is staying here. Could you take care of tweety? Make sure he does not get coled. The man who solld him to me said he is the mowst wonderful bird he ever met. Please be sure, tho, that he does not fly away.

Ana

Proofreading Marks

¶	Indent
∧	Add
ℐ	Delete
≡	Capital letter
/	Small letter

Basic
load
open
told
yellow
soak
shadow
foam
follow
glow
sold
window
coach
! sew
! though

Review
cold
most

Challenge
tomorrow
clothes

Write an E-mail Message

prewrite → draft → revise → proofread → publish

Write an e-mail message to a friend. Tell about something that happened to you.

- Write a greeting, a message, and your name.
- Use some Spelling Words and names of people or pets.
- Proofread your work.

Power Proofreading
www.eduplace.com/kids/sv/

Test Tip If you have time, check your answers again.

Test Format Practice

Directions This test will show how well you can spell.

- Many of the questions in this test have spelling mistakes. Some do not have any mistakes at all.
- Look for mistakes in spelling.
- If there is a mistake, fill in the answer space on your answer sheet that has the same letter as the **line** with the mistake.
- If there is no mistake, fill in the last answer space.

Example:

Ⓐ Ⓑ Ⓒ Ⓓ Ⓔ

Answer Sheet

1. Ⓐ Ⓑ Ⓒ Ⓓ Ⓔ
2. Ⓙ Ⓚ Ⓛ Ⓜ Ⓝ
3. Ⓐ Ⓑ Ⓒ Ⓓ Ⓔ
4. Ⓙ Ⓚ Ⓛ Ⓜ Ⓝ
5. Ⓐ Ⓑ Ⓒ Ⓓ Ⓔ
6. Ⓙ Ⓚ Ⓛ Ⓜ Ⓝ

Example:
A told
B soke
C most
D front
E No mistakes

1. **A** cold
    B broke
    C glowe
    D though
    E No mistakes

2. **J** load
    K sew
    L yellow
    M sold
    N No mistakes

3. **A** koach
    B neighbor
    C cone
    D spoke
    E No mistakes

4. **J** shadoh
    K weigh
    L eight
    M window
    N No mistakes

5. **A** open
    B those
    C leave
    D folow
    E No mistakes

6. **J** done
    K tho
    L today
    M these
    N foam

More Practice
Now write all the misspelled words correctly on a separate sheet of paper.

Spelling Games
www.eduplace.com/kids/sv/
Review for your test.

Real-World Vocabulary

Recreation: Swim Meet

Write the words from the box to complete the article from a school newspaper. Use your Spelling Dictionary.

Spelling Word Link

coach

goggles
scoreboard
starter
relay
platform

NEW RECORD SET!

The Harris County swim meet was last Saturday. The final event was the team _____(1)_____ race. Our team had not yet won an event.

The first swimmer for each team climbed up on the _____(2)_____. The racers put on their _____(3)_____ and got ready. Then the _____(4)_____ blew her whistle, and the race began.

Our last swimmer set a new record. The coach cheered when he saw the time on the _____(5)_____.

1. _____
2. _____
3. _____
4. _____
5. _____

eWord Game
www.eduplace.com/kids/sv/

Try This — CHALLENGE

Fix It! Replace each underlined word with a word from the box.

6. I wore <u>earmuffs</u> to protect my eyes.

7. I was swimming in a <u>foot</u> race.

8. The <u>finisher</u> gave the signal for the race to begin.

6. _____

7. _____

8. _____

PART 1 Spelling and Phonics

Read the Spelling Words and sentences.

Basic Words

1.	bright	bright	The sun is very **bright**.
2.	mild	mild	Enjoy the **mild** weather.
3.	sight	sight	Look at that pretty **sight**.
4.	pie	pie	We ate the whole **pie**.
5.	shiny	shiny	Gold and silver are **shiny**.
6.	mind	mind	What idea is in her **mind**?
7.	tie	tie	He wore a shirt and a **tie**.
8.	pilot	pilot	A **pilot** flies a plane.
9.	might	might	We **might** go swimming.
10.	lie	lie	I will not tell a **lie**.
11.	tight	tight	His shoes are too **tight**.
12.	blind	blind	Is the old horse **blind**?
13.	fight	fight	My cats **fight** at times.
14.	die	die	Will this broken bush **die**?

Review

15. find   16. night

Challenge

17. silent   18. frightening

Think about the Spelling Strategy.

Each word has the long *i* sound. This sound is shown as /ī/. The /ī/ sound can be spelled *igh*, *i*, or *ie*.

/ī/ br**igh**t, m**i**ld, p**ie**

Sort and write the words.

Write each Basic Word under its spelling of the /ī/ sound. Circle the letter or letters that spell the /ī/ sound.

Sort for *igh*

1. _____
2. _____
3. _____
4. _____
5. _____

Sort for *i*

6. _____
7. _____
8. _____
9. _____
10. _____

Sort for *ie*

11. _____
12. _____
13. _____
14. _____

Phonics

Write Basic Words to answer the questions.

15. Which word begins with the /sh/ sound?
16. Which word rhymes with *child*?
17. Which word begins with the same two sounds you hear at the beginning of *brown*?
18–19. Which two words begin like *much* or *black* and rhyme with *kind*?

Vocabulary: Context Paragraph

Write Basic Words to complete this paragraph.

Clover the Clown is a curious _____(20). Her _____(21) is too long, and her belt is too _____(22). Throw a _____(23) at her face, and watch her ears wiggle. When you see her perform, you _____(24) get a case of the giggles!

Challenge Words

Write the Challenge Word that belongs in each group. Use your Spelling Dictionary.

25. quiet, calm, _____   26.   scary, horrible, _____

bright   mild   pie

Phonics

15.

16.

17.

18.

19.

Context Paragraph

20.

21.

22.

23.

24.

Challenge Words

25.

26.

At Home — With a family member, write each Spelling Word on a separate slip of paper. Work together to arrange the words in ABC order.

43

ind Words

1. _____

2. _____

3. _____

ight Words

4. _____

5. _____

6. _____

Dictionary

7. _____

8. _____

9. _____

10. _____

11. _____

12. _____

Word Families: Rhyming Words

Practice 1–6. Make rhyming words that have the long *i* vowel sound. Use the letters in the pictures. Write each word under *ind* Words or *ight* Words.

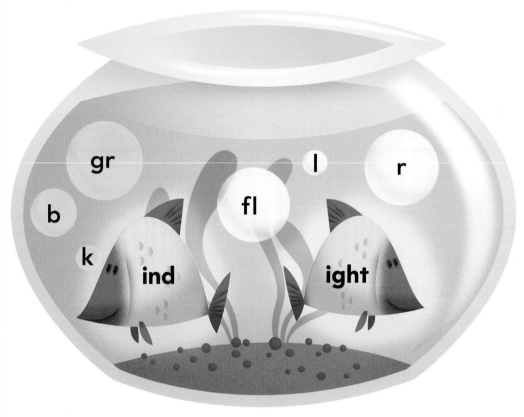

Dictionary: Parts of a Dictionary

A dictionary lists words in ABC order. How could you find the word *blind* quickly? Turn to the beginning, where you will find the words starting with *b*.

BEGINNING	MIDDLE	END
abcdefg	hijklmnopq	rstuvwxyz

Practice Write *beginning*, *middle*, or *end* to tell the part of the dictionary where you would find each word below.

7. find
8. tie
9. pilot
10. bright
11. lie
12. wind

PART 3 Spelling and Writing

Proofread a Travel Ad

Spelling and Proper Nouns Proofread this travel ad. Use proofreading marks to fix **four** spelling mistakes and **four** missing capital letters in the names of places.

Example: A ~~pilote~~ *pilot* could fly you to Italy or japan!

Tours for You!

We can help you make up your mind where to go on your next vacation. You miht decide to see the united states. In florida, you can li in the hot sun. In New york, there are lots of museums to visit. You can probably fynd a wonderful sighte in your own state!

Write a Travel Ad

| prewrite → draft → revise → proofread → publish |

Write a travel ad about a place you would like to visit.
- Write some facts and details about the place.
- Use some Spelling Words and the names of places.
- Proofread your work.

Proofreading Marks

¶	Indent
∧	Add
⌐	Delete
≡	Capital letter
/	Small letter

Basic
bright
mild
sight
pie
shiny
mind
tie
pilot
might
lie
tight
blind
fight
die

Review
find
night

Challenge
silent
frightening

Power Proofreading
www.eduplace.com/kids/sv/

45

Test Tip If you change an answer, erase your first answer completely.

Test Format Practice

Directions Read each group of sentences. Decide if one of the underlined words is spelled wrong or if there is *No mistake*. Fill in the space for the answer you have chosen.

Example: ○ Who sent this <u>gift</u>?
○ That bug is <u>blinde</u>.
○ I <u>might</u> go home.
○ No mistake

1. ○ I like apple <u>pie</u>.
   ○ This penny is <u>shiny</u>.
   ○ The fish did not <u>dy</u>.
   ○ No mistake

2. ○ Feel the <u>mild</u> breeze.
   ○ We do not like to <u>fite</u>.
   ○ The tomatoes are <u>ripe</u>.
   ○ No mistake

3. ○ The lamp is <u>bright</u>.
   ○ Did you <u>find</u> the key?
   ○ He did not tell a <u>ly</u>.
   ○ No mistake

4. ○ He can <u>tie</u> a bow.
   ○ I will <u>invite</u> you.
   ○ We do not <u>mind</u>.
   ○ No mistake

5. ○ She is a <u>pillot</u>.
   ○ This shirt feels <u>tight</u>.
   ○ They have a happy <u>life</u>.
   ○ No mistake

6. ○ The moon shines at <u>nihgt</u>.
   ○ We ran a <u>mile</u>.
   ○ That is a funny <u>sight</u>.
   ○ No mistake

7. ○ What is the <u>price</u>?
   ○ We <u>mite</u> go.
   ○ This dog helps the <u>blind</u>.
   ○ No mistake

8. ○ Try to <u>tye</u> a knot.
   ○ I saw him last <u>night</u>.
   ○ Do you know the <u>pilot</u>?
   ○ No mistake

More Practice
Now write all the misspelled words correctly on a separate sheet of paper.

Spelling Games
www.eduplace.com/kids/sv/
Review for your test.

Real-World Vocabulary

Science: Stars

Write the words from the box to complete this passage from a book about stars. Use your Spelling Dictionary.

Long ago, the Greeks began to ___(1)___ the stars in the night sky. They wondered how ___(2)___ the twinkling lights were from Earth. They also thought that certain groups of stars formed pictures.

The Greeks used their ___(3)___ to name these different groups of stars. One early ___(4)___ decided that one ___(5)___ of stars looked like Leo, the lion. Another was thought to look like the hunter Orion. He was wearing a belt of three bright stars. Today we still use these names for certain groups of stars.

1. _____

2. _____

3. _____

4. _____

5. _____

eWord Game
www.eduplace.com/kids/sv/

Try This CHALLENGE

Complete It! Write a word from the box that completes each sentence.

6. How many stars are in that _____?

7. Use your _____ to tell an exciting story.

8. Would you like to travel to _____ lands?

6. _____

7. _____

8. _____

Spelling Review

Unit 1

1. _____
2. _____
3. _____
4. _____
5. _____
6. _____
7. _____

Unit 2

8. _____
9. _____
10. _____
11. _____
12. _____
13. _____
14. _____

Unit 1	Short Vowels		pages 18–23
plan	smell	pumpkin	clock
gift	⚠ head	⚠ friend	

Spelling Strategy In most words, the short vowel sounds are spelled **a**, **e**, **i**, **o**, or **u**.

Rhyme Time Write the Spelling Word that rhymes with each word.

  1. bread   **2.** man   **3.** bell

Fill-in-the-Blank Write the missing words.

  4. Set the alarm _____.

  5. Give her a _____ for her birthday.

  6. Can you carve a _____?

  7. You are my best _____.

Unit 2	Vowel-Consonant-e		pages 24–29
cone	cube	price	erase
ripe	skate	⚠ done	

Spelling Strategy A long vowel sound is often spelled vowel-consonant-**e**.

Word Clues Write a word for each clue.

  8. how much something costs

  9. a shape with six sides

 10. this might have wheels

 11. ice cream holder

 12. fruit that is ready to eat

 13. remove from the chalkboard

 14. finished

Unit 3 More Long *a* and Long *e* Words   pages 30–35

trail	sweet	today	dream
always	❗eight	❗neighbor	

Spelling Strategy In many words, the /ā/ sound is spelled **ay** or **ai**. The /ē/ sound may be spelled **ea** or **ee**.

Fill-in-the-Blank Write the missing words.

My birthday is ___(15)___. Now I am ___(16)___ years old. I have ___(17)___ wanted a puppy. Guess what? My ___(18)___ came true! My next-door ___(19)___ gave me a puppy. I finally have a pet of my own!

Word Pairs Write a word to finish the second sentence in each pair.

20. A *pepper* is *spicy*. *Pineapple* is _____.

21. You *drive* on a *street*. You *hike* on a _____.

Unit 4   More Long *o* Words   pages 36–41

told	yellow	foam	glow
coach	❗sew	❗though	

Spelling Strategy The /ō/ sound can be spelled **oa**, **o**, or **ow**.

Letter Math Add and take away letters to write Spelling Words.

22. th + rough − r =

23. foal − l + m =

24. t + mold − m =

25. g + blow − b =

26. s + chew − ch =

27. y + mellow − m =

28. coat − t + ch =

Unit 3

15. _____

16. _____

17. _____

18. _____

19. _____

20. _____

21. _____

Unit 4

22. _____

23. _____

24. _____

25. _____

26. _____

27. _____

28. _____

Spelling Review

Unit 5

29.

30.

31.

32.

33.

34.

35.

Challenge Words

36.

37.

38.

39.

40.

Unit 5	More Long *i* Words		pages 42–47
bright	mild	sight	mind
tie	pilot	die	

Spelling Strategy The /ī/ sound can be spelled **igh**, **i**, or **ie**.

Letter Swap Change the letters in dark print. Write Spelling Words.

29. **w**ild   **30.** **l**ight   **31.** min**e**   **32.** di**m**

Word Clues Write the word for each clue.

33. This person flies a plane.

34. what you do when you make a knot

35. the opposite of dull

Challenge Words	Units 1–5	pages 18–47
fantastic	surprise	yesterday
tomorrow	silent	

Fill-in-the-Blank Write the missing words.

I can hardly wait for ___(36)___. Dad promised me a ___(37)___. I know it will be something really ___(38)___. I saw him carry a big box into the house ___(39)___. I will not tell him what I saw. I think it is best to keep ___(40)___.

Spelling (and) Writing

Proofread a Personal Narrative

Spelling and Grammar Mixed Review Proofread this personal narrative. Use proofreading marks to fix **five** spelling mistakes, **one** missing end mark, and **two** missing capital letters.

Example: The ~~theng~~ I liked best was my trip to florida.
(thing added above; florida underlined for capital)

What a Trip!

I thought my flight to miami would be dull. I was wrong Before we took off, the pilot decided to inviet Dad and me to see the front cabin. He thought I mite enjoy learning about the plane. He spoak about each button and knob. I did not want to leeve, but soon it was time to take off. What a great treet this was! I can hardly wait to tell my friend jim.

Write a Personal Narrative

prewrite → draft → revise → proofread → publish

Think about an interesting experience you had. Write a personal narrative to tell what happened.

- Use some Spelling Words from Units 1–5.
- Proofread your work.

Tips

- List interesting things you have done. Then choose one to write about.
- Include details that will bring the experience to life.

Power Proofreading
www.eduplace.com/kids/sv/

Spelling Test Practice

Test Format Practice

> **Test Tip** Read the sentence and all the answer choices.

Directions Find the word that is spelled correctly and best completes this sentence.

Example: The point of my pencil _____.

brocke	browk	broke	brooke
○	○	○	○

1. The glue is very _____.

stickey	sticky	stiky	stickee
○	○	○	○

2. I walk a _____ every day.

mille	myle	miel	mile
○	○	○	○

3. How much does this melon _____?

waigh	weiye	weigh	waye
○	○	○	○

4. The tree makes a _____ on the wall.

shaadow	shadow	shado	shadoe
○	○	○	○

5. My favorite dessert is apple _____.

piye	pi	pie	pye
○	○	○	○

6. They _____ to be good friends.

seeme	seme	sem	seem
○	○	○	○

Spelling Games
www.eduplace.com/kids/sv/
Review for your test.

Test Tip Think about what each answer choice means.

Directions Choose the word or group of words that means almost the same as the underlined word. Fill in the space on your answer sheet for the answer you have chosen.

Test Format Practice

Example: **To <u>follow</u> means**
- ○ trip
- ○ go after
- ○ believe
- ○ cheat

1. To <u>save</u> means
- ○ give
- ○ spend
- ○ keep
- ○ take

2. To <u>lay</u> means
- ○ stop
- ○ run
- ○ hold
- ○ put

3. A <u>crop</u> is a
- ○ farm
- ○ plant
- ○ barn
- ○ tractor

4. To <u>soak</u> means
- ○ snow
- ○ wet
- ○ drip
- ○ dry

5. A <u>lunch</u> is a
- ○ promise
- ○ wish
- ○ plan
- ○ meal

6. An <u>excuse</u> is a
- ○ reason
- ○ job
- ○ riddle
- ○ song

7. A <u>chain</u> is
- ○ branches
- ○ cups
- ○ links
- ○ footsteps

8. To <u>load</u> means
- ○ take out
- ○ to put in
- ○ jump on
- ○ go through

UNIT 7

Short and Long Vowels

Basic Words

1.	math	math	My best subject is **math**.
2.	toast	toast	We eat **toast** and butter.
3.	flame	flame	The **flame** is very hot.
4.	easy	easy	Is the puzzle **easy** to do?
5.	socks	socks	I am wearing blue **socks**.
6.	Friday	Friday	Will you leave on **Friday**?
7.	stuff	stuff	What is all this **stuff**?
8.	paid	paid	They **paid** their bills.
9.	cheese	cheese	Please eat this **cheese**.
10.	thick	thick	The pizza crust is **thick**.
11.	elbow	elbow	An arm bends at the **elbow**.
12.	huge	huge	That mountain is **huge**.
13.	program	program	I saw a great TV **program**!
14.	shell	shell	A turtle has a hard **shell**.

Review

15. each   16. both

Challenge

17. comb   18. holiday

Sort for Short Vowel Sound

1. _____
2. _____
3. _____
4. _____
5. _____

Sort for Long Vowel Sound

6. _____
7. _____
8. _____
9. _____
10. _____
11. _____
12. _____
13. _____
14. _____

Think about the Spelling Strategy.

Each word has a short or a long vowel sound.

/ă/ m**a**th   /ē/ **ea**sy   /ō/ pr**o**gram   /ā/ fl**a**me

Sort and write the words.

Write each Basic Word under its vowel sound. Write *program* and *Friday* under the first vowel sound in each word. Write *elbow* under the second vowel sound.

Phonics

Write the Basic Word that has the same beginning sound or sounds as each group of words.

15. thin, think, _____
16. flag, fly, _____
17. price, press, _____

18. chin, check, _____
19. ship, sharp, _____
20. man, mine, _____

Vocabulary: Word Clues

Write the Basic Word that fits each clue.

21. You wear these on your feet.
22. When you gave money for something, you did this.
23. This describes something that is very large.
24. This is part of your arm.

Challenge Words

Write the Challenge Word that completes each sentence. Use your Spelling Dictionary.

25. We invited our friends to celebrate the _____ with us.
26. I will _____ my hair a new way to surprise them!

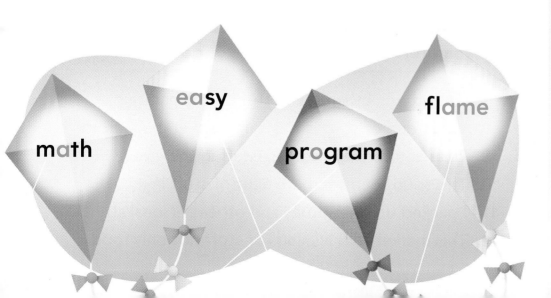

easy

flame

math

program

15. _____
16. _____
17. _____
18. _____
19. _____
20. _____

Word Clues

21. _____
22. _____
23. _____
24. _____

Challenge Words

25. _____
26. _____

At Home With a family member, take turns writing the last two letters of a Spelling Word. The other person finishes the word.

Word Meaning: Shortened Words

Some words have shortened forms. The word *photo* is short for *photograph*.

Practice Write the word from the box that is the shortened form of each underlined word.

math	gas	gym
phone	plane	exam

1. We played basketball in the <u>gymnasium</u>.
2. This car will need more <u>gasoline</u> soon.
3. The <u>airplane</u> to Dallas left Chicago at noon.
4. What did you learn today in <u>mathematics</u> class?
5. Everyone studied for the <u>examination</u>.
6. Please <u>telephone</u> us when you arrive!

Dallas

Thesaurus: Exact Words for *stuff*

Practice Write the exact word for *stuff* that best fits each sentence. Use your Thesaurus.

ingredients	equipment	belongings
material	junk	goods

7. Get rid of all the useless <u>stuff</u> in the garage.
8. What kind of <u>stuff</u> is this soft blanket made from?
9. Please store your camping <u>stuff</u> in the garage.
10. This soup seems to have a lot of <u>stuff</u> in it.
11. I packed up my clothes and other personal <u>stuff</u>.
12. This market sells all kinds of <u>stuff</u> not only food.

Word Meaning

1. _____
2. _____
3. _____
4. _____
5. _____
6. _____

Thesaurus

7. _____
8. _____
9. _____
10. _____
11. _____
12. _____

PART 3 Spelling and Writing

Proofread a Museum Brochure

Spelling and Proper Nouns Proofread this museum brochure. Use proofreading marks to fix **five** spelling mistakes and **three** missing capital letters in the names of holidays, months, and days of the week.

Example: We have a special ~~programe~~ every labor day.
program

Proofreading Marks
¶	Indent
∧	Add
ℰ	Delete
≡	Capital letter
/	Small letter

WELCOME TO THE SCIENCE MUSEUM!

It is easey to move around eache floor. See a huge planet show! Learn how to make chease and ice cream! Discover the stuf that nests are made of! We are open tuesday through Fryday in November and december. Visit us often, but do not come on thanksgiving Day. We are closed!

Basic
math
toast
flame
easy
socks
Friday
stuff
paid
cheese
thick
elbow
huge
program
shell

Review
each
both

Challenge
comb
holiday

Write a Brochure

prewrite → draft → revise → proofread → publish

Write a brochure about a place you like to visit.
- Tell about some things to see or do there.
- Use some Spelling Words and the names of holidays, months, and days of the week.
- Proofread your work.

Power Proofreading
www.eduplace.com/kids/sv/

57

Test Tip Do not spend too much time on one question.

Test Format Practice

Directions Find the phrase containing an underlined word that is not spelled correctly. If all the underlined words are spelled correctly, mark "All correct."

Example: <u>tight</u> boot   low <u>flaim</u>   <u>huge</u> load   All correct
⃝   ⃝   ⃝   ⃝

1. <u>bothe</u> feet   our <u>socks</u>   <u>each</u> person   All correct
    ⃝   ⃝   ⃝   ⃝

2. <u>thick</u> mat   burnt <u>toste</u>   soft <u>cheese</u>   All correct
    ⃝   ⃝   ⃝   ⃝

3. <u>Friday</u> night   <u>math</u> test   new <u>program</u>   All correct
    ⃝   ⃝   ⃝   ⃝

4. <u>pade</u> for   some <u>stuff</u>   sore <u>elbow</u>   All correct
    ⃝   ⃝   ⃝   ⃝

More Practice
Now write all the misspelled words correctly on a separate sheet of paper.

5. apple <u>pie</u>   <u>bright</u> star   clam <u>schell</u>   All correct
    ⃝   ⃝   ⃝   ⃝

6. <u>shiny</u> coin   <u>easey</u> work   <u>mild</u> day   All correct
    ⃝   ⃝   ⃝   ⃝

Spelling Games
www.eduplace.com/kids/sv/
Review for your test.

Real-World Vocabulary

Social Studies: Chinese New Year

Write the words from the box to complete the post card that Jake sent to his pen pal, Derek. Use your Spelling Dictionary.

Dear Derek,

Happy New Year from Hong Kong! On the Chinese ___(1)___, February starts a new year. It is a Chinese ___(2)___ to celebrate for days. Family and friends get together for a big ___(3)___ with lots of delicious food. Everyone watches the noisy ___(4)___ in the street. I saw a giant ___(5)___ with huge eyes. I wish you could have seen it.

Your pal,

Jake

Spelling Word Link

holiday

feast
dragon
calendar
custom
procession

1. _____
2. _____
3. _____
4. _____
5. _____

eWord Game
www.eduplace.com/kids/sv/

Try This CHALLENGE

Word Groups Write the word from the box that belongs in each group.

6. parade, march, _____
7. date, month, _____
8. dinner, meal, _____

6. _____

7. _____

8. _____

Read the Spelling Words and sentences.

Basic Words

1.	three	*three*	Lil has **three** brothers.
2.	scrap	*scrap*	A **scrap** of food is left over.
3.	street	*street*	Is it safe to cross the **street**?
4.	spring	*spring*	Flowers bloom in the **spring**.
5.	thrill	*thrill*	Did the circus act **thrill** you?
6.	scream	*scream*	He thinks he heard a **scream**.
7.	strange	*strange*	What a **strange** movie this is!
8.	throw	*throw*	We **throw** bones to our dog.
9.	string	*string*	This **string** has a knot in it.
10.	scrape	*scrape*	Please **scrape** off the paint.
11.	spray	*spray*	I **spray** water on the plant.
12.	stream	*stream*	Do fish swim in that **stream**?
13.	threw	*threw*	Matt **threw** the ball to me.
14.	strong	*strong*	The hockey player is **strong**!

Review

15. think   16. they

Challenge

17. straight   18. scramble

Sort for *thr*

1. _____
2. _____
3. _____
4. _____

Sort for *scr*

5. _____
6. _____
7. _____

Sort for *str*

8. _____
9. _____
10. _____
11. _____
12. _____

Sort for *spr*

13. _____
14. _____

Think about the Spelling Strategy.

Each Basic Word begins with the consonant cluster *thr, scr, str,* or *spr*. A consonant cluster is made up of two or more consonants written together that have different sounds. You can hear the different consonant sounds in the cluster.

three   **scr**ap   **str**eet   **spr**ing

Sort and write the words.

Write each Basic Word under its beginning consonant cluster.

Phonics

Write the Basic Word that rhymes with each word.

15. mill **18.** trap

16. tray **19.** flew

17. tape **20.** change

Vocabulary: Word Pairs

Write the Basic Word that completes each pair of sentences.

21. It turns *colder* in the *fall*.
It turns *warmer* in the _____.

22. You *whisper* in a *soft* voice.
You _____ in a *loud* voice.

23. You *swing* a baseball *bat*.
You _____ a *ball*.

24. A *boat* travels on the *water*.
A *car* travels on the _____.

Challenge Words

Write the Challenge Word that fits each meaning. Use your Spelling Dictionary.

25. not bent **26.** mix up

Phonics

15. _____

16. _____

17. _____

18. _____

19. _____

20. _____

Word Pairs

21. _____

22. _____

23 _____

24. _____

Challenge Words

25. _____

26. _____

three   **scrap**   **street**   **spring**

At Home   Make word crosses with a family member. Write one Spelling Word across a page. Take turns writing Spelling Words that cross any word you wrote.

Word Building

1. _____

2. _____

3. _____

4. _____

5. _____

6. _____

Dictionary

7. _____

8. _____

9. _____

10. _____

11. _____

12. _____

Word Building: *scr, spr, str,* and *thr*

Practice For each word, think of the missing letters, *scr, spr, str,* or *thr*. Write each word.

1. ___?___ + een

4. ___?___ + ead

2. ___?___ + oat

5. ___?___ + apbook

3. ___?___ + aw

6. ___?___ + ain

Dictionary: Guide Words

Entry words are the main words in a dictionary. They are in ABC Order. Two **guide words** at the top of each page help you find entry words quickly. The guide words tell the first and last entry words on the page.

Practice 7–12. Write the six words from the box that would be on the same dictionary page as the guide words *stray/thrill.*

stream	strong	think	sunshine
thunder	threw	skate	thank

Proofread a Newspaper Article

Spelling and Plural Nouns Proofread this newspaper article. Use proofreading marks to fix **five** spelling mistakes and **two** mistakes in nouns that name more than one thing.

Example: Sometimes ~~animal~~ animals do very ~~strainge~~ strange things.

TRAFFIC STOPPERS

Two pig sat down in the middle of the road yesterday. The animals stopped traffic on Broadway for thre hour.

People began to screem at them, but thay would not get up. Finally, someone threw a skrap of food. The idea worked. The first pig got up to eat the food. It moved out of the streat. The second pig followed. Happy drivers were able to move their cars again.

Proofreading Marks

¶	Indent
∧	Add
ℱ	Delete
≡	Capital letter
/	Small letter

Basic
three
scrap
street
spring
thrill
scream
strange
throw
string
scrape
spray
stream
threw
strong

Review
think
they

Challenge
straight
scramble

Write a Newspaper Article

prewrite → draft → revise → proofread → publish

Write a newspaper article about something that happened this week.

- Tell who, what, where, when, why, and how.
- Use some Spelling Words and plural nouns.
- Proofread your work.

Power Proofreading
www.eduplace.com/kids/sv/

✔ **Test Tip** If you have time, check your answers again.

Test Format Practice

Directions Find the word that is spelled correctly and best completes the sentence.

Example: I _____ that we are ready to go now.

| thinke | theenk | think | tink |
| ○ | ○ | ○ | ○ |

---

1. We like to play baseball in the _____.

| sprieng | sping | spring | springe |
| ○ | ○ | ○ | ○ |

2. Drew has a _____ on his knee.

| scape | skrap | skrape | scrape |
| ○ | ○ | ○ | ○ |

3. Pull this _____ to turn on the light.

| string | streeng | streng | strinng |
| ○ | ○ | ○ | ○ |

4. How far will the hose _____ the water?

| spraye | spray | spraiy | sprae |
| ○ | ○ | ○ | ○ |

5. Did you _____ a penny into the fountain?

| trow | throw | thro | throwe |
| ○ | ○ | ○ | ○ |

6. It was a _____ to jump off the diving board!

| thrille | thriwl | thrill | thril |
| ○ | ○ | ○ | ○ |

More Practice
Now write each correctly spelled word on a sheet of paper.

Spelling Games
www.eduplace.com/kids/sv/
Review for your test.

Phonics

Write a Basic Word to answer each question.

15. Which word rhymes with *lap*?
16. Which word rhymes with *strong*?
17. Which word begins with the consonant cluster *scr*?
18. Which word rhymes with *neck*?

Vocabulary: Context Sentences

Write the Basic Word that completes each sentence.

19. This red jacket does not _____ these purple pants.
20. My bug bites _____!
21. If I _____ this elastic band too far, it will break.
22. This blue _____ will cover the hole in my jeans.
23. Can you tie a _____ in this string?
24. Please eat with a spoon, a fork, and a _____.

Challenge Words

Write the Challenge Word that matches each clue. Use your Spelling Dictionary.

25. This connects a finger to the rest of the hand.
26. You might have this little fold in your shirt collar.

Phonics

15.

16.

17.

18.

Context Sentences

19.

20.

21.

22.

23.

24.

Challenge Words

25.

26.

At Home With a family member, take turns "finger spelling" a Spelling Word into the other's hand and guessing the word.

Word Meaning

1. _____

_____

2. _____

_____

3. _____

_____

4. _____

_____

5. _____

_____

🔍 Word Meaning: Watch Words

The words in the house all have *watch* in them. How are their meanings alike?

Practice Write a word from the house to complete each sentence.

1. My class is _____ a film about a rain forest.

2. We climbed to the top of the old _____.

3. Please keep a _____ eye on the baby.

4. This _____ barks at strangers to scare them away.

5. The crossing guard stood as a _____ on the busy street.

| watch |
| watching |
| watcher |
| watchful |
| watchdog |
| watchtower |

Dictionary: Definitions

A dictionary entry has one or more **definitions**, or meanings, for the entry word. A **sample sentence** helps to make the meaning clear.

┌─definition

knee (nē) *n., pl.* **knees** The place where the thigh bone and lower leg bone come together: *The dancer bent his knee and then straightened his leg.* ◄─

└── sample sentence

Practice Use your Spelling Dictionary to complete the exercises. Write your answers on a separate sheet of paper.

6. Look up *knock*. Write the definition.

7. Look up *wrap*. Write the sample sentence.

8. Look up *strong*. Write the definition.

9. Look up *find*. Write the sample sentence.

Proofread a List

Spelling and Nouns with 's Proofread this list. Use proofreading marks to fix **five** spelling mistakes and **two** missing apostrophes in singular nouns that show ownership.

Example: It is ~~rong~~ *wrong* to skateboard in your dad's driveway.

Proofreading Marks

¶	Indent
∧	Add
℘	Delete
≡	Capital letter
/	Small letter

Do You Want to Skateboard?

- Find a good place to start, like your school track.

- Be sure to watsh for anything that will stop your board.

- Expect to fall and get a scratch or two.

- A helmet is a skateboarders friend.

- Wear nee and elbow pads. Do not nock into people.

- Talk with another skateboarder. Get an experts advice.

- If you cach skateboarding fever, you will soon knowe many skateboarding tricks!

Basic
itch
wreck
knee
patch
wrap
knot
watch
knife
stretch
write
scratch
knock
match
wrong

Review
know
catch

Challenge
wrinkle
knuckle

Write a List

prewrite → draft → revise → proofread → publish

Write a list of rules or tips about a sport you like.
- Start each sentence on a new line.
- Use some Spelling Words and singular nouns that show ownership.
- Proofread your work.

Power Proofreading
www.eduplace.com/kids/sv/

Test Tip Be sure to read all the answer choices. Then choose the correct one.

Test Format Practice

Directions Read each group of sentences. Decide if one of the underlined words is spelled wrong or if there is *No mistake*. Fill in the space for the answer you have chosen.

Example:
- ○ I <u>spent</u> one dollar.
- ○ These socks <u>matsh</u>.
- ○ My shirt has a <u>patch</u>.
- ○ No mistake

1.
- ○ I bend my <u>knee</u>.
- ○ We have a good <u>plan</u>.
- ○ He did not <u>reck</u> it.
- ○ No mistake

2.
- ○ Please <u>knock</u> on the door.
- ○ Cats like to <u>stretch</u>.
- ○ She tied a <u>nott</u>.
- ○ No mistake

3.
- ○ He used a sharp <u>nife</u>.
- ○ Where does the <u>trail</u> go?
- ○ I opened the <u>window</u> in the bedroom.
- ○ No mistake

4.
- ○ Please <u>wrap</u> the box.
- ○ Did you <u>catch</u> the ball?
- ○ Nothing is <u>wrong</u>.
- ○ No mistake

5.
- ○ I <u>know</u> her name.
- ○ He will <u>writ</u> a letter.
- ○ Does your hand <u>itch</u>?
- ○ No mistake

6.
- ○ We will <u>watsh</u> the play.
- ○ Do not <u>scratch</u> the new floor.
- ○ We ate <u>cheese</u> for lunch.
- ○ No mistake

More Practice
Now write all the misspelled words correctly on a separate sheet of paper.

Spelling Games
www.eduplace.com/kids/sv/
Review for your test.

Real-World Vocabulary

Language Arts: Friendly Letter

Write the words from the box to label the friendly letter.
Use your Spelling Dictionary.

Spelling Word Link

write

body
signature
heading
greeting
closing

1. _____

2. _____

3. _____

4. _____

5. _____

Camp Harmony
Winston, CT 33218
July 15, 2006

Dear Mom and Dad,

I'm having a great time at camp.
I really like all the girls in my cabin.
Today we learned how to paddle
a canoe. Ana and I did very well
together. We didn't splash too much
when we used the oars.
Tomorrow we are going to learn
how to set up a tent. I can't wait!

Love,
Becky

eWord Game
www.eduplace.com/kids/sv/

Try This CHALLENGE

Questions and Answers Write a word from
the box to answer each question.

6. Which part contains the date in a letter?

7. Which part contains the name?

8. Which part contains the message?

6. _____

7. _____

8. _____

Read the Spelling Words and sentences.

Basic Words

1.	clown	*clown*	See the funny **clown** juggle!
2.	round	*round*	A basketball is **round**.
3.	bow	*bow*	We will **bow** to the audience.
4.	cloud	*cloud*	Is that a rain **cloud** in the sky?
5.	power	*power*	The king used his **power** well.
6.	crown	*crown*	The queen wore a gold **crown**.
7.	thousand	*thousand*	The bike cost a **thousand** dollars!
8.	crowd	*crowd*	The large **crowd** was noisy.
9.	sound	*sound*	Did you hear that squeaky **sound**?
10.	count	*count*	Please **count** your tickets.
11.	powder	*powder*	Where is the can of **powder**?
12.	blouse	*blouse*	Deb will wear her new **blouse**.
13.	frown	*frown*	The sad movie made him **frown**.
! 14.	would	*would*	I **would** like to sing for you.

/ou/ Sound Spelled *ow*

1.

2.

3.

4.

5.

6.

7.

/ou/ Sound Spelled *ou*

8.

9.

10.

11.

12.

13.

Other Sound

14.

Review

15. *house*   16. *found*

Challenge

17. *mountain*   18. *coward*

Think about the Spelling Strategy.

Most of the words have the vowel sound you hear in *clown*. This sound is shown as /ou/. The /ou/ sound is often spelled *ow* or *ou*.

/ou/ cl**ow**n, r**ou**nd

! How is the Memory Word different?

Sort and write the words.

Write each Basic Word under the correct heading.

Phonics

Write the Basic Words that rhyme with the words below.

15. how   **18.** mouse

16. flower   **19–20.** found

17. mount

Vocabulary: Fill-in-the-Blank

Write the missing Basic Words.

I __(21)__ like to go to the Fourth of July parade today. The weather is perfect. There is not a single __(22)__ in the sky. I heard that one __(23)__ people will line Main Street to hear the music and see the sights. What a huge __(24)__ that will be! I can hardly wait!

Challenge Words

Write the Challenge Word that fits each clue. Use your Spelling Dictionary.

25. a person who is not brave

26. a piece of land that rises very high

clown   round

Phonics

15. _____

16. _____

17. _____

18. _____

19. _____

20. _____

Fill-in-the-Blank

21. _____

22. _____

23. _____

24. _____

Challenge Words

25. _____

26. _____

At Home   With a family member, take turns thinking of a clue for a Spelling Word. The other person guesses the word and spells it correctly.

73

Word Meaning

1. _____

2. _____

3. _____

4. _____

5. _____

6. _____

7. _____

8. _____

9. _____

10. _____

🔍 Word Meaning: Homographs

Homographs are words that are spelled the same but have different meanings. They may also have different pronunciations. The words in each group below are homographs.

  a. bow /bou/   to bend the body, head, or knee
  b. bow /bou/   the front part of a ship or a boat
  c. bow /bō/   a weapon for shooting arrows

  d. wind /wĭnd/   air that is in motion
  e. wind /wīnd/   to wrap around something

  f. bark /bärk/   the short, gruff sound a dog makes
  g. bark /bärk/   the outer covering of trees

Practice Write the letter of the meaning of each homograph.

1. Please walk with me to the <u>bow</u> of the boat.

2. After I play my violin, I will <u>bow</u> to the audience.

3. He dropped the <u>bow</u> after he shot the arrow.

4. She could not <u>bow</u> because she hurt her knee.

5. I forgot to <u>wind</u> the string around my yo-yo.

6. A sailboat cannot sail without <u>wind</u>.

7. See the <u>wind</u> blow the leaves around!

8. My puppy has a squeaky <u>bark</u>!

9. The <u>bark</u> of this tree is very rough.

10. Buddy will <u>bark</u> at strangers.

✏ Proofread an Ad

Spelling and Nouns with s' Proofread this ad. Use proofreading marks to fix **six** spelling mistakes and **two** missing apostrophes in plural nouns that show ownership.

Example: We ~~founde~~ found a great place to buy parents' gifts!

Proofreading Marks

¶	Indent
∧	Add
⌒	Delete
≡	Capital letter
/	Small letter

Yard Sale

Do you need a blowse or a skirt? You will find lots of girls clothing. Do you need belts or boys shirts? We have a thousand for sale. You will find face pouder and paint. You can even buy a funny glass cloun or a gold crowne. Join the croud! Come to our howse on 3 Main Street at 2:00 P.M. on Friday.

Basic

clown
round
bow
cloud
power
crown
thousand
crowd
sound
count
powder
blouse
frown
❗ would

Review

house
found

Challenge

mountain
coward

✏ Write an Ad

prewrite → draft → revise → proofread → publish

Write an ad to sell some things from your house.

- Tell what is for sale. Tell where and when people can come to buy.
- Use some Spelling Words and some plural nouns that show ownership.
- Proofread your work.

Power Proofreading
www.eduplace.com/kids/sv/

PART 4

Spelling Test Practice

Test Tip Read the directions carefully.

Test Format Practice

Directions This test will show how well you can spell.

- Many of the questions in this test have spelling mistakes. Some do not have any mistakes at all.
- Look for mistakes in spelling.
- If there is a mistake, fill in the answer space on your answer sheet that has the same letter as the **line** with the mistake.
- If there is no mistake, fill in the last answer space.

Example:

Ⓐ Ⓑ Ⓒ Ⓓ Ⓔ

Example: **A** clowd
           B wrong
           C thousand
           D powder
           E (No mistakes)

Answer Sheet

1. Ⓐ Ⓑ Ⓒ Ⓓ Ⓔ
2. Ⓙ Ⓚ Ⓛ Ⓜ Ⓝ
3. Ⓐ Ⓑ Ⓒ Ⓓ Ⓔ
4. Ⓙ Ⓚ Ⓛ Ⓜ Ⓝ
5. Ⓐ Ⓑ Ⓒ Ⓓ Ⓔ
6. Ⓙ Ⓚ Ⓛ Ⓜ Ⓝ

1. **A** crowd
   B fownd
   C follow
   D sound
   E (No mistakes)

4. **J** bow
   K coach
   L rownd
   M shadow
   N (No mistakes)

2. **J** would
   K strong
   L blouse
   M window
   N (No mistakes)

5. **A** clown
   B cownt
   C though
   D elbow
   E (No mistakes)

3. **A** frowne
   B yellow
   C crown
   D glow
   E (No mistakes)

6. **J** sew
   K know
   L power
   M howse
   N (No mistakes)

More Practice
Now write all the misspelled words correctly on a separate sheet of paper.

Spelling Games
www.eduplace.com/kids/sv/
Review for your test.

Real-World Vocabulary

Music: A Musical Show

Write the words from the box to complete the poster.
Use your Spelling Dictionary.

Spelling Word Link

sound

guitar
musician
recital
concert hall
melody

A MUSICAL TREAT

The Garden City Arts Club is proud to present Clifton Asato, a world-famous ___(1)___. If the ___(2)___ is one of your favorite instruments, you won't want to miss this show. Mr. Asato will give a ___(3)___ on January 15th at 2:30 P.M. He will play a number of pieces, including one ___(4)___ that he wrote.

The show will be in the ___(5)___ at 89 Oak Street.

TICKETS ARE ON SALE NOW!
CALL 555-7976

1. _____
2. _____
3. _____
4. _____
5. _____

Try This
CHALLENGE

Clues Write a clue for each of the words in the box on a separate sheet of paper. Trade papers with a partner. Have your partner guess the words.

eWord Game
www.eduplace.com/kids/sv/

Read the Spelling Words and sentences.

Basic Words

1.	talk	*talk*	I like to **talk** to my friends.
2.	cross	*cross*	We can **cross** the street now.
3.	awful	*awful*	When I am sick, I feel **awful**.
4.	almost	*almost*	They **almost** won the race.
5.	law	*law*	I think this **law** is very fair.
6.	cloth	*cloth*	The **cloth** is made of wool.
7.	cost	*cost*	The kites **cost** five dollars.
8.	crawl	*crawl*	That baby can **crawl** fast!
9.	chalk	*chalk*	Is there **chalk** at the board?
10.	also	*also*	He **also** swam with us.
11.	raw	*raw*	The rabbits like **raw** carrots.
12.	salt	*salt*	Please put **salt** in the soup.
13.	wall	*wall*	A photo hung on the **wall**.
14.	lawn	*lawn*	Their **lawn** is bright green.

Review

15. soft   16. *small*

Challenge

17. *often*   18. *strawberry*

Sort for *a* before *l*

1. _____

2. _____

3. _____

4. _____

5. _____

6. _____

Sort for *o*

7. _____

8. _____

9. _____

Sort for *aw*

10. _____

11. _____

12. _____

13. _____

14. _____

Think about the Spelling Strategy.

Each word has the vowel sound you hear in *lawn*. This sound is shown as /ô/. The /ô/ sound can be spelled *a* before *l*. It can also be spelled *o* or *aw*.

/ô/ t**a**lk, cr**o**ss, **aw**ful

Sort and write the words.

Write each Basic Word under its spelling of the /ô/ sound.

Phonics

Write Basic Words to answer the questions.

15. Which word begins like *chin*?

16. Which word rhymes with *moth*?

17. Which word ends with a vowel?

18. Which word rhymes with *lost*?

19–20. Which two words end with a double consonant?

Vocabulary: Synonyms

Write a Basic Word that means the same or almost the same as each word below.

21. rule   **23.** uncooked

22. terrible   **24.** nearly

Challenge Words

Write the Challenge Word that completes each sentence. Use your Spelling Dictionary.

25. Most _____, my family eats fruit for dessert.

26. When we have ice cream, though, my favorite flavor is _____.

Phonics

15.

16.

17.

18.

19.

20.

Synonyms

21.

22.

23.

24.

Challenge Words

25.

26.

talk   cross   awful

At Home With a family member, take turns writing two Spelling Words on a piece of paper. Cut all the letters apart and mix them up. The other person puts the letters together to spell the words.

awn Words

1. _____

2. _____

3. _____

oss Words

4. _____

5. _____

6. _____

Dictionary

7. _____

8. _____

9. _____

10. _____

11. _____

Word Families: Rhyming Words

Practice 1–6. Follow each path of letters to make new words that rhyme with *yawn* and *loss*. Not all the letters will work.

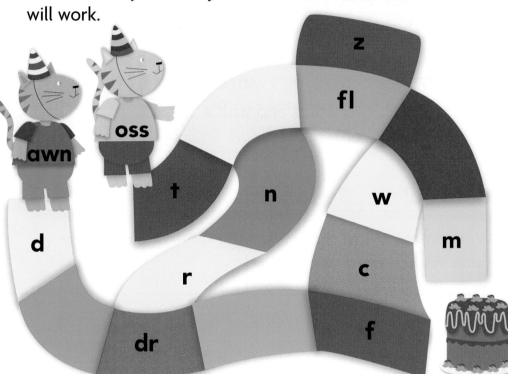

Dictionary: Pronunciation Key

A dictionary entry has a **pronunciation** that helps you say the entry word.

┌─ pronunciation

raw (rô) *adj.* **rawer, rawest** Uncooked: *I made a salad of raw vegetables.*

A **pronunciation key** tells what sounds the pronunciation symbols stand for. It gives a sample word for each sound. For example, *pat* has the vowel sound shown by ă.

Practice Write the word from the key below that helps you say the vowel sound in each pronunciation.

ă pat	ĕ pet	ē be	ĭ pit	ô paw

7. /lĭst/   **8.** /sôlt/   **9.** /wrăp/   **10.** /kēp/   **11.** /hĕd/

✎ Proofread a Journal Entry

Spelling and Using *I* and *me* Proofread this journal entry.
Use proofreading marks to fix **five** spelling mistakes and
two mistakes using *I* and *me*.

Example: ~~Me and Jake~~ were ~~allmost~~ finished playing.
Jake and I ~~almost~~

June 30

    Today my friends and me were outside
on the laun. We were playing checkers on a
sawft blanket. Suddenly, Cora and I saw a
bug crauwl toward us. I do not mind smal
bugs, but this one was huge. Just then
Dad came by to tawk to us. He said that
the bug was a praying mantis.
He also said that it was
harmless. Me and Dad laughed
as the bug went away.

Proofreading Marks

¶	Indent
∧	Add
⌐	Delete
≡	Capital letter
/	Small letter

Basic
talk
cross
awful
almost
law
cloth
cost
crawl
chalk
also
raw
salt
wall
lawn

Review
soft
small

Challenge
often
strawberry

✎ Write a Journal Entry

prewrite → draft → revise → proofread → publish

Write a journal entry about something that once surprised you.
- Tell what happened.
- Use some Spelling Words and the word *I*.
- Proofread your work.

Power Proofreading
www.eduplace.com/kids/sv/

Test Tip Make sure you fill in the whole circle.

Test Format Practice

Directions Find the phrase containing an underlined word that is not spelled correctly. If all the underlined words are spelled correctly, mark "All correct."

Example: cross quickly   brick waul   fluffy cloud   All correct
○   ○   ○   ○

1. my house   sawlt shaker   small rock   All correct
○   ○   ○   ○

2. talk softly   white chalk   crawl fast   All correct
○   ○   ○   ○

3. rau meat   red cloth   new blouse   All correct
○   ○   ○   ○

4. would go   soft fur   awfull itch   All correct
○   ○   ○   ○

More Practice
Now write all the misspelled words correctly on a separate sheet of paper.

5. high caust   almost done   two thousand   All correct
○   ○   ○   ○

6. not sold   good lawe   large crowd   All correct
○   ○   ○   ○

Spelling Games
www.eduplace.com/kids/sv/
Review for your test.

Real-World Vocabulary

Language Arts: Giving a Talk

Write the words from the box to complete the directions.
Use your Spelling Dictionary.

Spelling Word Link

talk

expression
subject
pause
rehearse
speech

HELPFUL HINTS

Many people are afraid to give a ___(1)___ in front of others. Here are some tips that can help you.

- Pick an interesting ___(2)___, something that your listeners will enjoy hearing about.

- Write down what you want to say in big letters. That way, it's easy to see.

- Give yourself time to ___(3)___ in front of a few friends. Did you speak with ___(4)___, or did you sound dull? Did you ___(5)___ at all, or did you race along?

1. _____
2. _____
3. _____
4. _____
5. _____

eWord Game
www.eduplace.com/kids/sv/

Try This — CHALLENGE

Complete It! Write a word from the box that completes each sentence.

6. I have to _____ some dance steps.

7. What is the _____ of that book?

8. Jim is giving a _____ at the youth center.

6. _____
7. _____
8. _____

UNIT 12

Review:
Units 7–11

Unit 7

1. _____

2. _____

3. _____

4. _____

5. _____

6. _____

7. _____

Unit 8

8. _____

9. _____

10. _____

11. _____

12. _____

13. _____

14. _____

Unit 7	Short and Long Vowels		pages 54–59
math	toast	thick	socks
Friday	elbow	huge	

Spelling Strategy The short vowel sound can be spelled with one letter. The long vowel sound can be spelled with one or two letters or with the vowel-consonant-**e** pattern.

Fill-in-the-Blank Write the missing words.

What a morning I had last ____(1)____! First, I couldn't find a pair of ____(2)____ to wear. Next, I banged my ____(3)____ on the door. I ate burnt ____(4)____ for breakfast, and I nearly missed the bus. At school I had a surprise quiz in ____(5)____. This turned out to be the best part of my day.

Antonyms Write the word that is the opposite of each word.

6. thin
7. small

Unit 8	Three-Letter Clusters		pages 60–65
scrap	street	scream	throw
spray	stream	strong	

Spelling Strategy Some words begin with the consonant clusters **thr**, **scr**, **str**, and **spr**.

Word Groups Write the word that belongs in each group.

8. road, avenue, _____
9. bit, piece, _____
10. yell, shout, _____
11. river, creek, _____
12. tough, powerful, _____
13. toss, pitch, _____
14. squirt, mist, _____

Unit 9   Unexpected Consonant Patterns   pages 66–71

wreck	knee	patch	knife
scratch	knock	wrong	

Spelling Strategy Some words have unexpected consonant patterns.

/n/ → **kn**ee   /r/ → **wr**eck   /ch/ → scra**tch**

Word Clues Write the word that matches each clue.

15. bend in the leg
16. not correct
17. rhymes with *neck*
18. _____ on the door.

19. covers a tear
20. done with a claw
21. goes with a fork

Unit 10   Vowel Sound in *clown*   pages 72–77

bow	power	crowd	sound
count	frown	⚠ would	

Spelling Strategy The /ou/ sound, as in *bow* or *count*, is often spelled **ow** or **ou**.

Word Pairs Write the word to finish the second sentence in each pair.

22. *Letters* are used to spell.
    Numbers are used to _____.
23. If you are *happy* you *smile*.
    If you are *sad* you _____.
24. A group of *birds* is a *flock*.
    A group of *people* is a _____.

Letter Swap Change the letters in dark print. Write Spelling Words.

25. bo**x**   26. **c**ould   27. sou**th**   28. **t**ower

Unit 9

15. _____
16. _____
17. _____
18. _____
19. _____
20. _____
21. _____

Unit 10

22. _____
23. _____
24. _____
25. _____
26. _____
27. _____
28. _____

Spelling Review

Unit 11

29. _____

30. _____

31. _____

32. _____

33. _____

34. _____

35. _____

Unit 11	Vowel Sound in *lawn*		pages 78–83
awful	almost	law	cloth
cost	chalk	lawn	

Spelling Strategy These patterns can spell the /ô/ sound: **a** before **l**, as in *almost;* **o**, as in *cost;* **aw**, as in *awful.*

Fill-in-the-Blank Write the missing words.

It did not rain for ___(29)___ two months this summer. This problem was not just bad, it was ___(30)___! Our town passed a new ___(31)___. People could not water their ___(32)___. Everyone had to save water.

Context Sentences Write the word that completes each sentence.

33. He used red _____ to write on the sidewalk.

34. How much money does this camera _____?

35. Please wipe the table with a wet _____.

Challenge Words

36. _____

37. _____

38. _____

39. _____

40. _____

Challenge Words	Units 7–11	pages 54–83
holiday	scramble	wrinkle
coward	often	

Word Meaning Write the word for each meaning.

36. to mix up
37. special day
38. a small fold
39. not brave
40. many times

Spelling (and) Writing

Proofread Instructions

Spelling and Grammar Mixed Review Proofread these instructions. Use proofreading marks to fix **five** spelling mistakes, **two** missing capital letters, and **two** errors in plural nouns.

Example: On monday we will ~~wach~~ ^watch^ the birds.

How to Make a Bird Feeder

Making a bird feeder is fun to do on a saturday. First, cut a rownd grapefruit in half. Then skrape out the fruit. Poke three hole near the edges. Next, tie a piece of streeng through each hole. Join the pieces on top with a nott. Finally, fill the shell with stuf like seeds and hang from a tree. In january, all the bird will really like it.

Proofreading Marks

¶	Indent
∧	Add
⌐	Delete
≡	Capital letter
/	Small letter

Write Instructions

prewrite → draft → revise → proofread → publish

Think of something you know how to do well. Write instructions that tell how to do it.

- Use some Spelling Words from Units 7–11.
- Proofread your work.

Tips

- Begin with a topic sentence.
- List all the steps in order.
- Use order words like **first, then, next,** and **finally**.

Power Proofreading
www.eduplace.com/kids/sv/

Spelling Test Practice

Test Tip Read all the words carefully.

Directions This test will show how well you can spell.

- Many of the questions in this test have spelling mistakes. Some do not have any mistakes at all.
- Look for mistakes in spelling.
- If there is a mistake, fill in the answer space on your answer sheet that has the same letter as the **line** with the mistake.
- If there is no mistake, fill in the last answer space.

Example:

Ⓐ Ⓑ Ⓒ Ⓓ Ⓔ

Answer Sheet

1. Ⓐ Ⓑ Ⓒ Ⓓ Ⓔ
2. Ⓙ Ⓚ Ⓛ Ⓜ Ⓝ
3. Ⓐ Ⓑ Ⓒ Ⓓ Ⓔ
4. Ⓙ Ⓚ Ⓛ Ⓜ Ⓝ
5. Ⓐ Ⓑ Ⓒ Ⓓ Ⓔ
6. Ⓙ Ⓚ Ⓛ Ⓜ Ⓝ

Example:
- **A** crown
- **B** stranje
- **C** life
- **D** program
- **E** (No mistakes)

1.
- **A** chease
- **B** crawl
- **C** thing
- **D** stretch
- **E** (No mistakes)

2.
- **J** spring
- **K** thousend
- **L** cross
- **M** sold
- **N** (No mistakes)

3.
- **A** blouse
- **B** tight
- **C** wall
- **D** window
- **E** (No mistakes)

4.
- **J** lie
- **K** spoke
- **L** threw
- **M** opin
- **N** (No mistakes)

5.
- **A** blind
- **B** clown
- **C** solt
- **D** itch
- **E** (No mistakes)

6.
- **J** excuz
- **K** real
- **L** write
- **M** paid
- **N** (No mistakes)

Spelling Games
www.eduplace.com/kids/sv/
Review for your test.

Test Tip Answer easy questions first.

Directions Read each sentence. Use the other words in the sentence to help you decide what the underlined word means.

Example: **The <u>cost</u> of milk keeps going up.**
<u>Cost</u> means –

- ○ price
- ○ weight
- ○ shelf
- ○ color

1. **The ride on the roller coaster gave us a <u>thrill</u>.**
   <u>Thrill</u> means –
   - ○ idea
   - ○ excitement
   - ○ present
   - ○ ticket

2. **You can bake apples or eat them <u>raw</u>.**
   <u>Raw</u> means –
   - ○ uncooked
   - ○ cut into pieces
   - ○ cold
   - ○ quickly

3. **The movie was so scary I was afraid to <u>watch</u> it.**
   <u>Watch</u> means –
   - ○ enjoy
   - ○ look at
   - ○ use
   - ○ buy

4. **She will <u>invite</u> ten friends to her party.**
   <u>Invite</u> means –
   - ○ send
   - ○ have
   - ○ ask
   - ○ bring

Sort for *oy*

1.

2.

3.

Sort for *oi*

4.

5.

6.

7.

8.

9.

10.

11.

12.

13.

14.

Read the Spelling Words and sentences.

Basic Words

1. joy	*joy*	The baby laughed with **joy**.
2. point	*point*	I can **point** to Mars.
3. voice	*voice*	Serena has a soft **voice**.
4. join	*join*	Will Don **join** the team?
5. oil	*oil*	Our car needs a quart of **oil**.
6. coin	*coin*	A dime is a small **coin**.
7. noise	*noise*	The bus makes a lot of **noise**!
8. spoil	*spoil*	Did the food **spoil** in the sun?
9. toy	*toy*	My puppy plays with a **toy**.
10. joint	*joint*	The knee is a **joint** in the leg.
11. boy	*boy*	We have a new **boy** in class.
12. soil	*soil*	I plant seeds in the **soil**.
13. choice	*choice*	Which movie is your **choice**?
14. boil	*boil*	Please **boil** these two eggs.

Review

15. come   16. are

Challenge

17. *poison*   18. *destroy*

Think about the Spelling Strategy.

Each Basic Word has the vowel sound you hear in *joy*. This sound is shown as /oi/. The /oi/ sound is spelled *oy* or *oi*.

/oi/ j**oy**, p**oi**nt

Sort and write the words.

Write each Basic Word under its spelling of the /oi/ sound. Circle the letters that spell the /oi/ sound.

Phonics

Write Basic Words to answer the questions.

15. Which word begins with *ch*?

16. Which word begins with *sp*?

17. Which word ends with the *z* sound?

18–19. Which two words begin with the same three letters as *joined*?

Vocabulary: Fill-in-the-Blank

Write the missing Basic Words.

Yesterday I was digging in the _(20)_. Suddenly, I saw a small metal circle. It looked like an old _(21)_. I called to my dad in a loud _(22)_. He asked me where I found it. I used my finger to _(23)_ to the spot. I had found something important! I felt a lot of _(24)_!

Challenge Words

Write a Challenge Word that fits each meaning. Use your Spelling Dictionary.

25. something that can cause illness or death

26. to ruin completely

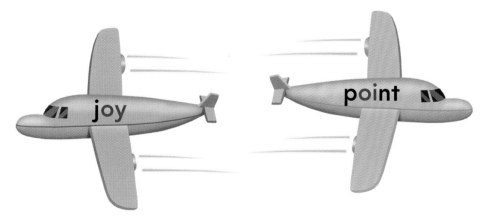

Phonics

15. _____

16. _____

17. _____

18. _____

19. _____

Fill-in-the-Blank

20. _____

21. _____

22. _____

23. _____

24. _____

Challenge Words

25. _____

26. _____

At Home With a family member, write each Spelling Word on a small piece of paper. Work together to arrange the words in ABC order.

Word Meaning

1. _____
2. _____
3. _____
4. _____
5. _____
6. _____
7. _____
8. _____
9. _____
10. _____
11. _____
12. _____

Word Meaning: Antonyms

An **antonym** is a word that means the opposite of another word.

The woods are **quiet** on this peaceful afternoon.

The mall is **noisy** with children shouting.

Practice Write the antonym for each word on the footballs. Use the words from the box. Use your Spelling Dictionary.

joy	melt	clean	wide
wake	smile	sick	dark
front	grow	empty	remember

1. full

5. forget

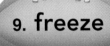
9. freeze

2. sleep

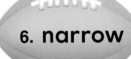
6. narrow

10. dirty

3. light

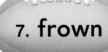
7. frown

11. healthy

4. sadness

8. back

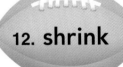
12. shrink

Proofread a Sign

Spelling and the Verb *be* Proofread this pool sign. Use proofreading marks to fix **four** spelling mistakes and **two** mistakes in the forms of the verb *be*.

Example: I ~~is~~ the first ~~bouy~~ to dive off the board.
(am) (boy)

Proofreading Marks

¶	Indent
∧	Add
⅋	Delete
≡	Capital letter
/	Small letter

Pool Information

We is happy that you have comm to our pool.

We hope you will join a swimming class.

Sunscreen oyl is free for anyone who needs it.

Babies can bring a toi into the baby pool.

Listen for the lifeguard's voise while you swim.

She are the boss.

Basic

joy
point
voice
join
oil
coin
noise
spoil
toy
joint
boy
soil
choice
boil

Review

come
are

Challenge

poison
destroy

Write a Sign

prewrite → draft → revise → proofread → publish

Write a sign for a library, a park, or another public place.
- Include some rules and helpful information.
- Use some Spelling Words and present tense forms of *be*.
- Proofread your work.

Power Proofreading
www.eduplace.com/kids/sv/

Test Tip If you change an answer, erase your first answer completely.

Test Format Practice

Directions Read each group of sentences. Decide if one of the underlined words is spelled wrong or if there is *No mistake*. Fill in the space for the answer you have chosen.

Example:
- ◯ I heard a loud <u>noise</u>.
- ◯ A nickel is a <u>koin</u>.
- ◯ Her <u>blouse</u> was pink.
- ◯ No mistake

---

1. ◯ He felt great <u>joy</u>.
   ◯ Please <u>boile</u> the potatoes.
   ◯ I <u>told</u> the truth.
   ◯ No mistake

2. ◯ They did not <u>point</u>.
   ◯ This is my new <u>toy</u>.
   ◯ Did the train <u>comme</u>?
   ◯ No mistake

3. ◯ Will the milk <u>spoil</u>?
   ◯ We <u>arr</u> all here.
   ◯ A tire is <u>round</u>.
   ◯ No mistake

4. ◯ She has a soft <u>voice</u>.
   ◯ Please <u>join</u> us.
   ◯ Did you <u>oil</u> the door?
   ◯ No mistake

5. ◯ Jack is a <u>pilot</u>.
   ◯ I know that <u>boi</u>.
   ◯ This is a good <u>choice</u>.
   ◯ No mistake

6. ◯ The elbow is a <u>joynt</u>.
   ◯ My <u>socks</u> got wet.
   ◯ A seed will grow in <u>soil</u>.
   ◯ No mistake

7. ◯ We are <u>almost</u> there.
   ◯ I saw a <u>thousend</u> birds.
   ◯ Try not to <u>frown</u>.
   ◯ No mistake

8. ◯ The <u>chalk</u> is gone.
   ◯ Do not <u>scratch</u> the car.
   ◯ I heard a <u>screem</u>.
   ◯ No mistake

More Practice
Now write all the misspelled words correctly on a separate sheet of paper.

Spelling Games
www.eduplace.com/kids/sv/
Review for your test.

Real-World Vocabulary

Health: Poison Ivy

Write the words from the box to complete the letter.
Use your Spelling Dictionary.

**Spelling
Word Link**

soil
harmful
calamine lotion
irritate
blister
contact

Dear Sarah,

Last week I got an itchy rash on my arms.
Then a ____(1)____ popped up. It was poison ivy!
Mom told me to stop scratching because it
would ____(2)____ the poison ivy and make it
worse. Then she put ____(3)____ on my arms, and
the itching stopped. Whew!

If you see a plant with shiny green and red
leaves that grow in sets of three, watch out!
It could be poison ivy, which is ____(4)____ to
many people. If you come in ____(5)____ with the
plant, you should wash right away.

Mike

1. _____

2. _____

3. _____

4. _____

5. _____

eWord Game
www.eduplace.com/kids/sv/

Try This CHALLENGE

Yes or No? Write *yes* or *no* to answer
each question.

6. Is good food harmful to your health?

7. Can smoke from a campfire irritate your eyes?

8. Can you get a blister if you burn your hand?

6. _____

7. _____

8. _____

Read the Spelling Words and sentences.

Basic Words

1.	horse	horse	She likes to ride on a **horse**.
2.	mark	mark	I made a **mark** with a pen.
3.	ear	ear	Can he hear with his sore **ear**?
4.	storm	storm	The **storm** left huge puddles.
5.	smart	smart	Our puppy is very **smart**!
6.	acorn	acorn	The squirrel ate an **acorn**.
7.	fear	fear	I used to **fear** the dark.
8.	artist	artist	The **artist** drew a picture.
9.	forest	forest	Deer live in the **forest**.
10.	March	March	My birthday is in **March**.
11.	clear	clear	The sky is **clear** today.
12.	north	north	Drive **north** to get home.
(!) 13.	heart	heart	I can feel my **heart** beat.
(!) 14.	fourth	fourth	My friend is in **fourth** grade.

Sort for /ôr/

1. _____

2. _____

3. _____

4. _____

5. _____

6. _____

Sort for /är/

7. _____

8. _____

9. _____

10. _____

11. _____

Sort for /îr/

12. _____

13. _____

14. _____

Review

15. year   16. story

Challenge

17. partner   18. fortune

Think about the Spelling Strategy.

Each word has a vowel sound + *r*. These sounds are shown as /ôr/, /är/, and /îr/.

/ôr/ h**or**se   /är/ m**ar**k   /îr/ **ear**

(!) How are the Memory Words different?

Sort and write the words.

Write each Basic Word under its vowel + /r/ sounds. Circle the letters that spell the /ôr/, /är/, or /îr/ sounds.

Phonics

Write Basic Words for your answers.

15–17. Write the three words that rhyme with *dear*.

18. Write the word that begins with the /ā/ sound.

19. Write the word that has the /ĭ/ sound spelled **i**.

Vocabulary: Classifying

Write the Basic Word that belongs in each group.

20. second, third, _____

21. east, south, _____

22. January, February, _____

23. elephant, cat, _____

24. jungle, park, _____

Challenge Words

Write the Challenge Word that completes each sentence. Use your Spelling Dictionary.

25. The treasure chest held a _____ in gold bars, old coins, and silver rings.

26. The man looked for a _____ to dance with.

Phonics

15. _____

16. _____

17. _____

18. _____

19. _____

Classifying

20. _____

21. _____

22. _____

23. _____

24. _____

Challenge Words

25. _____

26. _____

At Home — With a family member, take turns printing the first and last letters of a Spelling Word on a card. The other person writes the missing letters.

Word Meaning

1. _____
2. _____
3. _____
4. _____
5. _____

Word Meaning: Analogies

An **analogy** looks at pairs of words to see how they are alike. One kind of analogy compares antonyms, or words with opposite meanings.

Example: *Day* is to *night* as *hot* is to *cold*.

Practice Write the word from the box that completes each analogy. Use your Spelling Dictionary.

clear	thin	late	none	north

1. *Windy* is to *calm* as *cloudy* is to _____.
2. *East* is to *west* as *south* is to _____.
3. *Tall* is to *short* as *thick* is to _____.
4. *More* is to *less* as *all* is to _____.
5. *Fast* is to *slow* as *early* is to _____.

Dictionary

6. _____
7. _____
8. _____
9. _____
10. _____

Dictionary: More Than One Meaning

If an entry word has more than one meaning, the meanings are numbered. A sample sentence may also be given.

mark (märk) *n., pl.* **marks** **1.** A visible trace, such as a scratch on a surface: *The car had a mark on it.* **2.** A written symbol: *The sentence needs an exclamation mark.* **3.** Something, as a line, that shows position.

Practice Write the number to tell which meaning of *mark* is used in each sentence. Use your Spelling Dictionary.

6. The runners are at the starting <u>mark</u>.
7. What is that red <u>mark</u> on the wall?
8. I forgot to write a question <u>mark</u>.
9. My book has a big <u>mark</u> on the cover.
10. Each white <u>mark</u> shows how far you jumped.

Proofread a Weather Report

Spelling and the Verb *be* Proofread this weather report. Use proofreading marks to fix **five** spelling mistakes and **two** mistakes in the forms of the verb *be*.

Example: The storm ~~were~~ was awful in ~~Marche~~ March.

WEATHER ALERT!

The fourth hurricane of the yeer arrived this morning. The weatherman were right. The winds was powerful. The hurricane swept through the hart of town. It is clear that it will keep moving noth. Be smat! Stay inside and listen for more on this storey!

Proofreading Marks

¶	Indent
∧	Add
‿	Delete
≡	Capital letter
/	Small letter

Basic
horse
mark
ear
storm
smart
acorn
fear
artist
forest
March
clear
north
! heart
! fourth

Review
year
story

Challenge
partner
fortune

Write a Weather Report

prewrite → draft → revise → proofread → publish

Write a weather report about a storm or some unusual type of weather.

- Tell some facts about the weather and give some advice.
- Use some Spelling Words and forms of the verb *be*.
- Proofread your work.

Power Proofreading
www.eduplace.com/kids/sv/

✓ **Test Tip** Do not spend too much time on one question.

Test Format Practice

Directions Find the phrase containing an underlined word that is not spelled correctly. If all the underlined words are spelled correctly, mark "All correct."

Example: boil water   left eer   very smart   All correct
○   ○   ○   ○

---

1. huge storm   good artest   baby powder   All correct
○   ○   ○   ○

2. thick forast   not clear   fast horse   All correct
○   ○   ○   ○

3. brown acorn   no fear   long storrey   All correct
○   ○   ○   ○

4. next yere   this spring   last March   All correct
○   ○   ○   ○

More Practice
Now write all the misspelled words correctly on a separate sheet of paper.

5. red heart   crawl slowly   yellow marke   All correct
○   ○   ○   ○

Spelling Games
www.eduplace.com/kids/sv/
Review for your test.

6. forthe grade   go north   large crowd   All correct
○   ○   ○   ○

Real-World Vocabulary

Science: Seasons

Write the words from the box to complete the essay.
Use your Spelling Dictionary.

THE SEASONS GO BY

A new year begins on the first day in
____(1)____. I enjoy the winter snow, but by March
I am ready for warmer days. Spring showers
often begin in the month of ____(2)____. Then
showers bring us lovely flowers in ____(3)____.
Next come the hot, lazy days of summer.
I am sad when the summer ends. In ____(4)____
I'm back in school. I love the colorful days
of fall, too. The year comes to a close in
____(5)____ as winter returns. Another
wonderful year has gone by.

Spelling Word Link

March

May
December
April
September
January

1. _____

2. _____

3. _____

4. _____

5. _____

eWord Game
www.eduplace.com/kids/sv/

CHALLENGE

Fix It! Replace each underlined word with
a word from the box.

6. Fall begins in <u>February</u>.

7. New Year's Day is <u>August</u> 1.

8. The month before June is <u>October</u>.

6. _____

7. _____

8. _____

Read the Spelling Words and sentences.

Basic Words

1.	nurse	*nurse*	A **nurse** helps the sick man.
2.	work	*work*	They **work** in an office.
3.	shirt	*shirt*	My **shirt** has a pocket.
4.	hurt	*hurt*	Does your throat **hurt**?
5.	first	*first*	Tyler is in **first** grade.
6.	word	*word*	How do you spell this **word**?
7.	serve	*serve*	Dad likes to **serve** dinner.
8.	curly	*curly*	Does she have **curly** hair?
9.	dirt	*dirt*	Please wipe off the **dirt**.
10.	third	*third*	I am **third** in line.
11.	worry	*worry*	Do not **worry** about a mistake.
12.	turn	*turn*	Can you **turn** the knob?
13.	bird	*bird*	I see a **bird** in a nest.
! 14.	were	*were*	The children **were** happy.

Review
15. her 16. girl

Challenge
17. perfect 18. hamburger

Think about the Spelling Strategy.

Each word has the vowel + /r/ sounds that you hear in *nurse*. These sounds are shown as /ûr/. The /ûr/ sounds can be spelled *ur*, *or*, *ir*, or *er*.

/ûr/ n**ur**se, w**or**k, sh**ir**t, s**er**ve

! How is the Memory Word different?

Sort and write the words.

Write each Basic Word under its spelling of the /ûr/ sounds. Circle the letters that spell the /ûr/ sounds.

Sort for *ur*
1. _____
2. _____
3. _____
4. _____

Sort for *or*
5. _____
6. _____
7. _____

Sort for *ir* or *er*
8. _____
9. _____
10. _____
11. _____
12. _____
13. _____

Other Spelling
14. _____

Phonics

Write Basic Words to answer the questions.

15. Which word rhymes with *purse*?
16. Which word begins like *think*?
17. Which word begins with *w* and ends with *d*?
18. Which word rhymes with *burn*?
19–21. Which three words rhyme with *skirt*?

Vocabulary: Analogies

Write the Basic Word that completes each analogy.

22. *Go* is to *stop* as *play* is to _____.
23. *End* is to *beginning* as *last* is to _____.
24. *Long* is to *short* as *straight* is to _____.

Challenge Words

Write the Challenge Word that matches each clue. Use your Spelling Dictionary.

25. This can describe something that turned out exactly as you wanted.
26. Some people like to eat this on a bun.

Phonics

15.

16.

17.

18.

19.

20.

21.

Analogies

22.

23.

24.

Challenge Words

25.

26.

At Home — With a family member, take turns "finger spelling" a Spelling Word into the other's hand and guessing the word.

103

Word Meaning

1. _____
2. _____
3. _____
4. _____

🔍 Word Meaning: Bird Words

The words in the house all have *bird* in them. How are their meanings alike?

Practice Write the word from the house that completes each sentence.

1. A person who watches birds is called a _____.
2. That _____ sounds like the bird is laughing.
3. A pet bird usually lives in a _____.
4. What fun it is to watch birds splash and wash in a _____!

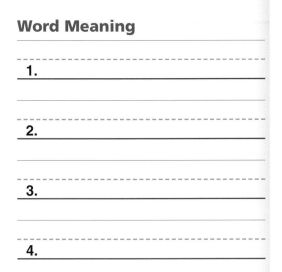

bird
---
birdcage
birdbath
birdcall
bird watcher

Thesaurus

5. _____
6. _____
7. _____
8. _____
9. _____
10. _____

Thesaurus: Exact Words for *bird*

Practice Write a word from the box in place of *bird* in each sentence. Use your Thesaurus.

parrot	penguin	woodpecker
owl	sea gull	peacock

5. The <u>bird</u> spread its blue and green feathers like a fan.
6. This black and white <u>bird</u> cannot fly and loves the cold temperatures.
7. Sean taught his <u>bird</u> to talk.
8. Watch the <u>bird</u> circle above the ocean waves.
9. That noisy <u>bird</u> is making a hole in the oak tree.
10. That <u>bird</u> flies at night and hunts for food.

PART 3 Spelling and Writing

✏️ Proofread a Diary Entry

Spelling and Subject-Verb Agreement Proofread this diary entry. Use proofreading marks to fix **five** spelling mistakes and **two** mistakes in correct verb form.

Example: Students ~~wants~~ *want* to spell every ~~wurd~~ *word* correctly.

Proofreading Marks

¶	Indent
∧	Add
ℐ	Delete
≡	Capital letter
/	Small letter

Dear Diary,

The spelling bee is today. I am trying not to worrey. Last year another gerl and I wer out in the first round. I studied with hur this year. We are in the therd grade now, and we are better spellers. Sometimes a teacher ask a hard word, though. Friends sends me good wishes. Wish me luck, too!

Basic
nurse
work
shirt
hurt
first
word
serve
curly
dirt
third
worry
turn
bird
⚠ were

Review
her
girl

Challenge
perfect
hamburger

✏️ Write a Diary Entry

prewrite → draft → revise → proofread → publish

Write a diary entry about something you are looking forward to.

- Tell about yourself and other people.
- Use some Spelling Words and correct verb forms.
- Proofread your work.

Power Proofreading
www.eduplace.com/kids/sv/

105

Test Tip If you have time, check your answers again.

Directions Find the word that is spelled correctly and best completes the sentence.

Example: Brian is wearing a plaid _____.

schirt	shurt	shirt	shert
○	○	○	○

1. I like his _____ hair.

kurly	curley	corley	curly
○	○	○	○

2. The waiter will _____ you soon.

serv	serve	sirve	surv
○	○	○	○

3. The _____ wanted to buy three dresses.

gurl	girle	girl	gril
○	○	○	○

4. We do not mind hard _____.

worke	wurke	werk	work
○	○	○	○

More Practice
Now write each correctly spelled word on a sheet of paper.

5. Julie gave _____ book report today.

her	herr	hir	har
○	○	○	○

6. Joe washed the _____ off his hands.

dirtt	derte	dirt	durt
○	○	○	○

Spelling Games
www.eduplace.com/kids/sv/
Review for your test.

Real-World ★ Vocabulary

Careers: Nursing

Write the words from the box to complete the ad.
Use your Spelling Dictionary.

HELP WANTED
Nurse

A nurse is needed to __(1)__ a doctor in a busy office. Special __(2)__ will be given to help you in this job. The nurse must be able to get a __(3)__ ready for an __(4)__ by the doctor. The nurse must also help the doctor give certain kinds of __(5)__ .

1. _____
2. _____
3. _____
4. _____
5. _____

eWord Game
www.eduplace.com/kids/sv/

Try This CHALLENGE

Clue Match Write a word from the box for each clue.

6. This is something you take to get better.
7. This is a checkup to see if you are healthy.
8. This is something you need to do some jobs.

6. _____
7. _____
8. _____

PART 1 Spelling and Phonics

Sort for *air*

1. _____

2. _____

3. _____

4. _____

5. _____

6. _____

Sort for *ear*

7. _____

8. _____

9. _____

Sort for *are*

10. _____

11. _____

12. _____

13. _____

Other Spelling

14. _____

Read the Spelling Words and sentences.

Basic Words

1.	air	*air*	The balloon is full of **air**.
2.	wear	*wear*	Please **wear** a warm coat.
3.	chair	*chair*	May I sit on this **chair**?
4.	bare	*bare*	Jan walks with **bare** feet.
5.	pear	*pear*	Do you want to eat a **pear**?
6.	stairs	*stairs*	Tony climbed the **stairs**.
7.	bear	*bear*	A **bear** has a very short tail.
8.	stare	*stare*	We **stare** at the strange sight.
9.	hair	*hair*	Did you comb your **hair**?
10.	care	*care*	I take good **care** of my gerbil.
11.	pair	*pair*	Tami has a new **pair** of shoes.
12.	share	*share*	Will the baby **share** his toys?
13.	fair	*fair*	She rode a pony at the **fair**.
(!) 14.	where	*where*	I know **where** he lives.

Review

15. buy   16. could

Challenge

17. *nightmare*   18. *compare*

Think about the Spelling Strategy.

Each Basic Word has the vowel + /r/ sounds that you hear in *air*. These sounds are shown as /âr/. The /âr/ sounds can be spelled *air*, *ear*, or *are*.

/âr/ **air**, w**ear**, b**are**

(!) How is the Memory Word different?

Sort and write the words.

Write each Basic Word under its spelling of the /âr/ sounds. Circle the letters that spell the /âr/ sounds.

Phonics

Write the Basic Word that has the same beginning sound as each group of words.

15. hand, horse, _____
16. fan, fish, _____
17. call, cape, _____
18. ship, sheep, _____
19. cheese, cherry, _____

cheese   cherry   ?

Vocabulary: Making Inferences

Write the Basic Word that matches each clue.

20. This is a fruit that tastes sweet.
21. This wild animal lives in the woods.
22. You cannot see this, but it is everywhere.
23. You can go up or down on these.
24. Two things make one of these.

Challenge Words

Write the Challenge Word that completes each sentence. Use your Spelling Dictionary.

25. I am going to _____ the main characters in these two books.
26. Each main character has a _____ about a forest fire.

air   wear   bare

Phonics

15. _____
16. _____
17. _____
18. _____
19. _____

Making Inferences

20. _____
21. _____
22. _____
23. _____
24. _____

Challenge Words

25. _____
26. _____

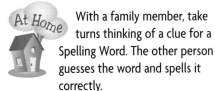

At Home   With a family member, take turns thinking of a clue for a Spelling Word. The other person guesses the word and spells it correctly.

Word Meaning

1.
2.
3.
4.

Dictionary

5.
6.
7.
8.
9.
10.

🔍 Word Meaning: Other Languages

Many animal names come from other languages.

Practice Write a word from the box that fits each clue. Use your Spelling Dictionary.

coyote	giraffe	panda	octopus

1. from Greek, a sea animal with eight arms
2. from Arabic, an animal with a very long neck
3. from Spanish, an animal that is like a wolf
4. from French, an animal that looks like a bear

Dictionary: Part of Speech

A dictionary entry shows if a word is a noun, a verb, or another **part of speech**. Abbreviations are used.

v. = verb

share (shâr) *v.* **shared, sharing** To have, use, or do together with another or others: *Let's share this last orange.* *n., pl.* **shares** A part; portion: *Everyone has an equal share of the pizza.*

n. = noun

Practice Write *verb* or *noun* to tell how *share* is used in each sentence.

5. I <u>share</u> almost all my toys.
6. Hannah ate her <u>share</u> of blueberries.
7. Marc is happy with his <u>share</u> of the reward.
8. Jen will <u>share</u> her markers with you.
9. My little brother does not <u>share</u> anything!
10. Your <u>share</u> of the work is larger than mine.

✎ Proofread a Story

Spelling and Using *good* and *bad* Proofread this story. Use proofreading marks to fix **four** spelling mistakes and **two** wrong forms of *good* or *bad*.

Example: The man hoped things ~~coud~~ get ~~gooder~~.
(*could*) (*better*)

> There once was a poor shoemaker. His cupboards had only air in them. He thought things could not be badder. Some friendly elves decided to help him. They made the goodest shoes the shoemaker ever saw. People came to steir at them. Soon everyone wanted to buye a par of his shoes. His cupboards were not bairre anymore!

Proofreading Marks

¶	Indent
∧	Add
⌷	Delete
≡	Capital letter
/	Small letter

Basic
air
wear
chair
bare
pear
stairs
bear
stare
hair
care
pair
share
fair
where

Review
buy
could

Challenge
nightmare
compare

✎ Write a Story

prewrite → draft → revise → proofread → publish

Write a story that you know, or make up a new one.
- Give details about what happens.
- Use some Spelling Words and forms of *good* and *bad*.
- Proofread your work.

Power Proofreading
www.eduplace.com/kids/sv/

Test Tip Skip the hard questions. Go back to them later.

Test Format Practice

Directions This test will show how well you can spell.

- Many of the questions in this test have spelling mistakes. Some do not have any mistakes at all.
- Look for mistakes in spelling.
- If there is a mistake, fill in the answer space on your answer sheet that has the same letter as the **line** with the mistake.
- If there is no mistake, fill in the last answer space.

Example:

Ⓐ Ⓑ Ⓒ Ⓓ Ⓔ

Answer Sheet

1. Ⓐ Ⓑ Ⓒ Ⓓ Ⓔ
2. Ⓙ Ⓚ Ⓛ Ⓜ Ⓝ
3. Ⓐ Ⓑ Ⓒ Ⓓ Ⓔ
4. Ⓙ Ⓚ Ⓛ Ⓜ Ⓝ
5. Ⓐ Ⓑ Ⓒ Ⓓ Ⓔ
6. Ⓙ Ⓚ Ⓛ Ⓜ Ⓝ

More Practice
Now write all the misspelled words correctly on a separate sheet of paper.

Spelling Games
www.eduplace.com/kids/sv/
Review for your test.

Example:
- **A** clear
- **B** fear
- **C** bear
- **D** kare
- **E** *(No mistakes)*

1.
- **A** chair
- **B** pair
- **C** share
- **D** were
- **E** *(No mistakes)*

2.
- **J** year
- **K** waer
- **L** stairs
- **M** heart
- **N** *(No mistakes)*

3.
- **A** stare
- **B** coud
- **C** are
- **D** pear
- **E** *(No mistakes)*

4.
- **J** hair
- **K** mark
- **L** buiy
- **M** air
- **N** *(No mistakes)*

5.
- **A** bare
- **B** treat
- **C** faire
- **D** stare
- **E** *(No mistakes)*

6.
- **J** wher
- **K** noise
- **L** serve
- **M** fourth
- **N** *(No mistakes)*

Real-World Vocabulary

Science: Wind

Write the words from the box to complete this article from an encyclopedia. Use your Spelling Dictionary.

Spelling Word Link

air

blizzard
motion
hurricane
breeze
tornado

WIND

Wind is the ___(1)___ of air on our planet. You cannot see wind, but you can feel it. A gentle wind is called a ___(2)___. A winter snowstorm with high winds and very cold temperatures is known as a ___(3)___. In warm weather, storms with strong winds and heavy rains often begin in the Atlantic Ocean or Caribbean Sea. This kind of storm is called a ___(4)___. A violent windstorm over land is called a ___(5)___.

1. _____

2. _____

3. _____

4. _____

5. _____

eWord Game
www.eduplace.com/kids/sv/

Try This CHALLENGE

What Am I? Write a word from the box to answer each riddle.

6. I am the opposite of stillness.

7. If you live near the ocean, you may worry about me.

8. I might blow the snow in big drifts.

6. _____

7. _____

8. _____

Read the Spelling Words and sentences.

Basic Words

#			
1.	spoon	spoon	I eat my soup with a **spoon**.
2.	wood	wood	Is this table made of **wood**?
3.	drew	drew	Al **drew** a ship on the paper.
4.	smooth	smooth	We skated on the **smooth** ice.
5.	blue	blue	Julia painted the sky **blue**.
6.	balloon	balloon	Her big **balloon** popped.
7.	flew	flew	The yellow bird **flew** away.
8.	true	true	Is that a **true** story?
9.	stood	stood	Luis **stood** on the ladder.
10.	chew	chew	Dogs like to **chew** bones.
11.	tooth	tooth	Did you just lose a **tooth**?
12.	shook	shook	The baby **shook** the rattle.
⚠ 13.	shoe	shoe	Where is my other **shoe**?
⚠ 14.	move	move	Please **move** your books.

Review
15. blew 16. foot

Challenge
17. loose 18. jewel

Think about the Spelling Strategy.

Each word has the vowel sound in *spoon* or the vowel sound in *wood*. These sounds are shown as /o͞o/ and /o͝o/.

/o͞o/ sp**oo**n, dr**ew**, bl**ue**   /o͝o/ w**oo**d

⚠ How are the Memory Words different?

Sort and write the words.

Write each Basic Word under its spelling of the /o͞o/ or the /o͝o/ sound. Circle the letters that spell the /o͞o/ or the /o͝o/ sound.

Sort for *oo*
1.
2.
3.
4.
5.
6.
7.

Sort for *ew*
8.
9.
10.

Sort for *ue*
11.
12.

Other Spellings
13.
14.

114 Unit 17

Phonics

Write Basic Words to answer the questions.

15. Which word rhymes with *booth*?
16. Which word starts and ends with the same consonants as *draw*?
17. Which word has a double consonant?

18–19. Which two words rhyme with *good*?

Vocabulary: Context Sentences

Write the Basic Word that completes each sentence.

20. We _____ the towel to get out the sand.
21. Please give a _____ to everyone at the table.
22. The United States flag is red, white, and _____.
23. Sandpaper is rough, but computer paper is _____.
24. The plane _____ out of Chicago on time.

Challenge Words

Write a Challenge Word for each clue. Use your Spelling Dictionary.

25. A ring may have this in it.
26. If the ring feels too big on your finger, it is this.

Phonics

15. _____
16. _____
17. _____
18. _____
19. _____

Context Sentences

20. _____
21. _____
22. _____
23. _____
24. _____

Challenge Words

25. _____
26. _____

spoon drew wood blue

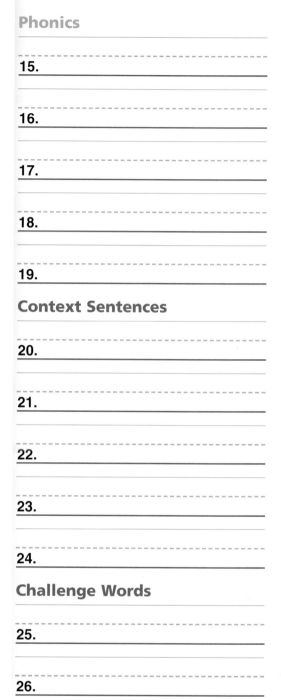

At Home Make word crosses with a family member. Write one Spelling Word across a page. Take turns writing Spelling Words that cross any word you wrote.

Word Families: Rhyming Words

Practice 1–6. Match the words on the board with the sounds on the erasers. Write the words under /o͞o/ or /o͝o/.

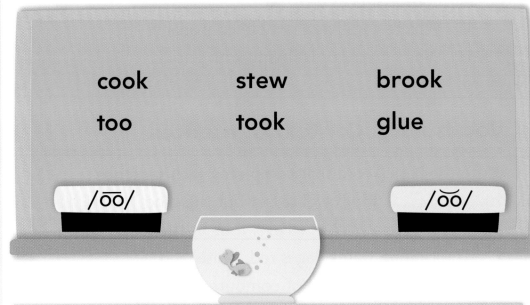

cook   stew   brook

too   took   glue

/o͞o/   /o͝o/

/o͞o/ Words

1. _____

2. _____

3. _____

/o͝o/ Words

4. _____

5. _____

6. _____

Dictionary: More Than One Meaning

This entry for *blue* gives three different meanings.

> **blue** (blo͞o) *adj.* **1.** Having the color of a clear sky. **2.** Having a gray or purplish color, as from cold or a bruise. **3.** Sad and gloomy.

Practice Write the number to tell which meaning of *blue* is used in each sentence. Use your Spelling Dictionary.

Dictionary

7. My fingers are turning <u>blue</u> from the cold.

8. Tina has a bad cold and is feeling <u>blue</u>.

9. Mix dark <u>blue</u> paint with white to lighten it.

10. Dan is wearing a red tie with his <u>blue</u> suit.

11. Seth is feeling <u>blue</u> because rain canceled the game.

12. My toe became <u>blue</u> after I banged it against the door.

7. _____

8. _____

9. _____

10. _____

11. _____

12. _____

Proofread a Poem

Spelling and Using -er and -est Proofread this poem. Use proofreading marks to fix **five** spelling mistakes and **two** mistakes in using -er and -est to compare things.

Example: I ~~shuk~~ *shook* my finger at the ~~smaller~~ *smallest* puppy of all.

Proofreading Marks

¶	Indent
∧	Add
ℴ	Delete
≡	Capital letter
/	Small letter

My Puppy

What I will tell you here is troo.

My puppy ate my new left shew.

He likes to chue things big and small,

And smooth, strong stuff is best of all.

He is the smarter dog of six.

And he does all the greatest tricks.

My left fut is coldest than my right one.

But I moove my toes and have great fun!

Basic
spoon
wood
drew
smooth
blue
balloon
flew
true
stood
chew
tooth
shook
! shoe
! move

Review
blew
foot

Challenge
loose
jewel

Write a Poem

prewrite → draft → revise → proofread → publish

Write a poem about an animal in your life.

- Try to make every two lines rhyme.
- Use some Spelling Words and -er and -est to compare things.
- Proofread your work.

Power Proofreading
www.eduplace.com/kids/sv/

Test Tip Make sure you fill in the whole circle.

Test Format Practice

Directions Read each group of sentences. Decide if one of the underlined words is spelled wrong or if there is *No mistake*. Fill in the space for the answer you have chosen.

Example:
- ○ The story is <u>trew</u>.
- ○ Go to the <u>nurse</u>.
- ○ He did not <u>move</u>.
- ○ No mistake

1.
- ○ I lost a <u>tooth</u>!
- ○ The <u>storm</u> passed.
- ○ A strong wind <u>bloo</u>.
- ○ No mistake

2.
- ○ She held a red <u>balloon</u>.
- ○ Please <u>chew</u> your food.
- ○ Go three blocks <u>north</u>.
- ○ No mistake

3.
- ○ He hurt his <u>fut</u>.
- ○ This stone is <u>smooth</u>.
- ○ Is the ink <u>blue</u>?
- ○ No mistake

4.
- ○ The birds <u>flew</u> south.
- ○ You may <u>erase</u> the answer.
- ○ We <u>stude</u> in line.
- ○ No mistake

5.
- ○ Please use a <u>spewn</u>.
- ○ I have <u>three</u> cats.
- ○ We chopped <u>wood</u>.
- ○ No mistake

6.
- ○ The branch <u>shook</u>.
- ○ She <u>drue</u> a picture.
- ○ Larry tied his <u>shoe</u>.
- ○ No mistake

7.
- ○ Pick up the <u>acorn</u>.
- ○ She is a great <u>artist</u>.
- ○ I was born in <u>March</u>.
- ○ No mistake

8.
- ○ Mel rode the <u>horse</u>.
- ○ You are <u>first</u> in line.
- ○ Try not to <u>wory</u>.
- ○ No mistake

More Practice
Now write all the misspelled words correctly on a separate sheet of paper.

Spelling Games
www.eduplace.com/kids/sv/
Review for your test.

Real-World Vocabulary

Social Studies: Moving West

Write the words from the box to complete this journal entry. Use your Spelling Dictionary.

Spelling Word Link

move

scout
wagon train
explore
oxen
pioneer

April 20, 1883

   Mama says that I should keep a journal on our journey to the West. My family is part of a long ___(1)___. As I write this, we are traveling through the Rocky Mountains. Our wagons are pulled by ___(2)___.

   My older brother is the ___(3)___ who rides ahead. He goes out to ___(4)___ the trail and make sure it is safe for us to travel. I am excited to be a ___(5)___, but I am a little scared, too. I will write more tomorrow.

Ellen Gillette

1. _____
2. _____
3. _____
4. _____
5. _____

Try This CHALLENGE

Clues Write a clue for each of the words in the box on a separate sheet of paper. Trade papers with a partner. Have your partner guess the words.

eWord Game
www.eduplace.com/kids/sv/

Spelling Review

Unit 13

1. _____

2. _____

3. _____

4. _____

5. _____

6. _____

7. _____

Unit 14

8. _____

9. _____

10. _____

11. _____

12. _____

13. _____

14. _____

Unit 13	Vowel Sound in *joy*		pages 90–95
joy	point	voice	oil
toy	joint	boil	

Spelling Strategy The /oi/ sound, as in *joy* and *point*, is spelled **oy** or **oi**.

Fill-in-the-Blank Write the missing words.

1. The guide will _____ the way to the park.
2. The water on the stove is starting to _____.
3. You can hear her loud _____ everywhere.
4. I felt great _____ when I found my lost dog.
5. The baby played with the new _____ for hours.
6. I could not wash the _____ stain out of my sock.
7. The runner rubbed her sore _____.

Unit 14	Vowel + /r/ Sounds		pages 96–101
horse	mark	smart	fear
forest	❗heart	❗fourth	

Spelling Strategy Remember these spelling patterns for the vowel + /r/ sounds:

/ôr/ *or*, as in h**or**se   /är/ *ar*, as in m**ar**k
/îr/ *ear*, as in f**ear**

Synonyms Write the Spelling Word that means the same as each word.

8. wise   9. worry   10. woods

Word Clues Write the word that matches each clue.

11. has four hooves and a mane
12. after third
13. beats in your chest
14. made with a pen or pencil

Unit 15 Vowel + /r/ Sounds in *nurse* pages 102–107

nurse	shirt	hurt	word
serve	bird	⚠ were	

Spelling Strategy The /ûr/ sounds can be spelled **ur**, **or**, **ir**, or **er**.

Letter Swap Change the letters in dark print. Write Spelling Words.

15. w**ire**   16. s**k**irt   17. bi**nd**   18. **n**erve

Fill-in-the-Blank Write the missing words.

My mother is a ___(19)___ at a doctor's office. She takes care of children who are sick or ___(20)___. She always has a kind ___(21)___ to say to every patient. My mother likes to help people.

Unit 16 Vowel + /r/ Sounds in *air* pages 108–113

air	chair	pear	bear
stare	fair	⚠ where	

Spelling Strategy The /âr/ sounds can have these patterns: **air**, as in *air*; **ear**, as in *pear*; **are**, as in *stare*.

Classifying Write the word that belongs in each group.

22. apple, orange, _____
23. table, sofa, _____
24. deer, fox, _____
25. land, water, _____
26. blink, look, _____
27. who, what, _____
28. parade, circus, _____

Unit 15

15. _____
16. _____
17. _____
18. _____
19. _____
20. _____
21. _____

Unit 16

22. _____
23. _____
24. _____
25. _____
26. _____
27. _____
28. _____

Spelling Review

Unit 17

29. _____

30. _____

31. _____

32. _____

33. _____

34. _____

35. _____

Unit 17	Vowel Sounds in *spoon, wood*		pages 114–119
smooth	blue	flew	true
stood	❗shoe	❗move	

Spelling Strategy The vowel sound /o͞o/ may be spelled **oo**, **ew**, or **ue**. The vowel sound /o͝o/ may be spelled **oo**.

Fill-in-the-Blank Write the missing words.

When I got to the beach, I took off my shoes and looked at the __(29)__ waves. Suddenly, a seagull grabbed the lace of my __(30)__! I did not know if I should stay still or __(31)__. Finally, I __(32)__ up. The seagull got scared and __(33)__ away. Lucky for me, it dropped my shoe.

Analogies Write the word that completes each analogy.

34. *Loud* is to *soft* as *rough* is to _____.

35. *Bad* is to *good* as *false* is to _____.

Challenge Words

36. _____

37. _____

38. _____

39. _____

40. _____

Challenge Words	Units 13–17	pages 90–119
destroy	fortune	hamburger
nightmare	loose	

Word Clues Write a word for each clue.

36. ruin

37. lots of money

38. not tight

39. found on a bun

40. a scream dream

Spelling and Writing

Proofread a Story

Spelling and Grammar Mixed Review Proofread this story. Use proofreading marks to fix **five** spelling mistakes, **two** mistakes in the forms of *be*, **one** wrong form of *good* or *bad*, and **one** mistake using *-er* and *-est*.

Example: The acorn were̶ in the fors̶t.
(was; forest)

Proofreading Marks

¶	Indent
∧	Add
ℐ	Delete
≡	Capital letter
/	Small letter

Squirrel's Big Find

One day, Squirrel found a giant acurn. It was tallest than Squirrel! Squirrel wanted to take it home, but it were clere that he could not move it. Squirrel shuk his head with wurry. Just then two chipmunks appeared. Squirrel said he would shair the acorn if they helped him. The big acorn were the goodest lunch they ever had.

Tips

- Include a main character and a setting.
- Include a problem that needs to be solved.
- Include details and some dialogue.

Write a Story

prewrite → draft → revise → proofread → publish

Write a story of your own.
- Use some Spelling Words from Units 13–17.
- Proofread your work.

Power Proofreading
www.eduplace.com/kids/sv/

Spelling Test Practice

Test Tip Make sure you fill in the whole circle.

Test Format Practice

Directions Read each group of sentences. Decide if one of the underlined words is spelled wrong or if there is *No mistake*. Fill in the space on your answer sheet for the answer you have chosen.

Example:
○ The <u>clown</u> is juggling.
○ Please <u>chew</u> your food.
● Adam painted the <u>woll</u>.
○ No mistake

---

1. ○ I sprinkled <u>powder</u>.
   ○ The baby's <u>ear</u> hurts.
   ○ The <u>baloon</u> popped.
   ○ No mistake

2. ○ Enjoy the <u>spring</u> weather!
   ○ I <u>waer</u> hats.
   ○ That <u>boy</u> runs fast.
   ○ No mistake

3. ○ <u>March</u> weather is cold.
   ○ Did you <u>joyn</u> the club?
   ○ Dawn has long <u>hair</u>.
   ○ No mistake

4. ○ Kim finished <u>furst</u>.
   ○ This is a shark <u>tooth</u>.
   ○ The plums are <u>ripe</u>.
   ○ No mistake

5. ○ Did you eat <u>toast</u>?
   ○ The <u>stairs</u> are slippery.
   ○ A rubber band can <u>stretch</u>.
   ○ No mistake

6. ○ Ann <u>droo</u> a picture.
   ○ Here is a plastic <u>spoon</u>.
   ○ We sat up <u>front</u>.
   ○ No mistake

Spelling Games
www.eduplace.com/kids/sv/
Review for your test.

Test Tip If you have time, check your answers again.

Directions For each question, decide which answer has almost the same meaning as the underlined word above it. Then, on your answer sheet, find the row of answer spaces numbered the same as the question. Fill in the answer space that has the same letter as your answer.

Test Format Practice

Example: <u>Shut</u> quietly

   A watch
   B close
   C open
   D lock

Example:

Ⓐ Ⓑ Ⓒ Ⓓ

Answer Sheet

1. Ⓐ Ⓑ Ⓒ Ⓓ
2. Ⓙ Ⓚ Ⓛ Ⓜ
3. Ⓐ Ⓑ Ⓒ Ⓓ
4. Ⓙ Ⓚ Ⓛ Ⓜ
5. Ⓐ Ⓑ Ⓒ Ⓓ
6. Ⓙ Ⓚ Ⓛ Ⓜ

1. <u>Talk</u> clearly

   A grow
   B laugh
   C speak
   D sing

4. <u>Bare</u> feet

   J covered
   K uncovered
   L sore
   M cold

2. Famous <u>artist</u>

   J painter
   K teacher
   L student
   M doctor

5. <u>Curly</u> hair

   A brown
   B straight
   C thick
   D wavy

3. Loud <u>noise</u>

   A people
   B sign
   C traffic
   D sound

6. A <u>real</u> diamond

   J expensive
   K true
   L large
   M fake

Read the Spelling Words and sentences.

Basic Words

1.	hole	*hole*	Max and I dug a **hole**.
2.	whole	*whole*	We ate the **whole** pizza.
3.	its	*its*	The bird is making **its** nest.
4.	it's	*it's*	Now **it's** time to begin.
5.	hear	*hear*	Did you **hear** the news?
6.	here	*here*	Please stop the car **here**.
7.	knew	*knew*	I **knew** the way home.
8.	new	*new*	They bought **new** bikes.
9.	our	*our*	The party is at **our** house.
10.	hour	*hour*	The play begins in one **hour**.
11.	their	*their*	Please hang up **their** coats.
12.	there	*there*	Your book is over **there**.
13.	they're	*they're*	I will go if **they're** going.

Review

14. *road*   15. *rode*

Challenge

16. *peace*   17. *piece*

Sort for Three Homophones

1. _____

2. _____

3. _____

Sort for Homophone Pairs

4. _____

5. _____

6. _____

7. _____

8. _____

9. _____

10. _____

11. _____

12. _____

13. _____

Think about the Spelling Strategy.

Each word is a homophone. **Homophones** are words that sound alike but have different spellings and meanings.

HOMOPHONE	MEANING
/hōl/ **h**ole	an opening into something
/hōl/ **wh**ole	complete

Sort and write the words.

Write the Basic Words under the correct heading.

Vocabulary: Context Sentences

Write the Basic Word that completes each sentence.

14. Do you like my (new, knew) jacket?
15. I (hear, here) the telephone ringing.
16. Dad drilled a (hole, whole) in the wall.
17. I think that (it's, its) a good movie.
18. Where is (their, they're, there) teacher?
19. My (whole, hole) class is going on the trip.
20. Ella (new, knew) the answer to the question.
21. We can pile the books right (hear, here).
22. I hope that (there, their, they're) at home.
23. The cat licks (it's, its) kittens.

Challenge Words

Write the Challenge Word that completes each sentence.
Use your Spelling Dictionary.

24. I need one more (piece, peace) of paper.
25. I am writing about (piece, peace) in the world.

Context Sentences

14. _____

15. _____

16. _____

17. _____

18. _____

19. _____

20. _____

21. _____

22. _____

23. _____

Challenge Words

24. _____

25. _____

At Home With a family member, take turns writing a Spelling Word. The other person writes its homophone.

127

Word Meaning

1. _____

2. _____

3. _____

4. _____

5. _____

6. _____

Word Meaning: Analogies

An analogy can compare synonyms, or words with the same or similar meanings.

Example: *Begin* is to *start* as *end* is to *finish*.

Practice Write the word from the box that best completes each analogy. Use your Spelling Dictionary.

hole	tale	road
kind	rug	close

1. *Lake* is to *pond* as *street* is to _____.
2. *Below* is to *under* as *near* is to _____.
3. *Big* is to *large* as *helpful* is to _____.
4. *Dirt* is to *soil* as *pit* is to _____.
5. *Song* is to *tune* as *story* is to _____.
6. *Animal* is to *creature* as *carpet* is to _____.

Dictionary

7. _____

8. _____

9. _____

10. _____

11. _____

12. _____

Dictionary: Homophones

Look at the dictionary entry below. Notice the ◆ in the last line. This points out the homophone for *hear*.

hear (hîr) *v.* **heard**, **hearing** To take in sounds through the ear: *We hear a dog barking.*
◆ *These sound alike* **hear**, **here**.

Practice Look up each word in your Spelling Dictionary. Write its homophone.

7. blue   9. way   11. sell

8. would   10. no   12. I

Proofread Directions

Spelling and Using *a* and *an* Proofread these directions. Use proofreading marks to fix **five** spelling mistakes and **two** mistakes using *a* and *an*.

it's an
Example: I think it's a easy walk to the park.

Directions to Green Park

Walk on the rode from hour house to town.

Go past a gas station. Keep going past the new

school. Turn right onto Berry Lane. The park is on

the right, after a art gallery. The walk should take

about an our. I once road my bike their. It took only

an few minutes.

Write Directions

| prewrite → draft → revise → proofread → publish |

Write directions from your home to another place.
- Tell how to get there and what places are on the way.
- Use some Spelling Words and the words *a* and *an*.
- Proofread your work.

Proofreading Marks

¶	Indent
∧	Add
℘	Delete
≡	Capital letter
/	Small letter

Basic
hole
whole
its
it's
hear
here
knew
new
our
hour
their
there
they're

Review
road
rode

Challenge
peace
piece

Power Proofreading
www.eduplace.com/kids/sv/

Test Format Practice

✓ **Test Tip** Decide which answer choices are wrong first.

Directions Find the word that is spelled correctly and best completes the sentence.

Example: Would you like to see _____ hats from Mexico?

oure	hour	our	houre
○	○	○	○

1. They _____ for miles before they found a gas station.

roade	rode	roode	road
○	○	○	○

2. I don't know where _____ going after school.

their	thier	there	they're
○	○	○	○

3. I like your _____ red backpack!

knew	knewe	new	newe
○	○	○	○

4. Is your _____ family going to the picnic?

whole	hwole	hole	hoele
○	○	○	○

More Practice
Now write each correctly spelled word on a sheet of paper.

5. The bird flew to _____ nest in the tree.

its'	itss	it's	its
○	○	○	○

6. Please put the vase of flowers _____.

heere	here	heare	hear
○	○	○	○

Spelling Games
www.eduplace.com/kids/sv/
Review for your test.

Real-World Vocabulary

Math: Numbers

Write the words from the box to complete the paragraph from a math textbook. Use your Spelling Dictionary.

Spelling Word Link

whole

decimal
odd
digit
even
fraction

Each of the symbols **0, 1, 2, 3, 4, 5, 6, 7, 8,** and **9** is called a ___(1)___. These symbols stand for whole numbers. The numbers **2, 4, 6,** and **8** are ___(2)___ numbers. The numbers **1, 3, 5, 7,** and **9** are ___(3)___ numbers. Some numbers stand for parts of a whole. For example, $\frac{1}{10}$ stands for one-tenth of a whole number. This is called a ___(4)___. This can also be written **0.1**, which is called a ___(5)___.

1. _____
2. _____
3. _____
4. _____
5. _____

eWord Game
www.eduplace.com/kids/sv/

Try This CHALLENGE

Questions and Answers Write a word from the box to answer each question.

6. What kind of numbers are 3 and 5?
7. What is $\frac{1}{9}$ called?
8. What is .25 called?

6. _____
7. _____
8. _____

Read the Spelling Words and sentences.

Basic Words

1. age	age	The baby's **age** is six months.
2. space	space	The rocket flew into **space**.
3. change	change	Did he **change** his mind?
4. jacket	jacket	Risa put on her **jacket**.
5. center	center	Mark the **center** of the circle.
6. giant	giant	That is a **giant** pumpkin!
7. pencil	pencil	My **pencil** has an eraser.
8. circle	circle	The class sat in a **circle**.
9. once	once	I saw that movie **once**.
10. large	large	Look at that **large** building!
11. dance	dance	We like to sing and **dance**.
12. jeans	jeans	Pedro is wearing new **jeans**.
13. bounce	bounce	That ball can **bounce** high!
14. orange	orange	I bit into a juicy **orange**.

Review
15. nice 16. page

Challenge
17. excited 18. gigantic

Sort for /j/ Spelled j
1. _____
2. _____

Sort for /j/ Spelled g
3. _____
4. _____
5. _____
6. _____
7. _____

Sort for /s/ Spelled c
8. _____
9. _____
10. _____
11. _____
12. _____
13. _____
14. _____

Think about the Spelling Strategy.

Each word has the /j/ sound, as in *jump*, or the /s/ sound, as in *sing*. The /j/ sound can be spelled with the consonant *j* or with the consonant *g* followed by *e* or *i*. The /s/ sound may be spelled *c* when the *c* is followed by *e* or *i*.

/j/ **j**acket, a**ge**, **gi**ant   /s/ spa**ce**, pen**ci**l

Sort and write the words.

Write each Basic Word under its spelling of the /j/ or /s/ sound.

Phonics

Write Basic Words to answer the questions.

15. Which word begins with the same sound as *dark*?

16. Which word rhymes with *barge*?

17. Which word has the /ī/ sound?

18–20. Which three words have the /ā/ sound?

Vocabulary: Analogies

Write the Basic Word that completes each analogy.

21. *First* is to *beginning* as *middle* is to _____.

22. *Hat* is to *cap* as *coat* is to _____.

23. *Hike* is to *walk* as *jump* is to _____.

24. *Shirt* is to *blouse* as *pants* is to _____.

Challenge Words

Write the Challenge Word that means the opposite of each underlined word. Use your Spelling Dictionary.

25. Her mouth fell open when she saw the <u>tiny</u> bug.

26. She was so <u>bored</u> that she started to yell.

jacket   age   giant   space   pencil

At Home With a family member, take turns thinking of a clue for a Spelling Word. The other person guesses the word and spells it correctly.

Phonics

15. _____

16. _____

17. _____

18. _____

19. _____

20. _____

Analogies

21. _____

22. _____

23. _____

24. _____

Challenge Words

25. _____

26. _____

Word Meaning

1. _____

2. _____

3. _____

4. _____

5. _____

Word Meaning: Regional Words

People in different parts of the United States sometimes use different words to name the same thing. For example, a *jacket* may be called a *parka* in some regions.

Practice Write a word from the box to replace the underlined word or words. Use your Spelling Dictionary.

pop	skillet	flapjacks
cellar	sofa	

1. We walked down the steps to the <u>basement</u>.
2. I like to sit on the <u>couch</u> and read a book.
3. Does this restaurant serve <u>soda</u> to drink?
4. Be careful! The <u>frying pan</u> is hot.
5. Brian likes syrup on his <u>pancakes</u>.

Thesaurus

6. _____

7. _____

8. _____

9. _____

10. _____

Thesaurus: Exact Words for *large*

Practice Write the exact word for *large* that best fits each sentence. Choose the word from the pair of words in ( ). Use your Thesaurus.

6. The sailor looked out over the *large* ocean. (heavy, huge)
7. Dinosaurs were *large* animals. (big, enormous)
8. I cannot pick up this *large* box. (heavy, deep)
9. The universe is *large*. (big, immense)
10. These pine trees are very *large*. (enormous, tall)

✏ Proofread an Assignment Sheet

Spelling and Abbreviations Proofread this assignment sheet. Use proofreading marks to fix **five** spelling mistakes and **four** mistakes in abbreviations for months and days.

Example: Get ~~redy~~ _ready_ for the trip on jan. 8.

Day	Assignment
Tues.	Read about whales in my oranje book. Answer questions wonce I am done.
wed	Study for the math test. Do not forget a pensil.
Thurs.	Read about giant apes. Draw a circul around any hard words. Reports are due feb 10. Do a paje of nice drawings.

Proofreading Marks

¶	Indent
∧	Add
൧	Delete
≡	Capital letter
/	Small letter

Basic
age
space
change
jacket
center
giant
pencil
circle
once
large
dance
jeans
bounce
orange

Review
nice
page

Challenge
excited
gigantic

✏ Write an Assignment Sheet

prewrite → draft → revise → proofread → publish

Write an assignment sheet for school.
- List things you have to do for two or three days.
- Use some Spelling Words and abbreviations for months and days of the week.
- Proofread your work.

Power Proofreading
www.eduplace.com/kids/sv/

135

Test Tip Read all the answer choices.
Then choose the correct one.

Directions This test will show how well you can spell.

- Many of the questions in this test have spelling mistakes. Some do not have any mistakes at all.
- Look for mistakes in spelling.
- If there is a mistake, fill in the answer space on your answer sheet that has the same letter as the **line** with the mistake.
- If there is no mistake, fill in the last answer space.

Example:

Ⓐ Ⓑ Ⓒ Ⓓ Ⓔ

Answer Sheet

1. Ⓐ Ⓑ Ⓒ Ⓓ Ⓔ
2. Ⓙ Ⓚ Ⓛ Ⓜ Ⓝ
3. Ⓐ Ⓑ Ⓒ Ⓓ Ⓔ
4. Ⓙ Ⓚ Ⓛ Ⓜ Ⓝ
5. Ⓐ Ⓑ Ⓒ Ⓓ Ⓔ
6. Ⓙ Ⓚ Ⓛ Ⓜ Ⓝ

Example: **A** giant
B cost
C chanje
D socks
E *(No mistakes)*

---

1. **A** center
   B aje
   C soil
   D spoil
   E *(No mistakes)*

2. **J** joint
   K orange
   L bownce
   M chalk
   N *(No mistakes)*

3. **A** jacket
   B horse
   C jeans
   D circle
   E *(No mistakes)*

4. **J** large
   K nize
   L clear
   M spoon
   N *(No mistakes)*

5. **A** joy
   B once
   C dance
   D payge
   E *(No mistakes)*

6. **J** pencil
   K nurse
   L spaice
   M artist
   N *(No mistakes)*

More Practice
Now write all the misspelled words correctly on a separate sheet of paper.

Spelling Games
www.eduplace.com/kids/sv/
Review for your test.

Real-World Vocabulary

Art: Colors

Read these instructions for painting a bird house. Then write the words from the box to complete the instructions. Use your Spelling Dictionary.

Spelling Word Link

orange

beige
aqua
violet
scarlet
olive green

Here is how to paint a bird house.

1. Paint the chimney a shade of red.

2. Paint the pole a shade of green.

3. Paint the walls a shade of brown.

4. Paint the roof a shade of blue and green.

5. Paint the perch a shade of purple.

1. _____
2. _____
3. _____
4. _____
5. _____

eWord Game
www.eduplace.com/kids/sv/

Try This CHALLENGE

Fix It! Replace each underlined word with a word from the box.

6. Water in a swimming pool looks <u>purple</u>.

7. <u>Black</u> is similar in color to red.

8. The sand on a beach looks <u>orange</u>.

6. _____
7. _____
8. _____

137

PART 1 Spelling and Phonics

Sort for /k/ Sound

1. _____
2. _____
3. _____
4. _____
5. _____
6. _____
7. _____
8. _____

Sort for /kw/ Sounds

9. _____
10. _____
11. _____
12. _____
13. _____
14. _____

Read the Spelling Words and sentences.

Basic Words

1.	shark	shark	A **shark** has a big fin.
2.	check	check	Please **check** your work.
3.	queen	queen	The **queen** wore a crown.
4.	circus	circus	Is the **circus** coming to town?
5.	flake	flake	See the first **flake** of snow!
6.	crack	crack	The blue bowl has a **crack**.
7.	second	second	My sister is in **second** grade.
8.	squeeze	squeeze	Please **squeeze** out the water.
9.	quart	quart	Mom bought a **quart** of milk.
10.	squeak	squeak	I heard a mouse **squeak**.
11.	quick	quick	The cat is too **quick** to catch.
12.	sink	sink	You can wash in the **sink**.
13.	quit	quit	He **quit** working at 6:00 p.m.
14.	school	school	We go to **school** to learn.

Review

15. black   16. thank

Challenge

17. correct   18. question

Think about the Spelling Strategy.

Each word has the /k/ sound, as in *shark*, or the /kw/ sounds, as in *queen*. The /k/ sound can be spelled *k*, *ck*, or *c*. The /kw/ sounds can be spelled *qu*.

/k/ shar**k**, che**ck**, cir**c**us   /kw/ **qu**een

How is the Memory Word different?

Sort and write the words.

Write each Basic Word under the /k/ or the /kw/ sounds. Write *squeak* and *quick* under the /kw/ sound.

Phonics

Write a Basic Word to answer each question.

15. Which word has the /k/ sound spelled both *c* and *ck*?

16. Which word begins like *flag*?

17. Which word rhymes with *pink*?

18. Which word begins with the first two letters of *quilt* and ends with the last three letters of *smart*?

19. Which word has the /ûr/ sound?

Vocabulary: Context Paragraph

Write Basic Words to complete this paragraph.

Fluffy got out of her cage again. This is the ___(20)___ time my gerbil has done that. I was ready to ___(21)___ everywhere to find Fluffy. Suddenly I heard a loud ___(22)___. Fluffy was about to ___(23)___ under my closet door. She was so ___(24)___ I almost did not see her!

Challenge Words

Write the Challenge Word that completes each sentence. Use your Spelling Dictionary.

25. Grandma can answer your _____.

26. Her answers are always _____.

shark   check   circus   queen

Phonics

15.

16.

17.

18.

19.

Context Paragraph

20.

21.

22.

23.

24.

Challenge Words

25.

26.

At Home With a family member, take turns writing the last three letters of a Spelling Word. The other person finishes the word.

139

Word Meaning: Onomatopoeia

Some words sound like what they mean. *Squeak* is one example. It means, "a high, thin cry or sound."

Practice Write a word from the box below to complete each sentence.

buzz	splash	boom
slurp	sizzle	

1. Justin jumped into the pool and made a big _____.
2. A loud _____ of thunder woke me up.
3. I heard a fly _____ as it flew past me.
4. Listen to the hot oil _____ in the pan!
5. Mom asked us not to _____ our soup.

Dictionary: Homographs

Some words are spelled the same but have different meanings. These words are numbered and listed separately in the dictionary.

second¹ (sĕk′ ənd) *n., pl.* **seconds** A unit of time equal to 1/60 of a minute: *I will be ready in one second.*

second² (sĕk′ ənd) *adj.* Coming after the first: *Elena won second prize.*

Practice Which meaning of *second* is used in each sentence? Write *second¹* or *second²*.

6. Lance won the race by one <u>second</u>.
7. Emma earned <u>second</u> prize in the spelling bee.
8. What fraction of a minute is one <u>second</u>?
9. Does this really cook in only one <u>second</u> in the microwave?
10. Do you remember the first and <u>second</u> book you ever read?

Word Meaning

1. _____
2. _____
3. _____
4. _____
5. _____

Dictionary

6. _____
7. _____
8. _____
9. _____
10. _____

Proofread a Post Card

Spelling and Abbreviations Proofread this post card. Use proofreading marks to fix **six** spelling mistakes and **one** missing capital letter. Add **one** missing period.

Example: I asked mr. Howe to ~~chek~~ *check* on the plants.

Dear mrs. Howe,

I am in Florida during scool vacation. Dr Stone is here, too. Today we saw a schark with blak eyes at the aquarium. After the aquarium, we quitt seeing the sights. Tomorrow we will see a clown king and kween at the circus. I want to thank you for feeding my cat.

Your friend,

Tim

Proofreading Marks

¶	Indent
∧	Add
⌐	Delete
≡	Capital letter
/	Small letter

Basic
shark
check
queen
circus
flake
crack
second
squeeze
quart
squeak
quick
sink
quit
! school

Review
black
thank

Challenge
correct
question

Write a Post Card

prewrite → draft → revise → proofread → publish

Write a post card to a neighbor about a real or made-up vacation.

- Write a greeting, a message, and a closing with your name.
- Use some Spelling Words and abbreviations for titles.
- Proofread your work.

Power Proofreading
www.eduplace.com/kids/sv/

✓ **Test Tip** Read the sentence and all the answer choices.

Test Format Practice

Directions Find the word that is spelled correctly and best completes the sentence.

Example: There are two pints in a _____.

quarte	quart	kwart	quwart
○	○	○	○

---

1. Please _____ out the last bit of toothpaste.

skweze	squeeze	squeze	squeez
○	○	○	○

2. I will _____ these two eggs into a bowl.

krack	crak	krak	crack
○	○	○	○

3. This _____ spot is ink from my pen.

blacke	black	blake	blac
○	○	○	○

4. Did I _____ you for helping me?

thank	thanc	thanke	thaenk
○	○	○	○

5. The dishes in the _____ are dirty.

sinke	seenk	sink	cink
○	○	○	○

6. Did you hear that high _____?

squeek	squeake	skweak	squeak
○	○	○	○

More Practice
Now write each correctly spelled word on a sheet of paper.

Spelling Games
www.eduplace.com/kids/sv/
Review for your test.

Real-World ★ Vocabulary

Careers: Circus

Write the words from the box to complete the poster. Use your Spelling Dictionary.

COME TO THE CIRCUS!

Hear the ___(1)___ announce each exciting act!

See **HANS**, the ___(2)___, keep seven balls in the air at one time!

Be amazed by **LILY**, the ___(3)___, as she stands on a galloping horse!

Thrill to **ALONZO**, as he walks on a ___(4)___ high above the ground!

Gasp as **JUN YEE**, the great ___(5)___ artist, flies high overhead from swing to swing!

1. _____
2. _____
3. _____
4. _____
5. _____

Try This CHALLENGE

Make a Poster! Make a poster for a neighborhood circus. Use the words in the box to label the circus acts.

eWord Game
www.eduplace.com/kids/sv/

Read the Spelling Words and sentences.

Basic Words

1. birthday   birthday   My **birthday** is in April.
2. anyone   anyone   Does **anyone** know the time?
3. sometimes   sometimes   I ride my bike **sometimes**.
4. everything   everything   Dad put **everything** away.
5. homework   homework   Mom helps me do **homework**.
6. afternoon   afternoon   What a busy **afternoon** this is!
7. airplane   airplane   Rafael flew in an **airplane**.
8. grandfather   grandfather   Isabel visits her **grandfather**.
9. something   something   I saw **something** in the tree.
10. himself   himself   He walks to school by **himself**.
11. faraway   faraway   They sailed to **faraway** lands.
12. grandmother   grandmother   My **grandmother** bakes a lot.
13. without   without   Please do not go **without** me.
14. herself   herself   She drew a picture of **herself**.

Review

15. someone   16. cannot

Challenge

17. scorekeeper   18. everybody

Think about the Spelling Strategy.

Each word is a compound word. A **compound word** is made up of two or more shorter words.

    birth + **day** = birthday   **any** + **one** = anyone

Sort and write the words.

Write each Basic Word. Draw a line between the two words that make up each compound word.

1.
2.
3.
4.
5.
6.
7.
8.
9.
10.
11.
12.
13.
14.

Phonics

Each word below is part of two Basic Words. Write the six Basic Words.

15–16. grand   **17–18.** self   **19–20.** thing

Vocabulary: Word Clues

Write the Basic Word that fits each clue.

21. the part of the day between noon and sunset

22. not close by

23. the day that a person was born

24. a machine that travels through the air

Challenge Words

Write the Challenge Word that completes each sentence. Use your Spelling Dictionary.

25. The coach wants _____ to listen carefully.

26. The _____ is saying that the game is tied.

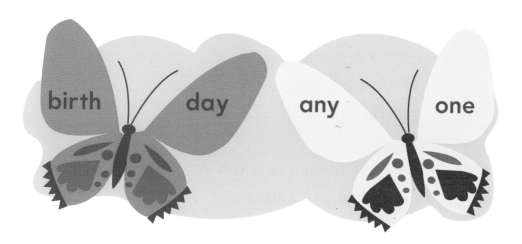

birth   day   any   one

15.

16.

17.

18.

19.

20.

Word Clues

21.

22.

23.

24.

Challenge Words

25.

26.

At Home   Make word crosses with a family member. Write one Spelling Word across a page. Take turns writing Spelling Words that cross any word you wrote.

Word Meaning

1. _____

2. _____

3. _____

4. _____

5. _____

6. _____

7. _____

8. _____

9. _____

10. _____

11. _____

12. _____

Word Meaning: Compound Words

Compound words are made by putting together two shorter words. The compound word has the meanings of both shorter words.

home + work = homework   "work that is done at home"

Train A

shoe	life	pea	snow
rain	hair	bed	out
pop	no	news	gold

Train B

spread	guard	paper	nut
flake	corn	body	lace
fish	doors	cut	coat

Practice Combine words from Train A with words from Train B to make compound words. Write a compound word for each clue.

1. something that an elephant likes to eat
2. something white that falls from the sky
3. an orange pet that swims
4. a person who watches over a beach
5. the opposite of *indoors*
6. something you read that tells what is happening
7. the opposite of *somebody*
8. This goes on a bed.
9. a string to tie your shoe
10. a tasty snack
11. Hair needs this when it gets too long.
12. This keeps you dry in a storm.

PART 3 Spelling and Writing

Proofread a Notice

Spelling and Correcting Run-on Sentences Proofread this notice. Use proofreading marks to fix **six** spelling mistakes and **four** mistakes in run-on sentences.

Example: Give yourself a ~~burthday~~ *birthday* present. join our club.

Study Club

Come join a study club it meets every afternoon. We canot do your homewurk for you, but we can help you with almost everything. If enyone wants to try the club, come talk to sumone here. Come with or witout a friend the club sommtimes meets in the library. We will see you there today!

Proofreading Marks

¶	Indent
∧	Add
℘	Delete
≡	Capital letter
/	Small letter

Basic
birthday
anyone
sometimes
everything
homework
afternoon
airplane
grandfather
something
himself
faraway
grandmother
without
herself

Review
someone
cannot

Challenge
scorekeeper
everybody

Write a Notice

prewrite → draft → revise → proofread → publish

Write a notice for a school bulletin board.
- Tell about a club or an event.
- Use some Spelling Words. Fix any run-on sentences.
- Proofread your work.

Power Proofreading
www.eduplace.com/kids/sv/

Test Tip Read the directions carefully.

Directions Read each group of sentences. Decide if one of the underlined words is spelled wrong or if there is *No mistake*. Fill in the space for the answer you have chosen.

Example: ◯ We play chess <u>sometimes</u>.
◯ Ted enjoyed the <u>program</u>.
◯ He scraped <u>hemself</u>.
◯ No mistake

---

1. ◯ She painted the room by <u>herself</u>.
   ◯ China is a <u>farraway</u> land.
   ◯ His <u>jacket</u> is red.
   ◯ No mistake

2. ◯ Joe is my <u>friend</u>.
   ◯ Is <u>anyone</u> going with us?
   ◯ My <u>grandmother</u> lives near us.
   ◯ No mistake

3. ◯ Today is my big brother's <u>birthday</u>.
   ◯ They have <u>homework</u>.
   ◯ Can <u>sumone</u> find it?
   ◯ No mistake

4. ◯ I <u>kannot</u> leave now.
   ◯ Look at my <u>shadow</u>.
   ◯ We did it <u>without</u> my father's help.
   ◯ No mistake

5. ◯ We leave this <u>afternoon</u>.
   ◯ Mom bought <u>something</u> at the store.
   ◯ Is your <u>gramfather</u> well?
   ◯ No mistake

6. ◯ The <u>airplain</u> landed.
   ◯ We will finish <u>everything</u> before we leave.
   ◯ Hold on to the <u>balloon</u>.
   ◯ No mistake

More Practice
Now write all the misspelled words correctly on a separate sheet of paper.

Spelling Games
www.eduplace.com/kids/sv/
Review for your test.

Real-World Vocabulary

Social Studies: Airplanes

Write the words from the box to complete this page from a book about airplanes. Use your Spelling Dictionary.

Airplanes are a useful form of ___(1)___. Some planes carry people from place to place. Depending on their size, these ___(2)___ planes can carry many people or just the pilot. Other planes transport ___(3)___ rather than people.

Airplanes can also help in an ___(4)___. Some carry medical supplies to people in need. Because it can land in a small space, a ___(5)___ is often used to rush injured people to a hospital.

Spelling Word Link

airplane

helicopter
freight
transportation
passenger
emergency

1. _____
2. _____
3. _____
4. _____
5. _____

e**Word Game**
www.eduplace.com/kids/sv/

Try This CHALLENGE

Yes or No? Is the word in dark print used correctly? Write *yes* or *no*.

6. The scary movie filled us with **freight**.
7. A building is a form of **transportation**.
8. Use the fire escape only in an **emergency**.

6. _____
7. _____
8. _____

Read the Spelling Words and sentences.

Basic Words

1.	I'd	I'd	I said **I'd** go with them.
2.	he's	he's	Zach knows **he's** smart.
3.	haven't	haven't	We **haven't** seen them.
4.	doesn't	doesn't	My aunt **doesn't** know him.
5.	let's	let's	Please **let's** go to the park.
6.	there's	there's	I will visit if **there's** time.
7.	wouldn't	wouldn't	The baby **wouldn't** go to sleep.
8.	what's	what's	Who knows **what's** for dinner?
9.	she's	she's	Emma says that **she's** tired.
10.	aren't	aren't	Why **aren't** you staying?
11.	hasn't	hasn't	The play **hasn't** begun yet.
12.	couldn't	couldn't	The hurt bird **couldn't** fly.
13.	won't	won't	This window **won't** close.
		o'clock	The game starts at four **o'clock**.

Challenge

17. we're   18. weren't

Spelling Strategy.

...tion. A **contraction** is a short way of ... more words. An apostrophe takes ... at are dropped.

... → **I'd**   he is → **he's**

What are the contractions for *will not* and *of the clock*?

Sort and write the words.

Write each Basic Word.

Basic Words

1. _____
2. _____
3. _____
4. _____
5. _____
6. _____
7. _____
8. _____
9. _____
10. _____
11. _____
12. _____
13. _____
14. _____

Phonics

Write Basic Words to answer the questions.

15. Which word begins with the /ī/ sound?

16. Which word begins with the /är/ sounds?

17–18. Which two words have the /ē/ sound?

Vocabulary: Context Sentences

Write the Basic Words that are contractions for the underlined words.

19. Who does not want to go on the picnic?

20. We are sorry we could not visit you last night.

21. She has not read this book yet.

22. Can you see what is inside the box?

23. I think there is an eraser in my backpack.

24. We have not been to the library this week.

Challenge Words

Write the Challenge Words that are contractions for the underlined words. Use your Spelling Dictionary.

25. I guess we are going shopping today.

26. The stores were not open yesterday.

I'd   he's

Context Sentences

19.

20.

21.

22.

23.

24.

Challenge Words

25.

26.

At Home — With a family member, take turns saying a silly sentence for each Spelling Word.

Word Building

1. _____

2. _____

3. _____

4. _____

5. _____

6. _____

Word Building: Contractions

Practice Write a contraction by solving each math problem below. Add an apostrophe to take the place of the letters you subtract.

1. I + have − ha = ___?___

2. here + is − i = ___?___

3. you + are − a = ___?___

4. did + not − o = ___?___

5. she + will − wi = ___?___

6. we + would − woul = ___?___

Dictionary

7. _____

8. _____

9. _____

10. _____

11. _____

12. _____

Dictionary: Spelling Table

How can you look up *doesn't* if you do not know how to spell the /ŭ/ sound? Turn to the **spelling table**, which shows the different ways a sound can be spelled. Check each spelling for /ŭ/ until you find the /ŭ/ spelling in *doesn't*.

Sound	Spellings	Sample Words
/ŭ/	**o, oe, u**	front, come, does, sun

Practice Write the correct spelling for each word below. Use the spelling table above and your Spelling Dictionary.

7. d + /ŭ/ + ne

8. /ŭ/ + nder

9. c + /ŭ/ + ver

10. s + /ŭ/ + me

11. j + /ŭ/ + st

12. l + /ŭ/ + ve

PART 3 Spelling and Writing

Proofread an Ad

Spelling and Commas Proofread this TV ad. Use proofreading marks to fix **five** spelling mistakes and **two** missing commas in compound sentences.

Example: This cleaner is great, and ~~Id~~ *I'd* buy it.

Let's say it is ten oclock in the morning. Your room is a mess! Your clothes are on the floor and games are everywhere. It wo'nt take long to clean but you cant do it. There is'nt anything easier than letting Robot-Cleaner clean your room. You wouldnt believe how fast it works! Buy one today!

Proofreading Marks

¶	Indent
∧	Add
℘	Delete
≡	Capital letter
/	Small letter

Basic
I'd
he's
haven't
doesn't
let's
there's
wouldn't
what's
she's
aren't
hasn't
couldn't
❗won't
❗o'clock

Review
can't
isn't

Challenge
we're
weren't

Write an Ad

prewrite → draft → revise → proofread → publish

Write a TV ad for a real or made-up product.
- Tell why people should buy it.
- Use some Spelling Words and compound sentences.
- Proofread your work.

Power Proofreading
www.eduplace.com/kids/sv/

153

Test Tip If you have time, check your answers again.

Test Format Practice

Directions This test will show how well you can spell.

• Many of the questions in this test have spelling mistakes. Some do not have any mistakes at all.

• Look for mistakes in spelling.

• If there is a mistake, fill in the answer space on your answer sheet that has the same letter as the **line** with the mistake.

• If there is no mistake, fill in the last answer space.

Example:

Ⓐ Ⓑ Ⓒ Ⓓ Ⓔ

Answer Sheet

1. Ⓐ Ⓑ Ⓒ Ⓓ Ⓔ
2. Ⓙ Ⓚ Ⓛ Ⓜ Ⓝ
3. Ⓐ Ⓑ Ⓒ Ⓓ Ⓔ
4. Ⓙ Ⓚ Ⓛ Ⓜ Ⓝ
5. Ⓐ Ⓑ Ⓒ Ⓓ Ⓔ
6. Ⓙ Ⓚ Ⓛ Ⓜ Ⓝ

Example:
- **A** wouldn't
- **B** anyone
- **C** squeak
- **D** shes
- **E** (*No mistakes*)

1.
- **A** whats'
- **B** faraway
- **C** won't
- **D** power
- **E** (*No mistakes*)

2.
- **J** awful
- **K** hasn't
- **L** ca'nt
- **M** everything
- **N** (*No mistakes*)

3.
- **A** haven't
- **B** let's
- **C** could'nt
- **D** himself
- **E** (*No mistakes*)

4.
- **J** o'clock
- **K** second
- **L** he's
- **M** are'nt
- **N** (*No mistakes*)

5.
- **A** isnt
- **B** herself
- **C** there's
- **D** squeeze
- **E** (*No mistakes*)

6.
- **J** doesn't
- **K** Id'
- **L** salt
- **M** frown
- **N** (*No mistakes*)

More Practice
Now write all the misspelled words correctly on a separate sheet of paper.

Spelling Games
www.eduplace.com/kids/sv/
Review for your test.

Real-World Vocabulary

Drama: A Play Review

Write the words from the box to complete the review.
Use your Spelling Dictionary.

Spelling Word Link

o'clock

lighting
comedy
applause
cast
makeup

It's a HIT!

Last night at eight o'clock, a new show opened called *Who's There?* I'm happy to say that the show is a very funny ___(1)___. The audience roared through every act. The wonderful ___(2)___ of actors did a great job. Whoever put on the monster's ___(3)___ should get an award. I've never seen such a silly face! It was too bad that the dim ___(4)___ often made it hard to see the action.

Who's There? is a sure hit. When the curtain came down, the ___(5)___ lasted for five minutes.

1. _____
2. _____
3. _____
4. _____
5. _____

eWord Game
www.eduplace.com/kids/sv/

Try This CHALLENGE

Clue Match Write a word from the box for each clue.

6. You should never be sad watching this.

7. Actors put this on and take it off, but it's not clothing.

8. The cast is very happy to hear this.

6. _____
7. _____
8. _____

Spelling Review

Unit 19

1. _____

2. _____

3. _____

4. _____

5. _____

6. _____

7. _____

Unit 20

8. _____

9. _____

10. _____

11. _____

12. _____

13. _____

14. _____

Unit 19	Homophones	pages 126–131

its	it's	our	hour
their	there	they're	

Spelling Strategy **Homophones** are words that sound alike but have different spellings and meanings.

Context Sentences Write the word that completes each sentence.

1. I hope (their, they're) coming to the fair.
2. The bus will pick us up in one (hour, our).
3. The tree has dropped all of (it's, its) leaves.
4. The children can write (their, they're) names.
5. Kurt will meet us (their, there) later.
6. Mom said that (it's, its) time for supper.
7. Have you seen (hour, our) new school?

Unit 20	Spelling /j/ and /s/	pages 132–137

jacket	center	giant	pencil
circle	jeans	orange	

Spelling Strategy The /j/ sound can be spelled with the consonant **j** or **g** followed by **e** or **i**. The /s/ sound may be spelled **c** when the **c** is followed by **e** or **i**.

Word Groups Write the word that fits with each group.

8. left, right, _____
9. big, huge, _____
10. pants, slacks, _____
11. coat, sweater, _____
12. pen, crayon, _____
13. square, triangle, _____
14. red, yellow, _____

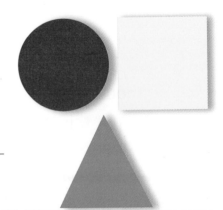

Unit 21 Spelling /k/ and /kw/ pages 138–143

crack	second	squeak	quick
sink	quit	ⓘ school	

Spelling Strategy The /k/ sound can be spelled **k**, **ck**, or **c**. The /kw/ sounds can be spelled **qu**.

Analogies Write the word that completes each analogy.

15. *Connect* is to *join* as *break* is to _____.

16. *Groan* is to *growl* as *squeal* is to _____.

17. *Smart* is to *clever* as *fast* is to _____.

Fill-in-the-Blank Write the missing words.

This morning I was in art class at ___(18)___. When it was time to ___(19)___, my hands were full of paint. I was ___(20)___ in line to wash them. When it was my turn, the drain in the ___(21)___ became clogged. What a mess!

Unit 22 Compound Words pages 144–149

birthday	anyone	homework	afternoon
airplane	grandfather	herself	

Spelling Strategy A **compound word** is made up of two or more shorter words.

Matching Add a word from the second column to each word in the first column. Write a compound word.

22. her   father
23. birth   work
24. home   self
25. air   day
26. grand   one
27. after   noon
28. any   plane

Unit 21

15. _____

16. _____

17. _____

18. _____

19. _____

20. _____

21. _____

Unit 22

22. _____

23. _____

24. _____

25. _____

26. _____

27. _____

28. _____

Spelling Review

29. _____

30. _____

31. _____

32. _____

33. _____

34. _____

35. _____

Challenge Words

36. _____

37. _____

38. _____

39. _____

40. _____

Unit 23	Contractions		pages 150–155
I'd	he's	let's	there's
what's	hasn't	! won't	

Spelling Strategy A **contraction** is a short way of saying or writing two or more words. An apostrophe takes the place of one or more letters.

I would   *I'd*

Word Meaning Write the Spelling Word that means the same as each group of words.

29. I would   33. there is

30. let us   34. will not

31. what is   35. has not

32. he is

Challenge Words	Units 19–23	pages 126–155
piece	excited	question
scorekeeper	we're	

Fill-in-the-Blank Write the missing words.

"The players are tied!" said the ___(36)___. "Now ___(37)___ going to start the final game."

What a thrilling chess match this is! Everyone watching us play is so ___(38)___. I moved my queen. That is an important chess ___(39)___. Who would win? That was the big ___(40)___ on everyone's mind.

Spelling (and) Writing

Proofread a Research Report

Spelling and Grammar Mixed Review Proofread this research report. Use proofreading marks to fix **five** spelling mistakes, **one** run-on sentence, and **one** compound sentence that needs a comma.

Example: ~~Lets~~ *Let's* not disturb the hive. let an expert collect the honey.

Proofreading Marks

¶	Indent
∧	Add
ℛ	Delete
≡	Capital letter
/	Small letter

The Busy Bee

Bee hives have thousands of worker bees but there is only one quene bee. Most of the time shes laying eggs. The worker bees take care of evrything in the hive they also collect pollen.

Bees tell each other where to find pollen in farway places. They do this with a special danse.

Other worker bees then go there to gather the pollen.

Write a Research Report Plan

prewrite → draft → revise → proofread → publish

Think of a topic that interests you. Write three things you want to learn about it.

- Use some Spelling Words from Units 19–23 in your plan.
- Proofread your work.

Tips

- Think about what you know about the topic and what you want to learn.
- Turn your sentences into questions.

Power Proofreading
www.eduplace.com/kids/sv/

Spelling Test Practice

Test Tip If you change an answer, erase your first answer completely.

Test Format Practice

Directions Find the word that is spelled correctly and best completes the sentence.

Example: Our cat likes to _____ the rug.

scratch ○   skrach ○   scrach ○   scretch ○

1. No one _____ the answer to the question.

new ○   noo ○   knue ○   knew ○

2. We saw many elephants at the _____.

cercus ○   circus ○   sercus ○   circas ○

3. The men _____ lift the heavy boxes.

couldn't ○   couldnt ○   could'nt ○   coudn't ○

4. The baby was not able to feed _____.

himsef ○   hymself ○   himself ○   himsalf ○

5. Please don't _____ the ball against the house.

bonce ○   bounce ○   bownce ○   bounse ○

6. They had to climb the _____ to get to the room.

stiars ○   stairs ○   stears ○   steres ○

Spelling Games
www.eduplace.com/kids/sv/
Review for your test.

Test Tip Read all the answer choices. Then choose the correct one.

Directions Choose the word that has the opposite meaning of the underlined word.

Example: <u>shut</u> the door

open ○   lock ○   break ○   touch ○

---

1. a <u>smooth</u> sea

strange ○   long ○   rough ○   calm ○

2. a <u>true</u> story

dull ○   false ○   long ○   unusual ○

3. <u>change</u> the plan

switch ○   go ○   keep ○   find ○

4. these <u>new</u> computers

large ○   fancy ○   small ○   old ○

5. <u>curly</u> hair

dark ○   straight ○   wavy ○   thick ○

6. <u>shiny</u> metal

dull ○   gold ○   bright ○   hard ○

PART 1 Spelling and Phonics

Read the Spelling Words and sentences.

Basic Words

1.	coming	coming	Is Lani **coming** to the party?
2.	swimming	swimming	The pool is open for **swimming**.
3.	dropped	dropped	He **dropped** a dime on the floor.
4.	wrapped	wrapped	Mom **wrapped** my sandwich.
5.	taping	taping	Are you **taping** the concert?
6.	invited	invited	They **invited** Kevin for dinner.
7.	saving	saving	We are **saving** our money.
8.	grinning	grinning	Why are you **grinning** at me?
9.	stared	stared	I **stared** at the movie screen.
10.	planned	planned	Uncle Pablo **planned** a vacation.
11.	changing	changing	The boys are **changing** places.
12.	tapping	tapping	Please stop **tapping** your foot!
13.	joking	joking	They are **joking** and laughing.
(!) 14.	fixing	fixing	Dad is **fixing** the fence.

Review

15. making   16. stopped

Challenge

17. scarred   18. scared

Think about the Spelling Strategy.

When a base word ends with one vowel and one consonant, the consonant is usually doubled before adding -ed or -ing. When a base word ends with e, drop the e before adding -ed or -ing.

drop + p + ed = drop**ped**   come − e + ing = com**ing**

(!) How is the Memory Word different?

Sort and write the words.

Write each Basic Word under the correct heading.

Double Final Consonant

1. _____

2. _____

3. _____

4. _____

5. _____

6. _____

Drop Final e

7. _____

8. _____

9. _____

10. _____

11. _____

12. _____

13. _____

No Spelling Change

14. _____

Phonics

Write the Basic Word that has the same beginning sound or sounds as each group of words.

15. sing, sand, _____

16. step, stone, _____

17. swing, swamp, _____

18. grass, grapes, _____

Vocabulary: Context Sentences

Write the Basic Word that completes each sentence.

19. Kaitlyn _____ Eva to a Fourth of July party.

20. My teacher is _____ our play so that we can see ourselves afterwards.

21. The present is _____ with green paper and a gold bow.

22. I tried _____ to make the audience laugh.

23. Someone is _____ on the window.

24. My little brother _____ his glass of milk.

Challenge Words

Write the Challenge Word that matches each clue. Use your Spelling Dictionary.

25. This is how you might feel at a creepy movie.

26. A tree that had marks or cuts in it would be called this.

coming   dropped

15. _____

16. _____

17. _____

18. _____

Context Sentences

19. _____

20. _____

21. _____

22. _____

23. _____

24. _____

Challenge Words

25. _____

26. _____

At Home Play charades with a family member. Take turns choosing a Spelling Word and acting it out. The other person writes the word.

163

Word Meaning

1. _____

2. _____

3. _____

4. _____

5. _____

🔍 Word Meaning: Analogies

An analogy can compare what someone or something does.

Example: _Dog_ is to _bark_ as _cat_ is to _meow_.

Practice Write the word from the box that best completes each analogy. Use your Spelling Dictionary.

swim	quack	roar	buzz	draw

1. _Author_ is to _write_ as _artist_ is to _____.
2. _Rabbit_ is to _hop_ as _fish_ is to _____.
3. _Snake_ is to _hiss_ as _bee_ is to _____.
4. _Horse_ is to _neigh_ as _duck_ is to _____.
5. _Mouse_ is to _squeak_ as _lion_ is to _____.

Dictionary

6. _____

7. _____

8. _____

9. _____

10. _____

Dictionary: More Than One Meaning

This dictionary entry shows that the word _wrap_ has a verb meaning and a noun meaning.

> **wrap** (răp) _v._ **wrapped, wrapping** To cover by winding or folding something. _n., pl._ **wraps** An outer garment, such as a coat, that is worn for warmth.

Practice Write _verb_ or _noun_ to tell how _wrap_ is used in each sentence. Use your Spelling Dictionary.

6. This shawl is a warm <u>wrap</u>.
7. Please <u>wrap</u> the baby in a blanket.
8. Mom wears a wool <u>wrap</u> when it is cold.
9. We have to <u>wrap</u> that gift right now!
10. Do not <u>wrap</u> the rope around the tree.

PART 3 Spelling and Writing

Proofread an E-mail Message

Spelling and Using *me* Proofread this e-mail message. Use proofreading marks to fix **six** spelling mistakes and **two** mistakes using *I* and *me*.

Example: Dad will go ~~swiming~~ *swimming* with Sara and ~~I~~ *me*.

Proofreading Marks

¶	Indent
∧	Add
⌇	Delete
☰	Capital letter
/	Small letter

Dear Aunt Nicole,

    I was so happy when you invited Dad and I to the beach. Dad and me will be comming in the morning. Sara will be makeing the trip later. Right now Dad is fixxing the car. It stoped running. We had pland to leave at 6 A.M. I hope our plans will not be changeing!

            Love,

            Sabrina

Basic
coming
swimming
dropped
wrapped
taping
invited
saving
grinning
stared
planned
changing
tapping
joking
fixing

Review
making
stopped

Challenge
scarred
scared

Write an E-mail Message

prewrite → draft → revise → proofread → publish

Write an e-mail message to a family member.
- Tell about some plans you have.
- Use some Spelling Words and the words *I* and *me*.
- Proofread your work.

Power Proofreading
www.eduplace.com/kids/sv/

165

Test Tip If you change an answer, erase your first answer completely.

Test Format Practice

Directions Find the word that is spelled correctly and best completes the sentence.

Example: Uncle Bob was only _____ about moving to Australia.

| joaking | jokking | jocking | joking |
| ○ | ○ | ○ | ○ |

---

1. The kite _____ to the ground.

| droped | dropd | dropped | drouped |
| ○ | ○ | ○ | ○ |

2. Jeremy was _____ from ear to ear.

| girning | grinning | grining | grrinning |
| ○ | ○ | ○ | ○ |

3. We are _____ these jars to recycle.

| saving | savving | saveing | saaving |
| ○ | ○ | ○ | ○ |

4. The train _____ for a long time at the station.

| stoped | stoppd | stopped | stopd |
| ○ | ○ | ○ | ○ |

5. What are you _____ with that clay?

| makking | makeing | macking | making |
| ○ | ○ | ○ | ○ |

6. The cat stood and _____ at the dog for a long time.

| starred | stared | staired | stareed |
| ○ | ○ | ○ | ○ |

More Practice
Now write each correctly spelled word on a sheet of paper.

Spelling Games
www.eduplace.com/kids/sv/
Review for your test.

Real-World Vocabulary

Social Studies: Planning a Trip

Write the words from the box to complete this checklist for planning a family trip. Use your Spelling Dictionary.

Spelling Word Link

planned

compass rose
scale of miles
route
interstate
speed limit

✔ Find the best _____(1)_____ to where you are going.

✔ Decide if using the _____(2)_____ highway will save some time.

✔ Use the _____(3)_____ printed on the map to find out how many miles you will need to travel.

✔ Look for signs telling the _____(4)_____ so you don't break the law.

✔ Find north, east, south, and west on the _____(5)_____ to see which direction you are going.

40 M.P.H.

1. _____
2. _____
3. _____
4. _____
5. _____

eWord Game
www.eduplace.com/kids/sv/

Try This CHALLENGE

Clue Match Write a word from the box for each clue.

6. It is a road from state to state.

7. You might think it's a flower, but it isn't.

8. On some roads, it's 35 miles per hour.

6. _____
7. _____
8. _____

Sort for *-ies*

1. _____
2. _____
3. _____
4. _____
5. _____
6. _____
7. _____
8. _____

Sort for *-ied*

9. _____
10. _____
11. _____
12. _____
13. _____
14. _____

Read the Spelling Words and sentences.

Basic Words

1.	cities	cities	I have visited many **cities**.
2.	cried	cried	My aunt **cried** tears of joy.
3.	puppies	puppies	These **puppies** are so cute!
4.	hurried	hurried	We **hurried** to catch the bus.
5.	stories	stories	Please read us some **stories**.
6.	dried	dried	Raisins are **dried** grapes.
7.	carried	carried	Dad **carried** the heavy box.
8.	flies	flies	The airplane **flies** fast.
9.	worried	worried	He **worried** when I was late.
10.	parties	parties	What fun the **parties** were!
11.	tried	tried	Have you ever **tried** to ski?
12.	pennies	pennies	I paid with all my **pennies**.
13.	ponies	ponies	We rode **ponies** at the fair.
14.	babies	babies	Those two **babies** are twins.

Review

15. pretty   16. very

Challenge

17. countries   18. libraries

Think about the Spelling Strategy.

Each Basic Word is made up of a base word and the ending *-es* or *-ed*. When a base word ends with a consonant and *y*, change the *y* to *i* before adding *-es* or *-ed*.

city − y + ies = cit**ies**   cry − y + ied = cr**ied**

Sort and write the words.

Write each Basic Word under its ending.

Phonics

Write Basic Words to answer the questions.

15. Which word rhymes with *married*?

16. Which word rhymes with *guppies*?

17. Which word has the /ûr/ sounds spelled *ur*?

18. Which word has the /ûr/ sounds spelled *or*?

19. Which word has the /ī/ sound and begins with *tr*?

20. Which word has the /ō/ sound?

Vocabulary: Analogies

Write the Basic Word that completes each analogy.

21. *Ponds* are to *lakes* as *towns* are to _____.

22. *Whale* is to *swims* as *eagle* is to _____.

23. *Whispered* is to *screamed* as *laughed* is to _____.

24. *Walk* is to *children* as *crawl* is to _____.

Challenge Words

Write the Challenge Word that completes each sentence. Use your Spelling Dictionary.

25. This city has two public _____.

26. We can read books about many different _____.

Phonics

15.

16.

17.

18.

19.

20.

Analogies

21.

22.

23.

24.

Challenge Words

25.

26.

cities

cried

At Home With a family member, take turns "finger spelling" a Spelling Word into the other's hand and guessing the word.

169

Word Meaning

1. _____
2. _____
3. _____
4. _____
5. _____

Dictionary

6. _____
7. _____
8. _____
9. _____
10. _____
11. _____
12. _____

🔍 Word Meaning: Homographs

You know that homographs are words that are spelled the same but have different meanings. Here are two meanings for the word *fly*.

a. to move through the air with wings

b. an insect, such as the common housefly, that has a single pair of thin, clear wings

Practice Which meaning of *fly* is used in each sentence? Write the letter of the meaning.

1. Geese <u>fly</u> south for the winter.
2. A <u>fly</u> landed on my sandwich.
3. Do you see that giant <u>fly</u> on the window?
4. The airplane will <u>fly</u> to Texas this morning.
5. I wish I had wings so that I could <u>fly</u>.

Dictionary: Base Words

How can you find out how to spell a word that ends with *-ies* or *-ied*? Look up its base word in a dictionary.

> **dry** (drī) *v.* **dried, drying** To make or become free from water or moisture: *Jill dried the wet puppy with a towel.*

Practice Write the base word you would look up in a dictionary to find each word below. Use your Spelling Dictionary.

6. hurried   8. pennies   10. stories   12. carried
7. cities   9. tried   11. worried

Proofread an Ad

Spelling and Abbreviations Proofread this magazine ad. Use proofreading marks to fix **five** spelling mistakes and **three** mistakes in abbreviations of addresses.

Example: Have you tryed our other store? It is on Mountain ave. in Arlington, va 22203.

Gifts for Kids

95 Caldwell st

Springfield, nj 07081

These are our specials this week!

- books, comics, and mystery storys

- rare penneys and other coins

- very prety cups for babies

- dryed flowers for partys and art projects

Basic
cities
cried
puppies
hurried
stories
dried
carried
flies
worried
parties
tried
pennies
ponies
babies

Review
pretty
very

Challenge
countries
libraries

Write an Ad

prewrite → draft → revise → proofread → publish

Write an ad for a store. The store can be real, or you can make it up.

- Write the name and address of the store. Tell what it sells.
- Use some Spelling Words and abbreviations in addresses.
- Proofread your work.

Power Proofreading
www.eduplace.com/kids/sv/

Test Tip Read all the words carefully.

Directions Find the phrase containing an underlined word that is not spelled correctly. If all the underlined words are spelled correctly, mark "All correct."

Example: cryed loudly   two pennies   big box   All correct
○   ○   ○   ○

1. hurryed home   not worried   saving money   All correct
○   ○   ○   ○

2. busy cities   tapping feet   prettey doll   All correct
○   ○   ○   ○

3. cute puppies   our parties   tried twice   All correct
○   ○   ○   ○

4. just joking   dried fruit   verey hard   All correct
○   ○   ○   ○

More Practice
Now write all the misspelled words correctly on a separate sheet of paper.

5. stared at   cute babys   dropped it   All correct
○   ○   ○   ○

Spelling Games
www.eduplace.com/kids/sv/
Review for your test.

6. stopped here   one quart   six ponyes   All correct
○   ○   ○   ○

Technology: The Library

Write the words from the box to complete the poster.
Use your Spelling Dictionary.

There's a World of Fun at the Library!

You will find the latest ___(1)___ books, full of amazing facts.

Take a look at our popular ___(2)___ books, full of fun and fantasy.

Visit our ___(3)___, where you can borrow great movies on VHS and DVD.

You can also listen to our tapes and CDs.

Visit our ___(4)___ to search the exciting world of the Internet and our library catalog.

Stop by soon and be sure to say hello to Ms. Walker, our ___(5)___!

1. _____
2. _____
3. _____
4. _____
5. _____

eWord Game
www.eduplace.com/kids/sv/

Try This CHALLENGE

Where Is It? In which section of the library would you find each of the following? Write a word from the box.

6. a book on United States history
7. a website that gives the current weather
8. a videotape of a cartoon

6. _____
7. _____
8. _____

Read the Spelling Words and sentences.

Basic Words

1. unfold — unfold — How can we **unfold** the cot?
2. replay — replay — She will **replay** the song.
3. untie — untie — I have to **untie** these laces.
4. reheat — reheat — Please **reheat** the pizza if it is cold.
5. unfair — unfair — That trick question is **unfair**.
6. unclear — unclear — His directions were **unclear**.
7. rejoin — rejoin — When can we **rejoin** the team?
8. rewrite — rewrite — Sue will **rewrite** her poem.
9. unhurt — unhurt — I fell down but am **unhurt**.
10. recheck — recheck — Please **recheck** the spelling.
11. unlucky — unlucky — I felt **unlucky**, but then I won!
12. unwrap — unwrap — Will you **unwrap** the present?
13. reuse — reuse — We can **reuse** this glass jar.
14. unsure — unsure — I am **unsure** about my choice.

Review

15. reread   16. unsafe

Challenge

17. unbuckle   18. unknown

Sort for *re-*

1.
2.
3.
4.
5.
6.

Sort for *un-*

7.
8.
9.
10.
11.
12.
13.
14.

Think about the Spelling Strategy.

Each word has a prefix and a base word. A **prefix** is a word part added to the beginning of a base word. It adds meaning to the base word. The prefix *re-* means "again." The prefix *un-* can mean "not" or "opposite of."

un + fair = **un**fair   un + fold = **un**fold

re + play = **re**play

Sort and write the words.

Write each Basic Word under its prefix.

Phonics

Write a Basic Word to answer each question.

15. Which word ends with the /ā/ sound?

16. Which word has a silent *w* and ends with *p*?

17. Which word has the /ō/ sound?

18. Which word ends with the /k/ sound?

Vocabulary: Context Paragraph

Write the missing Basic Words.

Just when the game was tied, Mom called me in to do homework. It seemed so ___(19)___! Would my friends wait for me to ___(20)___ the game? I had to ___(21)___ my story. I finished and jumped up. Then I tripped. Luckily, I was ___(22)___. Somehow I had tied my sneakers together. I had to quickly ___(23)___ the knot. I thought I was having an ___(24)___ day. Then I got in the game and hit a home run!

Challenge Words

Write the Challenge Word that completes each sentence. Use your Spelling Dictionary.

25. Please do not _____ your seatbelt.

26. We explored an _____ part of the woods.

replay   unfair   unfold

Context Paragraph

19. _____

20. _____

21. _____

22. _____

23. _____

24. _____

Challenge Words

25. _____

26. _____

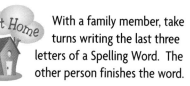

At Home   With a family member, take turns writing the last three letters of a Spelling Word. The other person finishes the word.

Word Building

_____
1. _____
_____
2. _____
_____
3. _____
_____
4. _____
_____
5. _____
_____
6. _____

Word Building: *re-* and *un-*

Practice Add *re-* or *un-* to a word from the chest. Write a new word to match each clue.

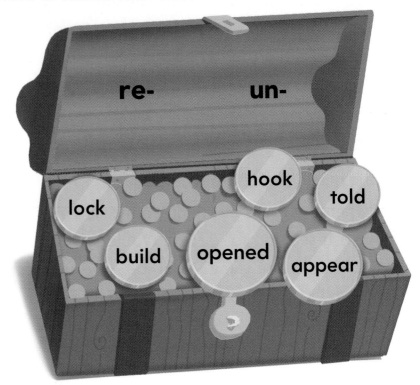

1. opposite of *hook*
2. not told
3. build again
4. opposite of *lock*
5. appear again
6. not opened

Dictionary: Prefixes

Not all words with prefixes are listed as entry words. If you want to find the meaning of *recheck*, look up the prefix *re-* and the base word *check*.

> **re-** A prefix that means "again": *refill*.

Practice Write the prefix and the base word you would look up to find the meaning of each word below.

7. unseal
8. rewrap
9. unmake
10. refold
11. repack
12. replay

Dictionary

_____
7. _____
_____
8. _____
_____
9. _____
_____
10. _____
_____
11. _____
_____
12. _____

PART 3 Spelling and Writing

✏ Proofread Instructions

Spelling and Verbs Proofread these instructions. Use proofreading marks to fix **five** spelling mistakes and **two** mistakes using verbs with pronouns.

Example: I ~~reads~~ _read_ the instructions before I ~~unrap~~ _unwrap_ the bag.

Proofreading Marks

¶	Indent
∧	Add
⌀	Delete
≡	Capital letter
/	Small letter

Making Microwave Popcorn

Important: It is unssafe to do this alone.

1. First, unfold the bag. It need to lie flat.

2. Next, set the timer and start the oven. If you are unshure about the timing, and the instructions are uncleare, turn off the oven when the popping stops.

3. Then you opens the bag after it cools.

4. Do not reheet unpopped kernels. Never reuze the bag.

Basic
unfold
replay
untie
reheat
unfair
unclear
rejoin
rewrite
unhurt
recheck
unlucky
unwrap
reuse
unsure

Review
reread
unsafe

Challenge
unbuckle
unknown

✏ Write Instructions

prewrite → draft → revise → proofread → publish

Write instructions about how to do something.
- Write steps and number them.
- Use some Spelling Words and pronouns.
- Proofread your work.

Power Proofreading
www.eduplace.com/kids/sv/

Test Tip Answer easy questions first.

Test Format Practice

Directions Choose the word that is spelled correctly and best completes the sentence.

Example: We are glad you are _____.

    A unhirt
    B unhurt
    C unhert
    D unhyrt

Example:

Ⓐ Ⓑ Ⓒ Ⓓ

Answer Sheet

1. Ⓐ Ⓑ Ⓒ Ⓓ
2. Ⓕ Ⓖ Ⓗ Ⓙ
3. Ⓐ Ⓑ Ⓒ Ⓓ
4. Ⓕ Ⓖ Ⓗ Ⓙ
5. Ⓐ Ⓑ Ⓒ Ⓓ
6. Ⓕ Ⓖ Ⓗ Ⓙ

1. Do you think she is being _____?

    A unfair
    B unfare
    C unfar
    D unfear

2. It is _____ to stand on this old ladder.

    F unsayfe
    G unnsafe
    H unsaf
    J unsafe

3. Please _____ these chairs and set them up.

    A unfolde
    B unfuld
    C unfold
    D unfoold

4. I will _____ this excellent book.

    F rered
    G rerede
    H reread
    J reeread

5. We will _____ our friends soon.

    A rejoyn
    B rejion
    C rejoine
    D rejoin

6. Did he _____ all of his answers?

    F rechek
    G recheck
    H recheke
    J rechec

More Practice
Now write each correctly spelled word on a sheet of paper.

Spelling Games
www.eduplace.com/kids/sv/
Review for your test.

Real-World Vocabulary

Health: Beach Safety

Write the words from the box to complete the sign.
Use your Spelling Dictionary.

Spelling Word Link

unsafe

undertow
lifeguard
partner
surf
whistle

!! BEACH RULES !!

Be safe as you play in the sand and ___(1)___, and follow these rules.

- Only swim where there is a ___(2)___ on duty.

- Young children may not swim alone. They must have an adult with them as a swimming ___(3)___.

- Do not swim too far from shore. If you hear a lifeguard's ___(4)___, you are out too far.

- Be careful of the ___(5)___. It can pull you out farther in the ocean than you want to be.

1. _____
2. _____
3. _____
4. _____
5. _____

eWord Game
www.eduplace.com/kids/sv/

Try This CHALLENGE

Riddles Write a word from the box to answer each riddle.

6. What crashes on the beach but never gets hurt?

7. What sends a signal without using words?

8. What can pull you but has no muscles?

6. _____
7. _____
8. _____

179

Read the Spelling Words and sentences.

Basic Words

1.	singer	singer	The **singer** sang a new song.
2.	loudly	loudly	Please speak **loudly**.
3.	joyful	joyful	I have **joyful** news to share.
4.	teacher	teacher	Who is your **teacher** this year?
5.	gladly	gladly	I will **gladly** help you clean up.
6.	fighter	fighter	The **fighter** lost the match.
7.	closely	closely	Look **closely** at this bug.
8.	powerful	powerful	The storm is very **powerful**.
9.	farmer	farmer	The **farmer** is planting wheat.
10.	quickly	quickly	They ran home **quickly**.
11.	careful	careful	I will be **careful** when I swim.
12.	friendly	friendly	What a **friendly** dog you have!
13.	speaker	speaker	The **speaker** gave a good speech.
14.	fearful	fearful	Are you **fearful** of heights?

Review

15. hopeful   16. safely

Challenge

17. listener   18. calmly

Think about the Spelling Strategy.

Each word is made up of a base word and a suffix. A **suffix** is a word part added to the end of a base word. The suffix *-ful* can mean "full of" or "having." The suffix *-ly* can mean "in a way that is." The suffix *-er* can mean "a person who."

joy + ful = joy**ful**   loud + ly = loud**ly**

sing + er = sing**er**

Sort and write the words.

Write each Basic Word under its suffix.

Sort for *-ful*

1. _____

2. _____

3. _____

4. _____

Sort for *-ly*

5. _____

6. _____

7. _____

8. _____

9. _____

Sort for *-er*

10. _____

11. _____

12. _____

13. _____

14. _____

Phonics

Write a Basic Word to answer each question.

15. Which word begins like *glue*?

16. Which word has the /ī/ sound spelled *igh*?

17. Which word rhymes with *stinger*?

18. Which word has the /oi/ sound spelled *oy*?

19. Which word begins like *clover*?

Vocabulary: Synonyms

Write the Basic Word that means the same or almost the same as each word below.

20. fast

21. instructor

22. strong

23. scared

24. planter

Challenge Words

Write the Challenge Word that completes each sentence. Use your Spelling Dictionary.

25. The class sat _____ during the TV star's talk.

26. Everyone wanted to be a good _____.

joyful   loudly   singer

Phonics

15. _____

16. _____

17. _____

18. _____

19. _____

Synonyms

20. _____

21. _____

22. _____

23. _____

24. _____

Challenge Words

25. _____

26. _____

At Home — Make word crosses with a family member. Write one Spelling Word across a page. Take turns writing Spelling Words that cross any word you wrote.

Word Building

1. _____

2. _____

3. _____

4. _____

5. _____

6. _____

Word Building: -er

You can build new words by adding a suffix to a base word. A suffix changes the meaning of the base word. Adding the suffix -er can change a verb into a noun.

sing + er = singer   "one who sings"

Practice Add the suffix -er to each base word in dark print. Write the new word.

1. one who **paint**s
2. one who **work**s
3. one who **buy**s
4. one who **play**s
5. one who **catch**es
6. one who **pitch**es

Dictionary

7. _____

8. _____

9. _____

10. _____

11. _____

12. _____

Dictionary: Suffixes

Not all words with suffixes are listed as entry words. If you want to find the meaning of *joyful*, look up the base word *joy* and the suffix *-ful*.

> **-ful** A suffix that forms adjectives. The suffix *-ful* means "full of" or "having": *beautiful*.

Practice Write the base word and the suffix you would look up to find the meaning of each word below.

7. sweetly
8. dreamer
9. tearful

10. motherly
11. walker
12. thoughtful

PART 3 Spelling and Writing

Proofread a Book List

Spelling and Book Titles Proofread this book list. Use proofreading marks to fix **four** spelling mistakes and **three** mistakes in book titles.

Example: The Lost and found by Mark Teague.

Proofreading Marks

¶	Indent
∧	Add
⌐	Delete
≡	Capital letter
/	Small letter

Must Read Book List

1. Chocolate touch by Patrick Skene Catling

   John has a powerfull gift. Everything his lips touch quickley turns to chocolate.

2. Miss Rumphius by Barbara Cooney

   Alice Rumphius is hopefule she can make the world more beautiful.

3. Raising dragons by Jerdine Nolen

   A little girl is joyful to have a pet dragon. Can she safeley keep it on her farm?

Basic
singer
loudly
joyful
teacher
gladly
fighter
closely
powerful
farmer
quickly
careful
friendly
speaker
fearful

Review
hopeful
safely

Challenge
listener
calmly

Write a Book List

prewrite → draft → revise → proofread → publish

Write a list of your favorite books.
- Tell a little about each book.
- Use some Spelling Words and book titles.
- Proofread your work.

Power Proofreading
www.eduplace.com/kids/sv/

183

Test Tip Do not spend too much time on one question.

Test Format Practice

Directions Read each group of sentences. Decide if one of the underlined words is spelled wrong or if there is *No mistake*.
Fill in the space for the answer you have chosen.

Example: ○ I like my <u>teacher</u>.
○ That story is <u>powerful</u>.
○ He has lived in many <u>cities</u>.
○ (*No mistake*)

1. ○ She knocked <u>lowdly</u>.
   ○ This is a <u>joyful</u> day!
   ○ We are not <u>fearful</u>.
   ○ (*No mistake*)

4. ○ We feel <u>hopefull</u> now.
   ○ He <u>dropped</u> his pencil.
   ○ I am not a <u>fighter</u>.
   ○ (*No mistake*)

2. ○ Please be very <u>cairful</u>.
   ○ They left <u>quickly</u>.
   ○ Marc has always been a good <u>neighbor</u>.
   ○ (*No mistake*)

5. ○ The <u>farmer</u> raises cows, sheep, and chickens.
   ○ Jenny is very <u>freindly</u>.
   ○ Lin wants to be a <u>singer</u>.
   ○ (*No mistake*)

More Practice
Now write all the misspelled words correctly on a separate sheet of paper.

3. ○ I will <u>replay</u> the movie.
   ○ Please watch me <u>closely</u>.
   ○ Who is the <u>speeker</u> tonight?
   ○ (*No mistake*)

6. ○ We will <u>gladly</u> help you.
   ○ They got home from the store <u>safelye</u>.
   ○ I can <u>reuse</u> that jar.
   ○ (*No mistake*)

Spelling Games
www.eduplace.com/kids/sv/
Review for your test.

Real-World ★ Vocabulary

Careers: Farm Worker

Write the words from the box to complete this essay.
Use your Spelling Dictionary.

My Farm
by Lisa Craig

I live on a big farm in the country. I help take care of our pigs, goats, and other ___(1)___. Our farm is a ___(2)___ farm, which means we ___(3)___ a lot of milk. We have over a hundred cows. They spend each day eating grass on our large ___(4)___. People often wonder how we milk so many cows. We use a ___(5)___ for each cow, which does all the work.

Spelling Word Link

farmer

machine
pasture
livestock
dairy
produce

1. _____
2. _____
3. _____
4. _____
5. _____

eWord Game
www.eduplace.com/kids/sv/

Try This CHALLENGE

Yes or No? Is the word in dark print in each sentence used correctly? Answer *yes* or *no*.

6. Hens **produce** eggs.
7. Jena wrote in her **dairy**.
8. You would hang a **pasture** on the wall.

6. _____
7. _____
8. _____

185

Read the Spelling Words and sentences.

Basic Words

1.	painless	*painless*	The ear exam was **painless**.
2.	sickness	*sickness*	A flu is an awful **sickness**.
3.	sadness	*sadness*	She felt alone in her **sadness**.
4.	helpless	*helpless*	A newborn baby is **helpless**.
5.	thankless	*thankless*	Is cleaning a **thankless** job?
6.	kindness	*kindness*	I thank you for your **kindness**.
7.	hopeless	*hopeless*	I am **hopeless** at sports.
8.	darkness	*darkness*	Candles lit up the **darkness**.
9.	fearless	*fearless*	A lion is a **fearless** animal.
10.	soundless	*soundless*	The empty room is **soundless**.
11.	thickness	*thickness*	See the **thickness** of the door.
12.	brightness	*brightness*	The **brightness** hurt my eyes.
13.	careless	*careless*	I made a **careless** mistake.
14.	softness	*softness*	Feel the **softness** of the blanket.

Sort for *-less*

1. _____
2. _____
3. _____
4. _____
5. _____
6. _____
7. _____

Sort for *-ness*

8. _____
9. _____
10. _____
11. _____
12. _____
13. _____
14. _____

Review

15. *useful*   16. *weakly*

Challenge

17. *breathless*   18. *eagerness*

Think about the Spelling Strategy.

Each word is made up of a base word and a suffix. The suffix *-less* means "without." The suffix *-ness* means "the condition of."

pain + less = pain**less**   sick + ness = sick**ness**

Sort and write the words.

Write each Basic Word under its suffix.

Phonics

Write Basic Words to answer the questions.

15. Which word has the /ō/ sound?
16. Which word has the /ā/ sound spelled *ai*?
17. Which word begins with *th* and ends with the suffix *-ness*?
18. Which word begins with *th* and ends with the suffix *-less*?

Vocabulary: Word Clues

Write the Basic Word that fits each clue.

19. means almost the same as *lightness*
20. measles, for example
21. the opposite of *gladness*
22. completely silent
23. the opposite of *careful*
24. brave and without fear

Challenge Words

Write the Challenge Word that completes each sentence. Use your Spelling Dictionary.

25. She ran very fast in her _____ to arrive.
26. She became _____ from running so quickly.

Phonics

15. _____
16. _____
17. _____
18. _____

Word Clues

19. _____
20. _____
21. _____
22. _____
23. _____
24. _____

Challenge Words

25. _____
26. _____

painless

sickness

At Home With a family member, take turns writing the first three letters of a Spelling Word. The other person finishes the word.

Word Meaning

1.

2.

3.

4.

5.

6

Word Meaning: Sick Words

Some words share the same base word. How are the words alike in spelling and meaning?

Practice Write a word from the house to complete each sentence.

1. I feel _____ today than I did yesterday.
2. This rocking boat is making me _____.
3. My older brother was _____ at camp.
4. This bird is not well. It looks _____.
5. Sara is absent because she has a _____.
6. Henry is the _____ one in the family.

sick
sickness
sicker
sickest
sickly
seasick
homesick

Thesaurus

7.

8.

9.

10.

11.

12.

Thesaurus: Exact Words for *sad*

Practice Write a more exact word for *sad* to complete each sentence. Choose a word from the box. You may use a word more than once. Use your Thesaurus.

gloomy	miserable	disappointed
unhappy	depressed	sorrowful

7. Marta tried to forget about her _____ weekend.
8. Why are you so _____ today?
9. We were _____ when the trip was canceled.
10. The sky is dark and _____ before a storm.
11. I felt _____ after my cat hurt its paw.
12. My sick aunt tries to be joyful rather than _____.

Proofread an Article

Spelling and End Marks Proofread this encyclopedia article. Use proofreading marks to fix **five** spelling mistakes, **one** incorrect end mark, and **two** missing end marks.

Example: The ~~thikness~~ *thickness* of their fur grows?

Proofreading Marks

¶	Indent
∧	Add
ℱ	Delete
≡	Capital letter
/	Small letter

Gerbil

Baby gerbils are born helplese. Their world is soundless It is full of darckness. The pups are blind and deaf at birth? They can squeak weakley right away, however.

Is the father gerbil usefull in taking care of the pups Yes, he usually treats them with kindniss.

Write an Article

prewrite → draft → revise → proofread → publish

Write a paragraph for an article about an animal.
- Give some facts about the animal.
- Use some Spelling Words. Check your end marks.
- Proofread your work.

Basic
painless
sickness
sadness
helpless
thankless
kindness
hopeless
darkness
fearless
soundless
thickness
brightness
careless
softness

Review
useful
weakly

Challenge
breathless
eagerness

Power Proofreading
www.eduplace.com/kids/sv/

Test Tip If you have time, check your answers again.

Test Format Practice

Directions Find the phrase containing an underlined word that is not spelled correctly. If all the underlined words are spelled correctly, mark "All correct."

Example:
A nearly <u>soundless</u>
B very <u>caireful</u>
C terrible <u>sickness</u>
D <u>anyone</u> home
E All correct

Example:
Ⓐ Ⓑ Ⓒ Ⓓ Ⓔ

Answer Sheet

1. Ⓐ Ⓑ Ⓒ Ⓓ Ⓔ
2. Ⓕ Ⓖ Ⓗ Ⓙ Ⓚ
3. Ⓐ Ⓑ Ⓒ Ⓓ Ⓔ
4. Ⓕ Ⓖ Ⓗ Ⓙ Ⓚ
5. Ⓐ Ⓑ Ⓒ Ⓓ Ⓔ
6. Ⓕ Ⓖ Ⓗ Ⓙ Ⓚ
7. Ⓐ Ⓑ Ⓒ Ⓓ Ⓔ
8. Ⓕ Ⓖ Ⓗ Ⓙ Ⓚ

More Practice
Now write all the misspelled words correctly on a separate sheet of paper.

Spelling Games
www.eduplace.com/kids/sv/
Review for your test.

1. A much <u>kindness</u>
   B long <u>stretch</u>
   C little <u>thickness</u>
   D no <u>sofness</u>
   E All correct

2. F some <u>sadness</u>
   G hardly <u>usefull</u>
   H <u>chew</u> slowly
   J too <u>careless</u>
   K All correct

3. A somewhat <u>powerful</u>
   B really <u>hopeless</u>
   C almost <u>painlass</u>
   D jumped <u>quickly</u>
   E All correct

4. F felt <u>thankless</u>
   G tiny <u>flake</u>
   H completely <u>fereless</u>
   J yelled <u>loudly</u>
   K All correct

5. A spoke <u>weaklye</u>
   B good <u>nurse</u>
   C sink <u>fast</u>
   D total <u>darkness</u>
   E All correct

6. F <u>swimming</u> back
   G never <u>worried</u>
   H yellow <u>brightness</u>
   J not <u>helpless</u>
   K All correct

7. A <u>without</u> a pen
   B <u>would'nt</u> move
   C red <u>balloon</u>
   D the <u>fourth</u> row
   E All correct

8. F <u>here</u> the sounds
   G large <u>circle</u>
   H this <u>afternoon</u>
   J a <u>thousand</u> words
   K All correct

Real-World Vocabulary

Health: Illness

Write the words from the box to complete this note. Use your Spelling Dictionary.

Dear Principal Raskin,

Please excuse Luis for not being in school last week. He was too sick to do his schoolwork. One minute he was burning up with a high ____(1)____. He also felt sore and seemed to ____(2)____ all over. The next minute he had ____(3)____ and shook, even with a blanket over him. His ____(4)____ was upset, so he had trouble eating. The doctor said Luis had the ____(5)____, but Luis is fine now.

Sincerely,

Olga Delgado

Spelling Word Link

sickness

fever
flu
stomach
ache
chills

1. _____

2. _____

3. _____

4. _____

5. _____

Try This
CHALLENGE

Clues Write a clue for each of the words in the box on a separate sheet of paper. Trade papers with a partner. Have your partner guess the word.

eWord Game
www.eduplace.com/kids/sv/

Spelling Review

Unit 25

1. _____

2. _____

3. _____

4. _____

5. _____

6. _____

7. _____

Unit 26

8. _____

9. _____

10. _____

11. _____

12. _____

13. _____

14. _____

Unit 25	Words with *-ed* or *-ing*	pages 162–167

| dropped | saving | grinning | stared |
| planned | joking | ⏺fixing | |

Spelling Strategy The spelling of some base words may change when **-ed** or **-ing** is added.

$$\text{drop} + p + ed = \textbf{dropped}$$
$$\text{save} - e + ing = \textbf{saving}$$

Letter Math Add and take away letters to write Spelling Words.

1. st + cared − c =
2. grin + n + ing =
3. plan + n + ed =
4. joke − e + ing =
5. save − e + ing =
6. fix + ing =
7. dr + stopped − st =

Unit 26	Changing Final *y* to *i*	pages 168–173

| cities | cried | puppies | stories |
| carried | flies | pennies | |

Spelling Strategy When a base word ends with a consonant and **y**, change the **y** to **i** before adding **-es** or **-ed**.

Classifying Write the word that completes each group.

8. dimes, nickels, _____
9. bees, spiders, _____
10. chicks, kittens, _____
11. poems, plays, _____

Synonyms Write the word that means the same or almost the same as each word below.

12. towns   13. sobbed   14. held

Unit 27   Prefixes *re-* and *un-*   pages 174–179

replay	untie	reheat	unfair
rejoin	rewrite	unwrap	

Spelling Strategy A **prefix** is a word part added to the beginning of a base word. **Re-** and **un-** are prefixes.

Fill-in-the-Blank Write the missing words.

15. Always _____ sneakers before taking them off.
16. It seemed _____ that it rained during vacation.
17. You should _____ your food if it is cold.
18. To see a movie again, you need to _____ it.
19. I will _____ the team after the first game.
20. We need to _____ the present to see what is inside.
21. If my essay has many errors, I will _____ it.

Unit 28   Suffixes *-ful*, *-ly*, and *-er*   pages 180–185

singer	loudly	joyful	teacher
gladly	powerful	farmer	

Spelling Strategy A **suffix** is a word part added to the end of a base word. **-Ful**, **-ly**, and **-er** are suffixes.

Rhyme Time Write the Spelling Word that rhymes with each word.

22. proudly   23. stinger   24. charmer   25. badly

Synonyms Write the word that means the same or almost the same as each word below.

26. strong   27. happy   28. coach

Unit 27

15. _____
16. _____
17. _____
18. _____
19. _____
20. _____
21. _____

Unit 28

22. _____
23. _____
24. _____
25. _____
26. _____
27. _____
28. _____

Spelling Review

Unit 29

29. _____

30. _____

31. _____

32. _____

33. _____

34. _____

35. _____

Challenge Words

36. _____

37. _____

38. _____

39. _____

40. _____

Unit 29	Suffixes *-less* and *-ness*	pages 186–191

painless	sickness	kindness	hopeless
darkness	fearless	soundless	

Spelling Strategy

fear + **less** = fear**less**

dark + **ness** = dark**ness**

Antonyms Write the word that means the opposite of each word.

29. brightness 30. meanness 31. wellness 32. noisy

Fill-in-the-Blank Write the missing words.

Rover is ___(33)___, but I could never get him into the tub. It seemed ___(34)___. Then one day I threw his ball into the tub. Rover jumped in after it. Now giving Rover a bath is ___(35)___.

Challenge Words	Units 25–29	pages 162–191

scared	libraries	unbuckle
listener	eagerness	

Fill-in-the-Blank Write the missing words.

36. We borrowed books from two _____.

37. The loud noise _____ us.

38. Do not _____ your seat belt until we stop.

39. My best friend is a good _____.

40. At dinner time, the dog jumped with _____.

Spelling (and) Writing

Proofread a Description

Spelling and Grammar Mixed Review Proofread this description. Use proofreading marks to fix **five** spelling mistakes, **one** incorrect end mark, and **two** mistakes using *I* and *me*.

Example: My sister and ~~me~~ ~~hurryed~~ outside~~?~~
I hurried .

Beth and me watched the soft, white flakes comming from the sky. We tryed to catch some on our tongues? The snow was icy cold, but its softness felt good. Everything was white. The briteness of the sun made me squint. I saw tiny animal tracks nearby. I was unshore which animal had made them. Then someone called out to Beth and I. We waved a frendly hello back.

Proofreading Marks

¶	Indent
∧	Add
⌐	Delete
≡	Capital letter
/	Small letter

Write a Description

prewrite → draft → revise → proofread → publish

Write a description of something you have seen or something you know very well.

- Use some Spelling Words from Units 25–29.
- Proofread your work.

Tips

- Begin by telling what you are describing.
- Use sense words and details.
- Use exact words and comparisons.

Power Proofreading
www.eduplace.com/kids/sv/

Spelling Test Practice

Test Tip Don't spend too much time on one question.

Directions Find the phrase containing an underlined word that is not spelled correctly. If all the underlined words are spelled correctly, mark "All correct."

Example:
  A eleven <u>o'clock</u>
  B long <u>word</u>
  C <u>bird</u> feathers
  D good <u>choyce</u>
  E All correct.

Example:

Ⓐ Ⓑ Ⓒ Ⓓ Ⓔ

Answer Sheet

1. Ⓐ Ⓑ Ⓒ Ⓓ Ⓔ
2. Ⓕ Ⓖ Ⓗ Ⓙ Ⓚ
3. Ⓐ Ⓑ Ⓒ Ⓓ Ⓔ
4. Ⓕ Ⓖ Ⓗ Ⓙ Ⓚ
5. Ⓐ Ⓑ Ⓒ Ⓓ Ⓔ
6. Ⓕ Ⓖ Ⓗ Ⓙ Ⓚ
7. Ⓐ Ⓑ Ⓒ Ⓓ Ⓔ
8. Ⓕ Ⓖ Ⓗ Ⓙ Ⓚ

1. **A** Tim's <u>birthday</u>
  B a <u>quick</u> move
  C <u>thankliss</u> job
  D big <u>squeeze</u>
  E All correct.

2. **F** lead <u>pencil</u>
  G a <u>smooth</u> ride
  H busy <u>street</u>
  J empty <u>shell</u>
  K All correct.

3. **A** run <u>quikly</u>
  B <u>blind</u> mice
  C <u>yellow</u> bananas
  D hiking <u>trail</u>
  E All correct.

4. **F** good <u>exkuse</u>
  G cuckoo <u>clock</u>
  H interesting <u>speaker</u>
  J passing <u>cloud</u>
  K All correct.

5. **A** <u>salt</u> shaker
  B <u>unhert</u> arm
  C special <u>toy</u>
  D one <u>mile</u>
  E All correct.

6. **F** cotton <u>shirt</u>
  G brick <u>wall</u>
  H rocking <u>chair</u>
  J black <u>shoe</u>
  K All correct.

7. **A** ballet <u>dance</u>
  B high <u>school</u>
  C <u>sumthing</u> special
  D corn <u>crop</u>
  E All correct.

8. **F** bubbly <u>foam</u>
  G <u>chease</u> pizza
  H <u>eight</u> days
  J <u>smart</u> answer
  K All correct.

Spelling Games
www.eduplace.com/kids/sv/
Review for your test.

Test Tip Read the directions carefully.

Example: Find the root word (base word) of the underlined word.

Test Format Practice

<u>careless</u>

car ○
care ○
less ○
ess ○

1. Find the word that has the suffix, and only the suffix, underlined.

thi<u>ck</u>ness ○
figh<u>ter</u> ○
ba<u>bies</u> ○
car<u>eful</u> ○

2. Find the root word (base word) of the underlined word.

<u>fearful</u>

ear ○
ful ○
fear ○
arful ○

3. Find the word that has the prefix, and only the prefix, underlined.

<u>re</u>check ○
<u>un</u>lucky ○
pon<u>ies</u> ○
<u>re</u>use ○

4. Find the word that dropped the final *e* before adding *-ing*.

parties ○
swimming ○
tapping ○
taping ○

5. Find the word that doubled a final consonant before adding *-ed*.

worried ○
wrapped ○
dried ○
unfold ○

6. Find the word that does <u>NOT</u> have a suffix.

helpless ○
speaker ○
unclear ○
sadness ○

197

Read the Spelling Words and sentences.

Basic Words

1. person   person   Michael is a kind **person**.
2. helmet   helmet   This **helmet** fits my head.
3. until   until   We can play **until** bedtime.
4. carpet   carpet   My room has a blue **carpet**.
5. napkin   napkin   I wipe my lips with a **napkin**.
6. Monday   Monday   The report is due on **Monday**.
7. enjoy   enjoy   I **enjoy** reading short stories.
8. forget   forget   Do not **forget** to call us!
9. problem   problem   We can solve this **problem**.
10. Sunday   Sunday   I went to the park on **Sunday**.
11. garden   garden   Tomatoes grow in our **garden**.
12. market   market   This **market** sells fresh fruit.
13. basket   basket   Are the papers in that **basket**?
14. order   order   Write the words in ABC **order**.

Review

15. after   16. under

Challenge

17. expect   18. wisdom

Think about the Spelling Strategy.

Each word has two syllables. Each word also has the vowel-consonant-consonant-vowel (VCCV) pattern. Divide a word between the two consonants to find the syllables. In each syllable look for spelling patterns you know.

VC | CV   VC | CV
per | son   **hel | met**

Sort and write the words.

Write the Basic Words. Divide them into syllables.

1. _____
2. _____
3. _____
4. _____
5. _____
6. _____
7. _____
8. _____
9. _____
10. _____
11. _____
12. _____
13. _____
14. _____

Phonics

Write Basic Words to answer the questions.

15. Which word begins with the /ŭ/ sound?
16. Which word rhymes with *border*?
17. Which word begins like *forever*?
18–19. Which two words begin with a capital letter?

Vocabulary: Context Sentences

Write the Basic Word that completes each sentence.

20. All bikers must wear a _____.
21. Please vacuum the _____.
22. Dad planted his _____.
23. May I have a _____ to wipe my face?
24. They collected flowers in a _____.

Challenge Words

Write the Challenge Word that completes each sentence. Use your Spelling Dictionary.

25. She answered the question with kindness and _____.
26. We _____ everyone to be happy with her answer.

per | son   hel | met

Phonics

15.

16.

17.

18.

19.

Context Sentences

20.

21.

22.

23.

24.

Challenge Words

25.

26.

At Home With a family member, take turns writing three Spelling Words on a piece of paper. Cut the syllables apart and mix them up. The other person puts the syllables together.

Word Building

1. _____
2. _____
3. _____
4. _____
5. _____
6. _____

🔍 Word Building: The VCCV Pattern

Practice Add a syllable on the left to a syllable on the right to make a word. Write the words.

1. tur
2. tar
3. ger
4. cor
5. dan
6. sig

nal
key
get
bil
ner
ger

Dictionary

7. _____
8. _____
9. _____
10. _____
11. _____
12. _____

Dictionary: Syllables

A syllable is a word part with one vowel sound. The dictionary uses dots (•) to separate the syllables of an entry word.

> **Sun•day** (sŭn′ dē) *or* (sŭn′ dā) *n., pl.* **Sundays** The first day of the week.

Practice Write each word below. Draw a line between the syllables. Use your Spelling Dictionary.

7. hornet
8. sandal
9. barber
10. picnic
11. lumber
12. monkey

✎ Proofread a Schedule

Spelling and Commas Proofread this activity schedule. Use proofreading marks to fix **five** spelling mistakes and **two** missing commas in dates and names of places.

Example: Do not ~~forgit~~ _forget_ the race in Cincinnati, Ohio.

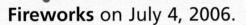

Proofreading Marks

¶	Indent
∧	Add
✎	Delete
≡	Capital letter
/	Small letter

Fireworks on July 4, 2006.

Come injoy the fireworks Munday night aftur dark at Byron Park. All are welcome.

Cleveland Ohio

Tours in the Park on July 9 2006.

Take a special bike tour for any persin undir twelve years of age. Bring a helmet.

Shaker Heights, Ohio

Basic

person
helmet
until
carpet
napkin
Monday
enjoy
forget
problem
Sunday
garden
market
basket
order

Review

after
under

Challenge

expect
wisdom

✎ Write a Schedule

prewrite→draft→revise→proofread→publish

Write an activity schedule for a newspaper.

- Describe at least two activities.
- Use some Spelling Words, dates, and names of places.
- Proofread your work.

Power Proofreading
www.eduplace.com/kids/sv/

Test Tip Skip the hard questions. Go back to them later.

Directions Find the phrase containing an underlined word that is not spelled correctly. If all the underlined words are spelled correctly, mark "All correct."

Example: A plastic <u>helmit</u>
B <u>window</u> ledge
C never <u>forget</u>
D dairy <u>farmer</u>
E All correct.

Example:

Ⓐ Ⓑ Ⓒ Ⓓ Ⓔ

Answer Sheet

1. Ⓐ Ⓑ Ⓒ Ⓓ Ⓔ

2. Ⓕ Ⓖ Ⓗ Ⓙ Ⓚ

3. Ⓐ Ⓑ Ⓒ Ⓓ Ⓔ

4. Ⓕ Ⓖ Ⓗ Ⓙ Ⓚ

5. Ⓐ Ⓑ Ⓒ Ⓓ Ⓔ

6. Ⓕ Ⓖ Ⓗ Ⓙ Ⓚ

7. Ⓐ Ⓑ Ⓒ Ⓓ Ⓔ

8. Ⓕ Ⓖ Ⓗ Ⓙ Ⓚ

More Practice
Now write all the misspelled words correctly on a separate sheet of paper.

Spelling Games
www.eduplace.com/kids/sv/
Review for your test.

1. A paper <u>napkin</u>
   B mail <u>order</u>
   C <u>almost</u> new
   D <u>circus</u> tent
   E All correct.

2. F <u>Sunday</u> morning
   G one <u>person</u>
   H famous <u>singer</u>
   J fruit <u>marcket</u>
   K All correct.

3. A great <u>artist</u>
   B small <u>problim</u>
   C tan <u>carpet</u>
   D left <u>elbow</u>
   E All correct.

4. F soft <u>powder</u>
   G <u>Monday</u> night
   H <u>undur</u> the bed
   J round <u>balloon</u>
   K All correct.

5. A <u>aftar</u> school
   B the <u>center</u>
   C large <u>basket</u>
   D <u>enjoy</u> the most
   E All correct.

6. F until <u>later</u>
   G no <u>excuse</u>
   H big <u>circle</u>
   J vegetable <u>gardin</u>
   K All correct.

7. A <u>powerful</u> storm
   B cute <u>puppys</u>
   C <u>grinning</u> child
   D <u>friendly</u> cat
   E All correct.

8. F warm <u>jacket</u>
   G loud <u>squeak</u>
   H one <u>o'clock</u>
   J <u>faraway</u> place
   K All correct.

Real-World Vocabulary

Life Skills: Eating Out

Write the words from the box to complete this personal narrative. Use your Spelling Dictionary.

Last weekend, my family went out to eat at a new _____(1)_____. A man gave each of us a _____(2)_____ that listed the foods we could order for dinner.

Mom, Dad, my brother, and I each picked our favorite food. Then a friendly _____(3)_____ came to our table and took our orders. We all enjoyed our meals. After dinner, we all had ice cream for _____(4)_____. Dad left some money on the table. This _____(5)_____ was his way of saying thank you for good service.

Spelling Word Link

order

menu
waiter
restaurant
tip
dessert

1. _____
2. _____
3. _____
4. _____
5. _____

Try This CHALLENGE

Fill-In-the-Blank Write a sentence for each of the words in the box on a separate sheet of paper. Leave a blank for the word. Have a partner guess the missing word.

eWord Game
www.eduplace.com/kids/sv/

Read the Spelling Words and sentences.

Basic Words

1. jelly — *jelly* — He puts **jelly** on his toast.
2. bottom — *bottom* — I can see the **bottom** of the lake.
3. pillow — *pillow* — Lay your head on the **pillow**.
4. happen — *happen* — Why did the accident **happen**?
5. butter — *butter* — I like to eat bread and **butter**.
6. lesson — *lesson* — My piano **lesson** is tomorrow.
7. cherry — *cherry* — Grandma made a **cherry** pie.
8. sudden — *sudden* — We heard a **sudden** shout.
9. arrow — *arrow* — Did the **arrow** hit the target?
10. dollar — *dollar* — I paid one **dollar** for the pen.
11. hello — *hello* — We called Dave to say **hello**.
12. rabbit — *rabbit* — The **rabbit** likes carrots.
13. letter — *letter* — A **letter** arrived in the mail.
14. button — *button* — My coat is missing a **button**.

Review
15. *funny*   16. *better*

Challenge
17. *stubborn*   18. *mirror*

Think about the Spelling Strategy.

Each word has the VCCV pattern and a double consonant. Divide between the consonants to find the syllables. Look for spelling patterns you know.

VC	CV		VC	CV
jel	**ly**		**bot**	**tom**

Sort and write the words.

Write the Basic Words. Divide them into syllables.

1.
2.
3.
4.
5.
6.
7.
8.
9.
10.
11.
12.
13.
14.

Phonics

Write the Basic Word that rhymes with each word below.

15. berry   **17.** collar   **19.** willow

16. flutter   **18.** sparrow

Vocabulary: Context Paragraph

Write Basic Words to complete this paragraph.

Today I was supposed to have a diving _(20)_. I am learning to dive to the _(21)_ of the pool. I was about to dive into the pool, when all of a _(22)_, thick gray clouds rolled in. I knew what would _(23)_ next. I went home before the storm began. I will write a _(24)_ instead of diving today!

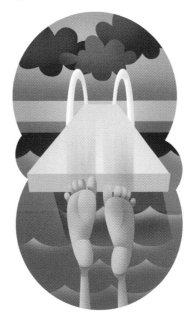

Challenge Words

Write the Challenge Word that completes each sentence. Use your Spelling Dictionary.

25. I looked in the _____ to comb my hair.

26. He agreed to the change because he is not _____.

jel | ly   bot | tom

At Home With a family member, take turns writing the first three letters of a Spelling Word. The other person finishes the word.

Phonics

15.

16.

17.

18.

19.

Context Paragraph

20.

21.

22.

23.

24.

Challenge Words

25.

26.

Word Meaning

1. _____

2. _____

3. _____

4. _____

5. _____

6. _____

Dictionary

7. _____

8. _____

9. _____

10. _____

11. _____

12. _____

Word Meaning: Analogies

An analogy can compare categories and things that belong in the categories.

Example: *Flower* is to *tulip* as *tree* is to *oak*.

Practice Write the word from the box that completes each analogy. Use your Spelling Dictionary.

cherry	robin	soccer
player	hammer	pants

1. *Class* is to *student* as *team* is to _____.
2. *Jewelry* is to *ring* as *clothing* is to _____.
3. *Vegetable* is to *carrot* as *fruit* is to _____.
4. *Ingredient* is to *sugar* as *tool* is to _____.
5. *Fish* is to *shark* as *bird* is to _____.
6. *Toy* is to *puzzle* as *sport* is to _____.

Dictionary: The Schwa Sound

Say *teacher*. The second syllable has a weak vowel sound called the **schwa** sound. The pronunciation key shows this sound as /ə/. The /ə/ sound can be spelled with any vowel.

/ə/ a**g**o, it**e**m, penc**i**l, lem**o**n, circ**u**s

Practice Look at each word and its pronunciation below. Write each word. Then underline the letter that spells the schwa sound. Use your Spelling Dictionary.

7. dollar /**dŏl'** ər/
8. joyful /**joi'** fəl/
9. tractor /**trăk'** tər/
10. nostril /**nŏs'** trəl/
11. better /**bĕt'** ər/
12. away /ə **wā'**/

Proofread a Menu

Spelling and Commas Proofread this lunch menu. Use proofreading marks to fix **five** spelling mistakes and **two** missing commas in a series.

Example: The soup, juice, and salad are a ~~doller~~ *dollar* each.

Lunch Menu

The cooks all say helloe. They hope you are hungry. You will feel beter after lunch.

The main dish for today is baked ziti. It comes with a salad and a roll with jelley, buter, or cheese cut in funney shapes. You may have pumpkin blueberry or cherry pie for dessert.

Write a Menu

prewrite → draft → revise → proofread → publish

Write a breakfast, lunch, or dinner menu.
- Name the foods that will be served.
- Use some Spelling Words and words in a series.
- Proofread your work.

Proofreading Marks

¶	Indent
∧	Add
˞	Delete
≡	Capital letter
/	Small letter

Basic
jelly
bottom
pillow
happen
butter
lesson
cherry
sudden
arrow
dollar
hello
rabbit
letter
button

Review
funny
better

Challenge
stubborn
mirror

Power Proofreading
www.eduplace.com/kids/sv/

Test Tip Make sure you fill in the whole circle.

Test Format Practice

Directions Find the word that is spelled correctly and best completes the sentence.

Example: All of a _____, the dog started to bark.

suden	sudun	sudden	suddon
○	○	○	○

---

1. A black _____ fell off my suit.

buton	butten	button	buttin
○	○	○	○

2. Jamal told a _____ story.

funni	funeye	funey	funny
○	○	○	○

3. Our class has a pet _____.

rabbet	rabbit	rabit	rabitt
○	○	○	○

4. Which book did you like _____?

bedder	bettar	better	betir
○	○	○	○

More Practice
Now write each correctly spelled word on a sheet of paper.

5. I cannot sleep without a _____.

pillow	pillo	pellow	pilow
○	○	○	○

6. We did an experiment during our science _____.

leson	lesen	lessin	lesson
○	○	○	○

Spelling Games
www.eduplace.com/kids/sv/
Review for your test.

Real-World Vocabulary

Language Arts: Fable

Write the words from the box to complete this fable. Use your Spelling Dictionary.

One day, a furry ___(1)___ named Flash quickly hopped past a ___(2)___ named Pokey as he slept in his shell.

"You are so slow!" Flash shouted.

"I may not be fast like you, but I could beat you in a race," said Pokey. "I never give up. I keep on going."

Flash liked a ___(3)___ so he agreed to race. Soon after the race began, Flash was far ahead. He was sure he would win, so he stopped to take a little nap. Pokey kept on going. He was slow but ___(4)___. Flash woke up just in time to hear the ___(5)___ announce that Pokey was the winner.

"See?" cried Pokey. "I never give up!"

Spelling Word Link

rabbit

judge
tortoise
steady
hare
challenge

1. _____
2. _____
3. _____
4. _____
5. _____

eWord Game
www.eduplace.com/kids/sv/

Try This CHALLENGE

Word Groups Write the word from the box that belongs in each group.

6. rabbit, bunny, _____
7. dare, test, _____
8. turtle, snail, _____

6. _____
7. _____
8. _____

Read the Spelling Words and sentences.

Basic Words

1.	taught	taught	My cousin **taught** me to juggle.
2.	thought	thought	I **thought** I knew the answer.
3.	rough	rough	How **rough** sandpaper feels!
4.	laugh	laugh	I always **laugh** at funny jokes.
5.	bought	bought	Mom **bought** pizza for supper.
6.	cough	cough	Ted has a cold and a **cough**.
7.	ought	ought	We **ought** to do our homework.
8.	caught	caught	They **caught** three fireflies.
9.	fought	fought	Firefighters **fought** the fire.
10.	daughter	daughter	Who is that woman's **daughter**?
11.	tough	tough	This piece of meat is **tough**.
12.	through	through	Please exit **through** the door.
13.	enough	enough	Do you have **enough** money?
14.	brought	brought	Who **brought** the picnic basket?

Review

15. was   16. warm

Challenge

17. sought   18. naughty

Think about the Spelling Strategy.

Each Basic Word is spelled with the pattern *ough* or *augh*. Each pattern spells more than one sound.

/ô/ t**augh**t, th**ough**t   /ă/ l**augh**

/ŭ/ r**ough**   /o͞o/ thr**ough**

Sort and write the words.

Write each Basic Word under its spelling pattern.

Sort for *ough*

1.
2.
3.
4.
5.
6.
7.
8.
9.
10.

Sort for *augh*

11.
12.
13.
14.

Phonics

Write the Basic Word that has the same beginning sound or sounds as each group of words.

15. road, rink, _____

16. fork, fist, _____

17. day, doll, _____

18. boat, bush, _____

19. bread, bridge, _____

Vocabulary: Word Clues

Write the Basic Word that fits each clue.

20. You do this when something is funny.

21. When you did this, you were thinking.

22. You should cover your mouth when you do this.

23. This describes something that cannot get away.

24. When you have all that you need, you have this.

Challenge Words

Write the Challenge Word that completes each sentence. Use your Spelling Dictionary.

25. The babysitter _____ a game for the kids.

26. They waited quietly without being _____.

Phonics

15.

16.

17.

18.

19.

Word Clues

20.

21.

22.

23.

24.

Challenge Words

25.

26.

taught

thought

rough

laugh

through

At Home
With a family member, write each Spelling Word on a small piece of paper. Work together to arrange the words in ABC order.

Word Meaning

1. _____

2. _____

3. _____

4. _____

5. _____

🔍 Word Meaning: Laugh Words

Words with the same base word are often alike in spelling and meaning.

Practice Write words from the house to complete the paragraph.

My family loves to read the Sunday comics. We spend the entire morning __(1)__ together. One character we like is always making silly mistakes. He is really __(2)__. You can hear our loud __(3)__ even outside our house. Our neighbor __(4)__ at us because he can hear us. He __(5)__ calls us a family of laughers!

laugh
laughs
laughing
laughter
laughingly
laughable

Thesaurus

6. _____

7. _____

8. _____

9. _____

10. _____

Thesaurus: Exact Words for *laugh*

Practice Write a word from the box that best fits each sentence. Use your Thesaurus.

roar	snicker	chuckle	giggle

6. As he read, the man would quietly _____ to himself.
7. The crowd began to _____ with delight when the player waved to the stands.
8. Do not _____ at someone's mistake.
9. The baby started to _____ when I tickled his foot.
10. Did she _____ quietly at the joke?

Proofread a Story

Spelling and Commas Proofread this short story. Use proofreading marks to fix **six** spelling mistakes and **two** missing commas after order words.

Example: First, Drew ~~thougt~~ *thought* about how tall the ladder was.

The Big Jump

Drew wuz ready to take his first jump off the diving board. First, he climbed the ladder. That was not tuffe. Next he stepped onto the board. It felt werm to his feet. He knew he awt to remember what his coach had tought him. He hoped he had learned enough. Finally he jumped. Everyone cheered when he was thruogh.

Proofreading Marks

¶	Indent
∧	Add
⸰	Delete
≡	Capital letter
/	Small letter

Basic

taught
thought
rough
laugh
bought
cough
ought
caught
fought
daughter
tough
through
enough
brought

Review

was
warm

Challenge

sought
naughty

Write a Story

prewrite → draft → revise → proofread → publish

Write a story about someone who learns to do something.

- Tell what the experience felt like.
- Use some Spelling Words and order words.
- Proofread your work.

Power Proofreading
www.eduplace.com/kids/sv/

Test Tip Answer easy questions first.

Test Format Practice

Directions Read each group of sentences. Decide if one of the underlined words is spelled wrong or if there is *No mistake*. Fill in the space for the answer you have chosen.

Example:
- ◯ They are in the <u>fourth</u> grade.
- ◯ This is a <u>tough</u> problem.
- ◯ Are there <u>enuff</u> eggs?
- ◯ No mistake

---

1. ◯ He <u>thought</u> for a while.
   ◯ A circle is <u>round</u>.
   ◯ She <u>wus</u> tired.
   ◯ No mistake

5. ◯ He <u>taught</u> us to sew.
   ◯ We <u>ought</u> to go now.
   ◯ We <u>faught</u> a bit.
   ◯ No mistake

2. ◯ Please <u>count</u> the pencils.
   ◯ Ann is her <u>doughter</u>.
   ◯ Who <u>caught</u> the ball?
   ◯ No mistake

6. ◯ The road is <u>rough.</u>
   ◯ We <u>broght</u> our lunch.
   ◯ Please do not <u>bounce</u>.
   ◯ No mistake

3. ◯ Do you have a <u>cough</u>?
   ◯ Climb <u>through</u> here.
   ◯ Please pass the <u>salt</u>.
   ◯ No mistake

7. ◯ We <u>reuse</u> the bags.
   ◯ My dog is <u>freindly</u>.
   ◯ Pass the <u>napkin</u>.
   ◯ No mistake

More Practice
Now write all the misspelled words correctly on a separate sheet of paper.

4. ◯ The sun is <u>warrm</u>.
   ◯ Did you <u>laugh</u> or cry?
   ◯ Joe <u>bought</u> a new bike.
   ◯ No mistake

8. ◯ I am not <u>worried.</u>
   ◯ Try to be <u>careful</u>.
   ◯ You are never <u>helpless</u>.
   ◯ No mistake

Spelling Games
www.eduplace.com/kids/sv/
Review for your test.

Real-World 🎀 Vocabulary

Life Skills: Lost Pet

Write the words from the box to complete the poster.
Use your Spelling Dictionary.

Help Me Find Curly!

My dog, Curly, is a white ___(1)___ with curly fur.
Around her neck, she wears a little red ___(2)___
with a ___(3)___ that tells her name and our phone
number.

I had let Curly off her ___(4)___ for a quick run in
the Hinkley Dog Park. There was a loud siren
nearby that scared her,
and she ran off. Please
help me find Curly. I miss
her a lot.

If you see Curly, please
call 555-3066. My
parents will pay a ___(5)___
for her return.

Spelling Word Link

sought

reward
collar
poodle
leash
tag

1. _____
2. _____
3. _____
4. _____
5. _____

eWord Game
www.eduplace.com/kids/sv/

Try This CHALLENGE

Label It! Draw a picture of a poodle on a separate
sheet of paper. Label the parts of the poodle, using
the words from the box and your own words.

215

Read the Spelling Words and sentences.

Basic Words

1.	apple	*apple*	I ate an **apple** for my snack.
2.	river	*river*	We sailed down the **river**.
3.	little	*little*	A kitten is a **little** cat.
4.	October	*October*	I was born in **October**.
5.	ladder	*ladder*	They climbed the **ladder**.
6.	summer	*summer*	My favorite season is **summer**.
7.	purple	*purple*	The **purple** tulips bloomed.
8.	later	*later*	Please finish this job **later**.
9.	November	*November*	We went hiking in **November**.
10.	number	*number*	What is your phone **number**?
11.	uncle	*uncle*	My aunt and **uncle** visited us.
12.	winter	*winter*	Did it snow here this **winter**?
⚠ 13.	travel	*travel*	They will **travel** by train.
⚠ 14.	color	*color*	What **color** is your bedroom?

Review

15. flower   16. people

Challenge

17. *whistle*   18. *character*

Sort for /ər/

1. _____

2. _____

3. _____

4. _____

5. _____

6. _____

7. _____

8. _____

9. _____

Sort for /əl/

10. _____

11. _____

12. _____

13. _____

14. _____

Think about the Spelling Strategy.

Each word ends with a schwa sound + *r* or a schwa sound + *l*. The schwa sound is shown as /ə/. In words with more than one syllable, the final /ər/ sounds are often spelled *er*. The final /əl/ sounds are often spelled *le*.

/ər/ riv**er**   /əl/ app**le**

⚠ How are the Memory Words different?

Sort and write the words.

Write each Basic Word under its ending sounds.

Phonics

Write Basic Words to answer the questions.

15. Which word rhymes with *liver*?

16. Which word begins with the /ŭ/ sound?

17. Which word has the /ā/ sound?

18–19. Which two words begin with a capital letter?

Vocabulary: Analogies

Write the Basic Word that completes each analogy.

20. *Vanilla* is to *flavor* as *blue* is to _____.

21. *W* is to *letter* as *ten* is to _____.

22. *Noisy* is to *loud* as *small* is to _____.

23. *Spring* is to *fall* as *summer* is to _____.

24. *Vegetable* is to *pea* as *fruit* is to _____.

Challenge Words

Write the Challenge Word that completes each sentence.
Use your Spelling Dictionary.

25. Aunt Charlotte is a _____ in my story.

26. She likes to _____ as she knits.

river   apple

Phonics

15. _____

16. _____

17. _____

18. _____

19. _____

Analogies

20. _____

21. _____

22. _____

23. _____

24. _____

Challenge Words

25. _____

26. _____

At Home Make word crosses with a family member. Write one Spelling Word across a page. Take turns writing Spelling Words that cross any word you wrote.

217

Word Meaning

1. _____
2. _____
3. _____
4. _____
5. _____

Word Meaning: Other Languages

Many food names come from other languages.

Practice Write a word from the box that fits each clue. Use your Spelling Dictionary.

cookie	spaghetti	yogurt
hamburger	potato	

1. an Italian word for long solid strings of dough that are boiled and often eaten with meatballs
2. a Turkish word for a thick, creamy dairy food
3. a Dutch word for a small, flat cake that can be a snack
4. a Spanish word for a starchy vegetable
5. a German word for a ground meat patty

Dictionary

6. _____
7. _____
8. _____
9. _____
10. _____
11. _____
12. _____

Dictionary: Stressed Syllables

Say *uncle*. Notice that the first syllable is said more strongly, or **stressed**. The dictionary pronunciation shows this syllable in dark print followed by an **accent mark** (').

un•cle (ŭng' kəl) *n., pl.* **uncles** the brother of one's mother or father.

Practice Write each word. Circle the stressed syllable. Use your Spelling Dictionary.

Example: river   ⃝river

6. purple
7. number
8. repeat
9. travel
10. ladder
11. unfold
12. summer

PART 3 Spelling and Writing

✏️ Proofread a Letter

Spelling, Greetings, and Closings Proofread this letter.
Use proofreading marks to fix **six** spelling mistakes, **two**
missing capital letters, and **one** missing comma.

Example: your favorite ~~uncel~~ *uncle*,

                                        August 7, 2006

dear Uncle Kevin

    The family party will be in Octobur. Most peaple do not

want it layter in the year. That awful storm almost ruined

our party last wintr! Please make traval plans soon. Next

summer we will have a party in the flouer garden.

                                        your niece,

                                        Toshiko

✏️ Write a Letter

| prewrite → draft → revise → proofread → publish |

Write a letter to a friend or a family member. Tell about
something you have planned.

- Include the five parts of a letter. Use Spelling Words.
- Use capital letters and commas correctly in the greeting
  and the closing of your letter.
- Proofread your work.

Proofreading Marks

¶	Indent
∧	Add
✍	Delete
≡	Capital letter
/	Small letter

Basic
apple
river
little
October
ladder
summer
purple
later
November
number
uncle
winter
❗ travel
❗ color

Review
flower
people

Challenge
whistle
character

Power Proofreading
www.eduplace.com/kids/sv/

219

Test Tip Read all the words carefully.

Test Format Practice

Directions Find the phrase containing an underlined word that is not spelled correctly. If all the underlined words are spelled correctly, mark "All correct."

Example: bright <u>color</u> ○   odd <u>numbir</u> ○   famous <u>singer</u> ○   All correct ○

1. <u>tried</u> hard ○   tall <u>lader</u> ○   faraway <u>travel</u> ○   All correct ○

2. pink <u>flowere</u> ○   calm <u>river</u> ○   loose <u>tooth</u> ○   All correct ○

3. long <u>letter</u> ○   <u>October</u> day ○   <u>littel</u> ant ○   All correct ○

4. <u>purpel</u> hat ○   melted <u>butter</u> ○   <u>their</u> books ○   All correct ○

5. your <u>uncle</u> ○   many <u>peeple</u> ○   <u>wrong</u> name ○   All correct ○

6. my <u>teacher</u> ○   much <u>later</u> ○   cold <u>winter</u> ○   All correct ○

7. new <u>carpet</u> ○   <u>careless</u> act ○   <u>sekond</u> grade ○   All correct ○

8. <u>without</u> us ○   many <u>stories</u> ○   look <u>closely</u> ○   All correct ○

More Practice
Now write all the misspelled words correctly on a separate sheet of paper.

Spelling Games
www.eduplace.com/kids/sv/
Review for your test.

Real-World Vocabulary

Social Studies: Amazon River Basin

Write the words from the box to complete the travel brochure. Use your Spelling Dictionary.

Spelling Word Link

river

rain forest
monkey
humid
parrot
crocodile

Take a Trip . . .
YOU WILL NEVER FORGET!

Let our trained guides show you the Amazon River and the beautiful ___(1)___ that surrounds it. This hot and ___(2)___ place has more plants and animals than anywhere else.

As you travel along the river, you might see a playful ___(3)___ call out as it swings through the branches of a tree. Perhaps a bright, colorful ___(4)___ will fly overhead. Don't be scared if you see a huge ___(5)___ sunning itself along the shore!

1. _____
2. _____
3. _____
4. _____
5. _____

eWord Game
www.eduplace.com/kids/sv/

Try This
CHALLENGE

What Am I? Write a word from the box to answer each riddle.

6. I have a big mouth full of sharp teeth.
7. People can teach me to say a few words.
8. I am a place filled with plants and animals.

6. _____
7. _____
8. _____

Read the Spelling Words and sentences.

Basic Words

1.	below	_below_	The river is **below** the bridge.
2.	about	_about_	Her poem is **about** friendship.
3.	belong	_belong_	Does this coat **belong** to you?
4.	around	_around_	The dog ran **around** the yard.
5.	again	_again_	We played the game **again**.
6.	alone	_alone_	I like to be **alone** sometimes.
7.	because	_because_	He slept **because** he was tired.
8.	above	_above_	The bird flew **above** the trees.
9.	between	_between_	Please sit down **between** us.
10.	ago	_ago_	The train left a minute **ago**.
11.	behind	_behind_	Zach is in line **behind** Derek.
12.	begin	_begin_	The concert will **begin** soon.
13.	alive	_alive_	Is that dry plant still **alive**?
14.	before	_before_	I wash my hands **before** I eat.

Review

15. away   16. want

Challenge

17. awhile   18. beyond

Sort for /ə/

1. _____
2. _____
3. _____
4. _____
5. _____
6. _____
7. _____

Sort for /bĭ/

8. _____
9. _____
10. _____
11. _____
12. _____
13. _____
14. _____

Think about the Spelling Strategy.

Each Basic Word has two syllables. The first syllable has the /ə/ sound spelled _a_ or the /bĭ/ sounds spelled _be_. The second syllable is stressed.

/ə/ **a**bout   /bĭ/ **be**low

Sort and write the words.

Write each Basic Word under the /ə/ sound or the /bĭ/ sounds.

Phonics

Write Basic Words to answer the questions.

15. Which word has the /ē/ sound spelled *ee*?
16. Which word has the /z/ sound?
17. Which word ends with the /ō/ sound spelled *ow*?
18. Which word ends with the /ō/ sound spelled *o*?
19–20. Which two words have the /ī/ sound?

Vocabulary: Context Sentences

Write the Basic Word that completes each sentence.

21. When does the school day _____?
22. I already saw the puppet show, but I would like to see it _____.
23. My older sister is allowed to stay home _____.
24. These puppies _____ to my aunt.

Challenge Words

Write the Challenge Word that completes each sentence. Use your Spelling Dictionary.

25. We drove _____ to find the restaurant.
26. We traveled _____ the town, and there it was!

about

below

Phonics

15. _____
16. _____
17. _____
18. _____
19. _____
20. _____

Context Sentences

21. _____
22. _____
23. _____
24. _____

Challenge Words

25. _____
26. _____

At Home — With a family member, take turns "finger spelling" a Spelling Word into the other's hand and guessing the word.

Word Building

1. _____
2. _____
3. _____
4. _____
5. _____
6. _____

Word Building: The Syllables *a* and *be*

Practice Build words that begin with the unstressed syllables *a* and *be*. Do the math. Write the new words.

1. a + sleep = ___?___
2. be + side = ___?___
3. a + wait = ___?___
4. be + come = ___?___
5. a + cross = ___?___
6. a + board = ___?___

Dictionary: Spelling Table

How can you look up *because* if you do not know how to spell the /ô/ sound? Turn to the **spelling table**, which shows the different ways a sound can be spelled. Check each spelling for /ô/ until you find *because*.

Sound	Spellings	Sample Words
/ô/	a, al, au, augh, aw, o, ough	w**a**ll, t**a**lk, p**au**se, t**augh**t, l**aw**n, s**o**ft, br**ough**t

Practice Write the correct spelling for each word below. Use the picture clues, the spelling table above, and your Spelling Dictionary.

Dictionary

7. _____
8. _____
9. _____
10. _____
11. _____
12. _____

7.  p + /ô/
8.  m + /ô/ + th
9.  c + /ô/
10.  ch + /ô/ + k
11. 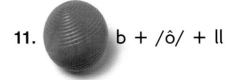 b + /ô/ + ll
12.  s + /ô/ + ce

Proofread a Newspaper Article

Spelling and Quotation Marks Proofread this newspaper article. Use proofreading marks to fix **five** spelling mistakes, **two** missing quotation marks, and **one** missing end mark.

Example: A witness said, "The whale is ~~elive~~ *alive*."

Proofreading Marks	
¶	Indent
∧	Add
⌒	Delete
≡	Capital letter
/	Small letter

Beached Whale

Two men found a small whale on a beach today at abowt 6 A.M. One man said, "I called for help right awae."

The other man said, We hoped to save it

Help came beefore 6:30. The area was roped off because a crowd had formed uround the whale.

Now rescuers wannt to keep the whale healthy until they can get it back into the sea.

Basic
below
about
belong
around
again
alone
because
above
between
ago
behind
begin
alive
before

Review
away
want

Challenge
awhile
beyond

Write a Newspaper Article

prewrite → draft → revise → proofread → publish

Write a newspaper article about an event. The event can be real, or you can make it up.
- Tell what happened, where, and when.
- Use some Spelling Words and quotation marks.
- Proofread your work.

Power Proofreading
www.eduplace.com/kids/sv/

Test Tip If you change an answer, erase your first answer completely.

Test Format Practice

Directions Choose the word that is spelled correctly and best completes the sentence.

Example: Please tell that funny story _____.

  A agen
  B agin
  C again
  D againe

Example:

Ⓐ Ⓑ Ⓒ Ⓓ

Answer Sheet

1. Ⓐ Ⓑ Ⓒ Ⓓ
2. Ⓕ Ⓖ Ⓗ Ⓙ
3. Ⓐ Ⓑ Ⓒ Ⓓ
4. Ⓕ Ⓖ Ⓗ Ⓙ
5. Ⓐ Ⓑ Ⓒ Ⓓ
6. Ⓕ Ⓖ Ⓗ Ⓙ

1. Look at the dark clouds _____ us.
  A abov
  B abuve
  C ubove
  D above

2. I hid _____ the big oak tree.
  F bihind
  G behind
  H beehind
  J behinde

3. Cameron woke up one hour _____.
  A aggo
  B agoe
  C ago
  D ugo

4. He did not _____ to eat a snack.
  F want
  G wawnt
  H waant
  J wante

5. Have those big dogs gone _____ yet?
  A awaye
  B away
  C awhay
  D awway

6. I like that puppy _____ it is so friendly.
  F becuz
  G becaus
  H becawz
  J because

More Practice
Now write each correctly spelled word on a sheet of paper.

Spelling Games
www.eduplace.com/kids/sv/
Review for your test.

Real-World Vocabulary

Science: Our Solar System

Write the words from the box to complete this
script for a TV show. Use your Spelling Dictionary.

**Spelling
Word Link**

beyond

orbit
planet
Jupiter
telescope
satellite

Narrator: **Where are we in the universe?**

I'll tell you. We live on the ___(1)___ Earth.
Earth is one of nine planets that ___(2)___ the
sun, and it is the third planet from the sun.
At night we can see other planets in our solar
system if we use a strong ___(3)___. We can see
the planet ___(4)___, which is the largest planet
in our solar system. We can also see a
weather ___(5)___ as it circles Earth.

1. _____

2. _____

3. _____

4. _____

5. _____

Try This CHALLENGE

Solar System Map Make a map of our solar system.
Label the planets that move around the sun.

eWord Game
www.eduplace.com/kids/sv/

Spelling Review

Unit 31

1. _____

2. _____

3. _____

4. _____

5. _____

6. _____

7. _____

Unit 32

8. _____

9. _____

10. _____

11. _____

12. _____

13. _____

14. _____

Unit 31	VCCV Pattern	pages 198–203

until	enjoy	forget	Sunday
garden	market	basket	

Spelling Strategy Divide a word with the VCCV pattern between the two consonants to find the syllables.

Fill-in-the-Blank Write the missing words.

My family plants a ___(1)___ every year. We ___(2)___ doing it. We grow vegetables, so we do not need to buy any from the ___(3)___. I try not to ___(4)___ to water the plants. I wait ___(5)___ the tomatoes are ripe to pick them. Then I collect them in a ___(6)___. Mom uses them to make tomato sauce for ___(7)___ dinner. It's delicious!

Unit 32	Double Consonants	pages 204–209

jelly	pillow	lesson	cherry
arrow	dollar	button	

Spelling Strategy A VCCV word may have double consonants. Divide between the consonants to find the syllables.

Letter Swap Change the letters in dark print. Write Spelling Words.

    8. a**ll**ow   **9.** less**er**   **10.** j**o**lly   **11.** **c**ollar

Classifying Write the word that completes each group.

12. zipper, snap, _____

13. grape, lemon, _____

14. bed, blanket, _____

Unit 33	Words with *ough* and *augh*	pages 210–215

thought	rough	laugh	bought
cough	caught	through	

Spelling Strategy Some words are spelled with the pattern **augh** or **ough**.

Verbs Write the word that tells the past time of each word.

15. think **16.** buy **17.** catch

Fill-in-the-Blank Write the missing words.

18. The silly joke made them _____.

19. I have a sore throat and a bad _____.

20. It looks too big to fit _____ the doorway.

21. The sandpaper felt _____.

Unit 34	Words Ending with *er* or *le*	pages 216–221

river	little	summer	later
uncle	! travel	! color	

Spelling Strategy In words with more than one syllable, the final /ər/ sounds are often spelled **er**. The final /əl/ sounds are often spelled **le**.

Analogies Write the word that completes each analogy.

22. *Quicker* is to *slower* as *earlier* is to _____.

23. *Hot* is to *cold* as *big* is to _____.

24. *Bird* is to *robin* as *season* is to _____.

25. *Car* is to *road* as *raft* is to _____.

26. *Mother* is to *father* as *aunt* is to _____.

27. *Triangle* is to *shape* as *red* is to _____.

28. *Scissors* is to *cut* as *plane* is to _____.

Unit 33

15. _____

16. _____

17. _____

18. _____

19. _____

20. _____

21. _____

Unit 34

22. _____

23. _____

24. _____

25. _____

26. _____

27. _____

28. _____

Spelling Review

Unit 35

29. _____

30. _____

31. _____

32. _____

33. _____

34. _____

35. _____

belong	alone	above	between
begin	alive	before	

Spelling Strategy In two-syllable words, the unstressed /ə/ sound may be spelled **a**. The unstressed /bĭ/ sounds may be spelled **be**.

Fill-in-the-Blank Write the missing words.

I found a tiny baby bird. It was __(29)__ and healthy. It was also scared because it was all __(30)__. Where was its mother? Where did it __(31)__? I spotted a small nest in the tree branches __(32)__ my head. The nest was tucked __(33)__ two branches. I put on gloves and gently put the bird back in its nest.

Antonyms Write the word that means the opposite of each word.

34. end   **35.** after

Challenge Words

36. _____

37. _____

38. _____

39. _____

40. _____

Challenge Words   Units 31–35   pages 198–227

expect	mirror	naughty
whistle	awhile	

Context Sentences Write the word to complete each sentence.

36. The _____ dog dug up the garden.

37. Chad looked in the _____ to check his new haircut.

38. We swam for _____, and then we ate lunch.

39. The race begins when the _____ is blown.

40. When do you _____ to finish your work?

Spelling (and) Writing

✎ ## Proofread a Persuasive Essay

Spelling and Grammar Mixed Review Proofread this persuasive essay. Use proofreading marks to fix **five** spelling mistakes, **two** missing commas in a series, and **one** missing comma after an order word.

person
Example: Every ~~person~~ should write, call, or e-mail the mayor.

Why We Need Sidewalks

Our town has streets without sidewalks. This is a real problm for several reasons. First we need sidewalks bicause walking in the street is unsafe. Second, we need sidewalks so kids can safely ride around on their scooters skateboards and bicycles. The town awght to put sidewalks along every street. If enough of us write a leter to show we care, it can hapen.

Tips

- Choose a topic that you have an opinion about.

- Write a topic sentence that states your opinion.

- List reasons that support your opinion.

✎ ## Write a Persuasive Essay

prewrite → draft → revise → proofread → publish

Write a persuasive essay that tells your opinion about something.

- Use some Spelling Words from Units 31–35.
- Proofread your work.

Power Proofreading
www.eduplace.com/kids/sv/

Spelling Test Practice

Test Tip Skip the hard questions. Come back to them later.

Directions Choose the word that is spelled correctly and best completes the sentence.

Example: The car made a _____ turn.

    A suden
    B suddan
    C sudden
    D suddin

Example:

Ⓐ Ⓑ Ⓒ Ⓓ

Answer Sheet

1. Ⓐ Ⓑ Ⓒ Ⓓ

2. Ⓙ Ⓚ Ⓛ Ⓜ

3. Ⓐ Ⓑ Ⓒ Ⓓ

4. Ⓙ Ⓚ Ⓛ Ⓜ

5. Ⓐ Ⓑ Ⓒ Ⓓ

6. Ⓙ Ⓚ Ⓛ Ⓜ

1. Please pass a clean _____.

    A knapken
    B napkin
    C nacken
    D napken

2. Spread the _____ on your pancakes.

    J buter
    K buttor
    L butter
    M buttir

3. I heard him _____ on our door.

    A tapping
    B taping
    C tapeing
    D tepping

4. Her favorite color is _____.

    J pirple
    K purple
    L purpil
    M perpal

5. I want to play the game _____.

    A aggen
    B agin
    C agen
    D again

6. Jeff _____ home after soccer practice.

    J hurried
    K hurryed
    L huried
    M hurreed

Spelling Games
www.eduplace.com/kids/sv/
Review for your test.

Vocabulary Test Practice

 Test Tip Read the sentences to yourself, using each answer choice to fill in the blanks.

Directions Find the word that fits in <u>both</u> of the sentences.

Test Format Practice

Example: **I needed _____ for a dollar.**
It is time to _____ these old, worn tires.

change   coin   patch   move
  ○   ○   ○   ○

_____

1. **I need a _____ to start the campfire.**
   Do these two socks _____ each other?

   flame   match   join   knife
     ○   ○   ○   ○

2. **Put the dirty dishes in the _____.**
   The high waves might _____ the little boat.

   knock   lawn   scrape   sink
     ○   ○   ○   ○

3. **The seeds were planted deep in the rich _____.**
   The spilled gravy will _____ the tablecloth.

   soil   smell   dirt   boil
    ○   ○   ○   ○

4. **The vet knew how to _____ the injured dog.**
   On hot days, ices are a cool _____.

   bounce   gift   treat   sweet
     ○   ○   ○   ○

5. **After dinner the waiter brought us the _____.**
   Please _____ to see if the door is locked.

   mark   surprise   watch   check
    ○   ○   ○   ○

233

Student's Handbook

Contents

Unit 1	Short Vowels		pages 18–23
crop	thing	shut	sticky
spent	lunch	⚠ front	

Spelling Strategy In most words, the short vowel sounds are spelled **a**, **e**, **i**, **o**, or **u**.

Missing Letters Write a word by adding the missing letters.

1. s__ut   2. sp__nt   3. fr__nt

Word Clues Write a word for each clue.

4. how maple syrup feels
5. not a person or a place
6. something a farmer grows
7. a meal eaten at noon

Unit 1

1. _____
2. _____
3. _____
4. _____
5. _____
6. _____
7. _____

Unit 2	Vowel-Consonant-e		pages 24–29
spoke	mile	save	excuse
invite	broke	life	

Spelling Strategy A long vowel sound is often spelled vowel-consonant-**e**.

Classifying Write the word that completes each group.

8. keep, collect, _____
9. foot, yard, _____
10. smashed, dropped, _____
11. party, guest, _____
12. said, talked, _____
13. living, alive, _____
14. reason, explanation, _____

Unit 2

8. _____
9. _____
10. _____
11. _____
12. _____
13. _____
14. _____

Unit 3

15. _____

16. _____

17. _____

18. _____

19. _____

20. _____

21. _____

Unit 3	More Long *a* and Long *e* Words	pages 30–35

lay	real	seem	treat
chain	leave	⏺weigh	

Spelling Strategy In many words, the /ā/ sound is spelled **ay** or **ai**. The /ē/ sound may be spelled **ea** or **ee**.

Rhyme Time Write the Spelling Word that rhymes with each word.

15. plain   16. heat   17. steal

Word Meaning Write the word for each meaning.

18. to go away

19. to put down

20. to measure how heavy something is

21. to appear to be

Unit 4

22. _____

23. _____

24. _____

25. _____

26. _____

27. _____

28. _____

Unit 4	More Long *o* Words	pages 36–41

load	open	soak	shadow
follow	sold	window	

Spelling Strategy The /ō/ sound can be spelled **oa**, **o**, or **ow**.

Context Sentences Write the missing words.

22. I got twenty dollars when I _____ my bike.

23. Help me _____ these boxes into my van.

24. The tree's _____ looks like a person.

25. I saw it through the _____.

26. You can _____ me so you don't get lost.

27. Can you _____ the door?

28. Go _____ your sore feet.

Unit 5   More Long *i* Words   pages 42–47

pie	shiny	might	lie
tight	blind	fight	

Spelling Strategy The /ī/ sound can be spelled **igh**, **i**, or **ie**.

Context Sentences Write the missing words.

29. A small dog picked a _____ with a big one.
30. I _____ win the race this time.
31. A new penny is _____.
32. An honest person does not tell a _____.
33. Shoes that are _____ hurt your feet.
34. A guide dog can help _____ people.
35. Cherry is my favorite kind of _____.

Challenge Words   Units 1–5   pages 18–47

hospital	decide	explain
clothes	frightening	

Synonyms Write the word that means the same.

36. choose   37. scary   38. outfits

Context Paragraph Write the missing words.

We bring our turtle to the animal __(39)__ when it is sick. The vet knows what to do. He can __(40)__ to us how to help Taffy feel better.

Unit 5

29. _____
30. _____
31. _____
32. _____
33. _____
34. _____
35. _____

Challenge Words

36. _____
37. _____
38. _____
39. _____
40. _____

Cycle 2 Extra Practice and Review

Unit 7

1. _____
2. _____
3. _____
4. _____
5. _____
6. _____
7. _____

Unit 7	Short and Long Vowels	pages 54–59

flame	easy	paid	stuff
cheese	program	shell	

Spelling Strategy The short vowel sound can be spelled with one letter. The long vowel sound can be spelled with one or two letters or with the vowel-consonant-**e** pattern.

Missing Letters Write a word by adding the missing letters.

1. pr__gr__m   2. p__ __d   3. st__ff

Word Clues Write a word for each clue.

4. This is what covers a turtle's body.
5. This is fire on the end of a match.
6. This goes on top of pizza.
7. This means not hard to do.

Unit 8

8. _____
9. _____
10. _____
11. _____
12. _____
13. _____
14. _____

Unit 8	Three-Letter Clusters	pages 60–65

three	spring	thrill	strange
string	scrape	threw	

Spelling Strategy Some words begin with the consonant clusters **thr**, **scr**, **str**, and **spr**.

Context Sentences Write the missing words.

8. Tony _____ the ball.
9. Did you _____ your knee?
10. Tie this _____ around the package.
11. My sister is two, but soon she will be _____.
12. It was a _____ to see a whale up close.
13. The _____ noise was my alarm clock.
14. Flowers bloom in _____.

238

Unit 9   Unexpected Consonant Patterns   pages 66–71

itch	wrap	knot	watch
stretch	write	match	

Spelling Strategy Some words have unexpected consonant patterns.

/n/ → **kn**ot   /r/ → **wr**ap   /ch/ → i**tch**

Context Paragraph Write the missing words.

I made a hat for my uncle. The yarn got a ____(15)____ in it. Now I will ____(16)____ the hat up and send it to him. I hope the wool doesn't ____(17)____ him. I will ____(18)____ a note about how to wash the hat. Then it won't ____(19)____ out of shape. Maybe I will make mittens to ____(20)____. You can ____(21)____ as I make them.

Unit 9

15. _____

16. _____

17. _____

18. _____

19. _____

20. _____

21. _____

Unit 10   Vowel Sound in *clown*   pages 72–77

clown	round	cloud	crown
thousand	powder	blouse	

Spelling Strategy The /ou/ sound, as in *crown* or *cloud*, is often spelled **ow** or **ou**.

Missing Letters Write a word by adding the missing letters.

22. p____der   23. r____nd   24. cr____n

Classifying Write the word that completes each group.

25. ten, hundred, _____   27. pants, dress, _____

26. circus, juggler, _____   28. sky, rain, _____

Unit 10

22. _____

23. _____

24. _____

25. _____

26. _____

27. _____

28. _____

Unit 11

29. _____

30. _____

31. _____

32. _____

33. _____

34. _____

35. _____

Unit 11	Vowel Sound in *lawn*		pages 78–83
talk	cross	crawl	also
raw	salt	wall	

Spelling Strategy These patterns can spell the /ô/ sound: **aw**, as in *raw*; **o**, as in *cross*; **a** before **l**, as in *wall*.

Word Pairs Write the word that completes each pair of sentences.

29. The *floor* is on the *bottom*.
    The _____ is on the *side*.

30. You *hear* when you *listen*.
    You *speak* when you _____.

Missing Letters Write a word by adding the missing letters.

31. cr__ __l
32. __ __so
33. s__ __t
34. cr__ss
35. r__ __

Challenge Words

36. _____

37. _____

38. _____

39. _____

40. _____

Challenge Words	Units 7–11	pages 54–83
comb	straight	knuckle
mountain	strawberry	

Word Clues Write a word for each clue.

36. not curly
37. to untangle hair
38. bigger than a hill
39. where your finger bends
40. a small, red fruit

Unit 13 Vowel Sound in *joy* pages 90–95

join	coin	noise	spoil
boy	soil	choice	

Spelling Strategy The /oi/ sound, as in *boy* and *coin*, is spelled **oy** or **oi**.

Missing Letters Write a word by adding the missing letters.

1. ch＿＿ce   2. sp＿＿l   3. j＿＿n

Word Clues Write a word for each clue.

4. This may hurt your ears.
5. This is what a gardener needs.
6. This person may be a brother.
7. This can go in a bank.

Unit 14 Vowel + /r/ Sounds pages 96–101

ear	storm	acorn	artist
March	clear	north	

Spelling Strategy Remember these spelling patterns for the vowel + /r/ sounds:

/ôr/ *or*, as in n**or**th   /är/ *ar*, as in **ar**tist
/îr/ *ear*, as in cl**ear**

Classifying Write the word that completes each group.

8. south, east, ＿＿＿
9. nut, seed, ＿＿＿
10. thunder, lightning, ＿＿＿
11. singer, actor, ＿＿＿
12. January, February, ＿＿＿
13. nose, eye, ＿＿＿
14. bright, sunny, ＿＿＿

Unit 13

1. _____
2. _____
3. _____
4. _____
5. _____
6. _____
7. _____

Unit 14

8. _____
9. _____
10. _____
11. _____
12. _____
13. _____
14. _____

241

Cycle 3 Extra Practice and Review

Unit 15

15. _____

16. _____

17. _____

18. _____

19. _____

20. _____

21. _____

Unit 15	Vowel + /r/ Sounds in *nurse*		pages 102–107
work	first	curly	dirt
third	worry	turn	

Spelling Strategy The /ûr/ sounds can be spelled **ur**, **or**, **ir**, or **er**.

Missing Letters Write a word by adding the missing letters.

15. d___t **16.** th___d **17.** w___ry **18.** t___n

Antonyms Write the word that means the opposite.

19. straight

20. last

21. play

Unit 16

22. _____

23. _____

24. _____

25. _____

26. _____

27. _____

28. _____

Unit 16	Vowel + /r/ Sounds in *air*		pages 108–113
wear	bare	stairs	hair
care	pair	share	

Spelling Strategy The /âr/ sounds can have these patterns: *air*, as in **hair**; *ear*, as in **wear**; *are*, as in **share**.

Word Clues Write a word for each clue.

22. Puppies need lots of this.

23. You should do this with your toys.

24. two

25. A tree in winter might be this.

26. You brush this.

27. Clothes are what you _____.

28. steps

Unit 17	Vowel Sounds in *spoon, wood*	pages 114–119

spoon	wood	drew	balloon
chew	tooth	shook	

Spelling Strategy The vowel sound /o͞o/ may be spelled **oo**, **ew**, or **ue**. The vowel sound /o͝o/ may be spelled **oo**.

Classifying Write the word that completes each group.

29. fork, knife, _____
30. kite, paper plane, _____
31. painted, sketched, _____
32. bite, swallow, _____
33. rubber, paper, _____
34. lip, tongue, _____
35. wiggled, rattled, _____

Unit 17

29. _____
30. _____
31. _____
32. _____
33. _____
34. _____
35. _____

Challenge Words	Units 13–17	pages 90–119

poison	partner	perfect
compare	jewel	

Context Sentences Write the missing words.

36. The green _____ is very sparkly.
37. Please choose a _____ to study with.
38. Let's _____ both chairs to see which is softer.
39. I know a _____ place for a picnic.
40. Was the bottle full of _____?

Challenge Words

36. _____
37. _____
38. _____
39. _____
40. _____

Cycle 4 Extra Practice and Review

Unit 19

1. _____

2. _____

3. _____

4. _____

5. _____

6. _____

Unit 19	Homophones	pages 126–131
hole	whole	hear
here	knew	new

Spelling Strategy **Homophones** are words that sound alike but have different spellings and meanings.

Context Sentences Write the missing words.

1. Does every donut have a _____?
2. I _____ the right answer.
3. Did you _____ the question?
4. I can't believe I ate the _____ thing.
5. Do you live near _____?
6. We got a _____ pet.

Unit 20

7. _____

8. _____

9. _____

10. _____

11. _____

12. _____

13. _____

Unit 20	Spelling /j/ and /s/	pages 132–137
age	space	change	once
large	dance	bounce	

Spelling Strategy The /j/ sound can be spelled with the consonant **j** or **g** followed by **e** or **i**. The /s/ sound may be spelled **c** when the **c** is followed by **e** or **i**.

Missing Letters Write a word by adding the missing letters.

7. chan___ ___   8. spa___ ___   9. lar___ ___

Word Clues Write a word for each clue.

10. one time
11. steps set to music
12. how old something is
13. what a ball does

242

Unit 21   Spelling /k/ and /kw/   pages 138–143

shark	check	queen	circus
flake	squeeze	quart	

Spelling Strategy The /k/ sound can be spelled **k**, **ck**, or **c**. The /kw/ sounds can be spelled **qu**.

Classifying Write the word that completes each group.

14. fair, zoo, _____

15. try, test, _____

16. whale, dolphin, _____

17. press, pinch, _____

18. cup, gallon, _____

Word Pairs Write the word that completes each pair of sentences.

19. *Rain* comes down in a *drop.*
    Snow comes down in a _____.

20. A *man* could be *king.*
    A *woman* could be _____.

Unit 22   Compound Words   pages 144–149

sometimes	everything	something	himself
faraway	grandmother	without	

Spelling Strategy A **compound word** is made up of two or more shorter words.

Word Building Write Spelling Words by adding words to the words below.

21. every_____

22. far_____

23. _____times

24. him_____

25. _____out

26. _____thing

27. grand_____

Unit 21

14. _____

15. _____

16. _____

17. _____

18. _____

19. _____

20. _____

Unit 22

21. _____

22. _____

23. _____

24. _____

25. _____

26. _____

27. _____

245

Cycle 4 Extra Practice and Review

Unit 23

28. _____

29. _____

30. _____

31. _____

32. _____

33. _____

34. _____

Unit 23	Contractions	pages 150–155
haven't doesn't wouldn't she's		
aren't couldn't ⚠ o'clock		

Spelling Strategy A **contraction** is a short way of saying or writing two or more words. An apostrophe takes the place of one or more letters.

are not   *aren't*

Word Meaning Write the word that means the same.

28. does not   **30.** are not

29. she is   **31.** have not

Context Paragraph Write the missing words.

The circus was coming to town. I ___(32)___ wait to go.
We were planning to leave at ten ___(33)___. I set my clock
for five A.M. so I ___(34)___ be late!

Challenge Words	Units 19–23	pages 126–155
peace gigantic correct		
everybody weren't		

Context Sentences Write the missing words.

35. We looked, but they _____ there.

36. I hope _____ can come to the party.

37. I want _____ and quiet!

38. The elephant was _____!

39. I knew the _____ answer.

Challenge Words

35. _____

36. _____

37. _____

38. _____

39. _____

Unit 25	Words with *-ed* or *-ing*	pages 162–167

coming	swimming	wrapped	taping
invited	changing	tapping	

Spelling Strategy The spelling of some base words may change when **-ed** or **-ing** is added.

wrap + p + ed = **wrapped**   come − e + ing = **coming**

Ending Swap Write Spelling Words by changing *-ed* to *-ing*.

1. changed   **2.** tapped   **3.** taped

Context Paragraph Write the missing words.

We ___(4)___ my cousin Anna to visit. She'll be ___(5)___ this afternoon. I can't wait to go ___(6)___ with Anna. Mom ___(7)___ up some sandwiches to bring to the lake.

Unit 26	Changing Final *y* to *i*	pages 168–173

hurried	dried	worried	parties
tried	ponies	babies	

Spelling Strategy When a base word ends with a consonant and **y**, change the **y** to **i** before adding **-es** or **-ed**.

Letter Math Add and take away letters to write Spelling Words.

8. dry − y + ied =

9. party − y + ies =

10. hurry − y + ied =

11. pony − y + ies =

12. try − y + ied =

13. baby − y + ies =

14. worry − y + ied =

Unit 25

1. _____

2. _____

3. _____

4. _____

5. _____

6. _____

7. _____

Unit 26

8. _____

9. _____

10. _____

11. _____

12. _____

13. _____

14. _____

Unit 27

15. _____

16. _____

17. _____

18. _____

19. _____

20. _____

21. _____

Unit 27	Prefixes *re-* and *un-*	pages 174–179

unfold	unclear	unhurt	recheck
unlucky	reuse	unsure	

Spelling Strategy A **prefix** is a word part added to the beginning of a base word. **Re-** and **un-** are prefixes.

Antonyms Write the word that means the opposite.

15. hurt   16. fold   17. sure   18. lucky

Context Sentences Write the missing words.

19. To cut down on pollution, please _____ your plastic bags.

20. To see if you did your homework right, _____ it.

21. Ask a question if the directions are _____.

Unit 28

22. _____

23. _____

24. _____

25. _____

26. _____

27. _____

28. _____

Unit 28	Suffixes *-ful*, *-ly*, and *-er*	pages 180–185

fighter	closely	quickly	careful
friendly	speaker	fearful	

Spelling Strategy A **suffix** is a word part added to the end of a base word. **-Ful**, **-ly**, and **-er** are suffixes.

Word Meaning Write a word for each meaning.

22. in a close way   26. one who speaks

23. full of care   27. in a quick way

24. one who fights   28. liking to meet people

25. full of fear

Unit 29	Suffixes *-less* and *-ness*	pages 186–191

| sadness | helpless | thankless | thickness |
| brightness | careless | softness | |

Spelling Strategy care + **less** = care**less**
bright + **ness** = bright**ness**

Word Pairs Write the word that completes each pair of sentences.

29. A *smile* shows *happiness.*
     A *tear* shows _____.

30. A *cloud* may bring *darkness.*
     The *sun* may bring _____.

31. *Being neat* is being *careful.*
     Dropping litter is being _____.

Ending Match Write Spelling Words by adding *-less* or *-ness* to each base word.

32. help   34. soft
33. thank   35. thick

Challenge Words	Units 25–29	pages 162–191

| scarred | countries | unknown |
| calmly | breathless | |

Word Clues Write a word for each clue.

36. the opposite of *known*
37. marked
38. what the United States and England are
39. how you feel after you run
40. in a quiet way

Unit 29

29. _____
30. _____
31. _____
32. _____
33. _____
34. _____
35. _____

Challenge Words

36. _____
37. _____
38. _____
39. _____
40. _____

Cycle 6 Extra Practice and Review

Unit 31

1. _____
2. _____
3. _____
4. _____
5. _____
6. _____
7. _____

Unit 32

8. _____
9. _____
10. _____
11. _____
12. _____
13. _____
14. _____

Unit 31   **VCCV Pattern**   **pages 198–203**

person	helmet	carpet	napkin
Monday	problem	order	

Spelling Strategy Divide a word with the VCCV pattern between the two consonants to find the syllables.

Missing Syllables Write Spelling Words by adding the missing syllables.

1. _____ | met
2. _____ | day
3. nap | _____
4. or | _____

Synonyms Write the word that means the same.

5. human   6. rug   7. trouble

Unit 32   **Double Consonants**   **pages 204–209**

bottom	happen	butter	sudden
hello	rabbit	letter	

Spelling Strategy A VCCV word may have double consonants. Divide between the consonants to find the syllables.

Context Sentences Write the missing words.

8. The storm began all of a _____.
9. I heard my neighbor say _____.
10. I like to have jam or _____ on my bread.
11. Please write me a _____.
12. I cleaned my room from top to _____.
13. What will _____ next?
14. My _____ likes to eat carrots.

Unit 33	**Words with *ough* and *augh***	**pages 210–215**

taught	ought	fought	daughter
tough	enough	brought	

Spelling Strategy Some words are spelled with the pattern **augh** or **ough**.

Verbs Write the past time of each word.

15. bring   **16.** teach   **17.** fight

Word Clues Write the word for each clue.

18. should

19. not a son

20. just the right amount

21. difficult

Unit 34	**Words Ending with *er* or *le***	**pages 216–221**

apple	October	ladder	purple
November	number	winter	

Spelling Strategy In words with more than one syllable, the final /ər/ sounds are often spelled **er**. The final /əl/ sounds are often spelled **le**.

Classifying Write the word that completes each group.

22. orange, pear, _____

23. letter, sign, _____

24. red, blue, _____

25. October, _____, December

26. summer, fall, _____

27. stairs, escalator, _____

28. August, September, _____

Unit 33

15. _____

16. _____

17. _____

18. _____

19. _____

20. _____

21. _____

Unit 34

22. _____

23. _____

24. _____

25. _____

26. _____

27. _____

28. _____

Cycle 6 Extra Practice and Review

Unit 35

29. _____

30. _____

31. _____

32. _____

33. _____

34. _____

35. _____

Unit 35	Beginning with *a* or *be*	pages 222–227
below about around again		
because ago behind		

Spelling Strategy In two-syllable words, the unstressed /ə/ sound may be spelled **a**. The unstressed /bĭ/ sounds may be spelled **be**.

Antonyms Write the word that means the opposite.

29. above   **30.** in front

Syllable Addition Write Spelling Words by adding *a* or *be* to the words below.

31. ____ | round   **34.** ____ | cause

32. ____ | gain   **35.** ____ | go

33. ____ | bout

Challenge Words

36. _____

37. _____

38. _____

39. _____

40. _____

Challenge Words	Units 31–35	pages 198–227
wisdom	stubborn	sought
character	beyond	

Context Paragraph Write the missing words.

The main __(36)__ in the story was a wise woman. She wanted to share her __(37)__ with others. She lived in a castle far __(38)__ a desert. A __(39)__ lion always guarded her door. Many people who __(40)__ knowledge came to visit the woman and her lion.

Capitalization and Punctuation Guide

Abbreviations

An abbreviation is a short way to write a word. Most abbreviations begin with a capital letter and end with a period.

Titles	<u>Mr.</u> Juan Albano	<u>Ms.</u> Leslie Clark
	<u>Mrs.</u> Janice Dodd	<u>Dr.</u> Frances Wong

Note: *Miss* is not an abbreviation and does not end with a period.

Days of the Week	Sun. (*Sunday*)	Thurs. (*Thursday*)
	Mon. (*Monday*)	Fri. (*Friday*)
	Tues. (*Tuesday*)	Sat. (*Saturday*)
	Wed. (*Wednesday*)	

Months of the Year	Jan. (*January*)	Sept. (*September*)
	Feb. (*February*)	Oct. (*October*)
	Mar. (*March*)	Nov. (*November*)
	Apr. (*April*)	Dec. (*December*)
	Aug. (*August*)	

Note: *May*, *June*, and *July* are not abbreviated.

Quotations

Quotation marks with commas and end marks	**Quotation marks (" ") set off someone's exact words from the rest of the sentence. The first word of a quotation begins with a capital letter. Use a comma to separate the quotation from the rest of the sentence. Put the end mark before the last quotation mark.**

Linda said, <u>"We</u> don't know where Danny went.<u>"</u>

Capitalization and Punctuation Guide

Capitalization

Rules for capitalization

Every sentence begins with a capital letter.

What a pretty color the roses are!

The pronoun *I* is always a capital letter.

What should I do next?

Begin each important word in the names of particular persons, places, or things (proper nouns) with a capital letter.

George Herman Ruth   New Jersey   Liberty Bell

Titles or their abbreviations when used with a person's name begin with a capital letter.

Doctor Garcia   Mrs. Lin

Begin the names of days, months, and holidays with a capital letter.

Labor Day is on the first Monday in September.

The first and last words and all important words in the titles of books begin with a capital letter. Titles of books are underlined.

The Hill and the Rock   The Bashful Tiger

Punctuation

End marks

A period (.) ends a statement or a command. A question mark (?) follows a question. An exclamation point (!) follows an exclamation.

The scissors are on my desk. (*statement*)
Look up the spelling of that word. (*command*)
How is the word spelled? (*question*)
This is your best poem so far! (*exclamation*)

Apostrophe	**Add an apostrophe (') and *s* to a singular noun to make it show ownership.**
	doctor's father's grandmother's family's
	For a plural noun that ends in *s*, add just an apostrophe to show ownership.
	sisters' families' Smiths' hound dogs'
	Use an apostrophe in contractions in place of missing letters.
	can't (*cannot*) we're (*we are*) I'm (*I am*)
Comma	**Use commas to separate three or more words in a series.**
	Rob bought apples, peaches, and grapes.
	Use commas after *Yes, No, Well,* and order words when they begin a sentence.
	First, set up the table. No, it is too early.
	Use a comma to separate the month and the day from the year.
	I was born on June 17, 1971.
	Use a comma between the names of a city and a state.
	Chicago, Illinois Miami, Florida
	Use a comma after the greeting and after the closing in a letter.
	Dear Uncle Rudolph, Your nephew,

Using the Thesaurus

How to Use This Thesaurus

This Thesaurus includes **main entries** for words you often use. The **main entry words** appear in purple. They are listed in ABC order. Each main entry includes

- the **part of speech**, a **definition**, and a **sample sentence** for the main entry word
- **subentry** words that could be used in place of the main entry word, with definitions and sample sentences
- **antonyms**, or opposites, for the main entry word.

 Imagine you wanted to find a more exact word for *loud* in this sentence:

*The **loud** train made it hard to hear.*

❶ Find the main entry for *loud* in your Thesaurus.

❷ Read the words, or subentries, that can be used in place of *loud: noisy* and *roaring*.

❸ Read the definition and the sample sentence for each subentry.

Now you can choose the best word for your sentence.

*The **roaring** train made it hard to hear.*

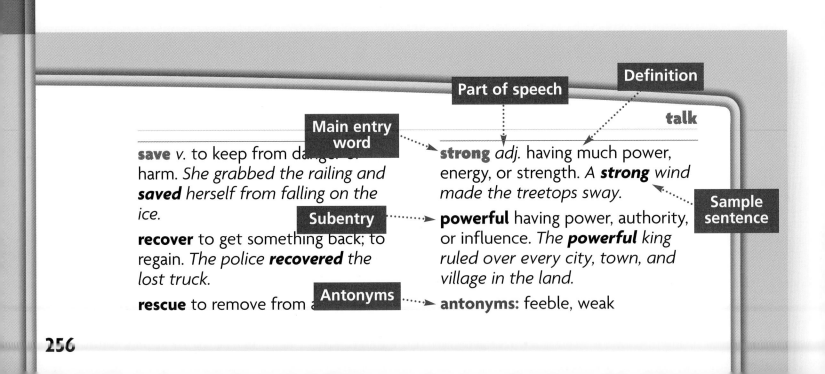

save *v.* to keep from danger or harm. *She grabbed the railing and **saved** herself from falling on the ice.*

recover to get something back; to regain. *The police **recovered** the lost truck.*

rescue to remove from a...

Main entry word

Part of speech

Definition

Subentry

Antonyms

Sample sentence

talk

strong *adj.* having much power, energy, or strength. *A **strong** wind made the treetops sway.*

powerful having power, authority, or influence. *The **powerful** king ruled over every city, town, and village in the land.*

antonyms: feeble, weak

Using the Thesaurus Index

The Thesaurus Index lists all the words in the Thesaurus in ABC order. The Thesaurus Index will help you find a word in this Thesaurus.

The Thesaurus Index lists all the main entry words, the subentries, and any antonyms included in the Thesaurus. The words in the Thesaurus Index are in alphabetical order.

When you look in the Thesaurus Index, you will see that words are shown in three ways.

Main entry words are shown in purple. For example, the word *laugh* is a main entry word.

Subentries are shown in dark print. For example, *lavender* is a subentry of *purple*.

laugh *v.*
lavender purple *adj.*
lawful **wrong** *adj.*

Antonyms are shown in regular print. For example, *lawful* is an antonym of *wrong*.

Practice Look up each word below in the Thesaurus Index. Write the main entry word for each word.

1. friendly   **2.** business   **3.** sketch   **4.** handy   **5.** unite

Use the Thesaurus to replace each underlined word. Rewrite each sentence, using the new word you chose.

6. I want to <u>hold</u> the kitten.
7. His <u>job</u> is to rake the leaves.
8. The board was <u>almost</u> three feet long.
9. The book about fixing things is very <u>useful</u>.
10. The <u>dirty</u> dog had played in the mud.

Thesaurus Index

A

about **almost** adv.
accurate **wrong** adj.
actual real adj.
admire like v.
adorable pretty adj.
adult **child** n.
ailing ill adj.
alarm frighten v.
almost adv.
amend improve v.
answer talk v.
appreciate like v.
approximately
  almost adv.
aqua blue adj.
argue talk v.
arid **wet** adj.
aroma smell n.
arrangement order n.
assignment job n.
attempt try v.
attractive pretty adj.
authentic real adj.

B

baby child n.
bake cook v.
bang knock v.
barbecue cook v.
barely **very** adv.
bawl **laugh** v.

beautiful pretty adj.
begin **end** v.
beige brown adj.
bellow yell v.
belongings stuff n.
better improve v.
big large adj.
bind fasten v.
bird n.
blend mix v.
blue adj.
boil cook v.
bony thin adj.
boulevard road n.
broil cook v.
brown adj.
bumpy **even** adj.
business work n.
button fasten v.

C

calm frighten v.
career work n.
carrot orange adj.
cheap **valuable** adj.
cheerful happy adj.
cheerful **sad** adj.
chestnut brown adj.
child n.
chop cut v.
chore job n.
chubby **thin** adj.
chuckle laugh v.
clasp hold v.

clean **dirty** adj.
clip cut v.
close fasten v.
close near adj.
clutch hold v.
common usual adj.
complete end v.
connect join v.
continue **end** v.
contract **grow** v.
convenient useful adj.
cook v.
correct **wrong** adj.
costly valuable adj.
cradle hold v.
criminal wrong adj.
crimson red adj.
cry **laugh** v.
cut v.
cute pretty adj.

D

dainty pretty adj.
damp wet adj.
decrease **grow** v.
deep large adj.
delicate soft adj.
depressed sad adj.
difficult hard adj.
dirty adj.
disagreeable **nice** adj.
disappointed sad adj.
dislike **like** v.
distant **near** adj.

divide **join** v.
divide **mix** v.
doodle draw v.
draw v.
drenched wet adj.
dripping wet adj.
drop **grab** v.
drum knock v.
dry **wet** adj.

easy **hard** adj.
enchanting pretty adj.
end v.
endanger **save** v.
enjoy like v.
enormous large adj.
equipment stuff n.
especially very adv.
even adj.
evil wrong adj.
exclaim say v.
expand grow v.
expensive valuable adj.
experiment try v.
extend grow v.
extra very adv.
extraordinary **usual** adj.
extremely very adv.

fair pretty adj.
fair **wrong** adj.

fake **real** adj.
false **real** adj.
false wrong adj.
familiar usual adj.
far **near** adj.
fasten v.
fat **thin** adj.
faulty wrong adj.
feeble **strong** adj.
filthy dirty adj.
finish end v.
fit **ill** adj.
flat even adj.
fluffy soft adj.
formation order n.
free **grab** v.
fresh new adj.
friendly nice adj.
frighten v.
fry cook v.

genuine real adj.
giggle laugh v.
glad happy adj.
glad **sad** adj.
gloomy **happy** adj.
gloomy sad adj.
gold yellow adj.
good **wrong** adj.
goods stuff n.
good-looking pretty adj.
gorgeous pretty adj.
gossip talk v.

grab v.
graceful pretty adj.
grasp grab v.
greatly very adv.
grimy dirty adj.
grow v.
grownup **child** n.
grubby dirty adj.

hack cut v.
hammer knock v.
handsome pretty adj.
handy useful adj.
happen v.
happy adj.
happy **sad** adj.
hard adj.
hardly **very** adv.
harm **improve** v.
hasty quick adj.
hate **like** v.
healthy **ill** adj.
heavy large adj.
help improve v.
helpful nice adj.
helpful useful adj.
highway road n.
hold v.
homely **pretty** adj.
hop jump v.
howl yell v.
hug hold v.
huge large adj.

Thesaurus Index

hurdle jump *v.*
hurry *v.*
hurt improve *v.*

ill *adj.*
illegal wrong *adj.*
immense large *adj.*
impractical **useful** *adj.*
improve *v.*
inaccurate wrong *adj.*
incorrect wrong *adj.*
inexact wrong *adj.*
inexpensive
　valuable *adj.*
infant child *n.*
ingredients stuff *n.*

job *n.*
join *v.*
jolly happy *adj.*
joyful happy *adj.*
jump *v.*
junk stuff *n.*
just **wrong** *adj.*

keep *v.*
knock *v.*
knot fasten *v.*

lane road *n.*
lanky thin *adj.*
large *adj.*
laugh *v.*
lavender purple *adj.*
lawful **wrong** *adj.*
lay put *v.*
lean thin *adj.*
leap jump *v.*
leisurely **quick** *adj.*
lemon yellow *adj.*
level even *adj.*
like *v.*
little **large** *adj.*
loosen **fasten** *v.*
lose **save** *v.*
loud *adj.*
love like *v.*
lovely pretty *adj.*

magnificent pretty *adj.*
march walk *v.*
material stuff *n.*
messy dirty *adj.*
mighty strong *adj.*
miserable **happy** *adj.*
miserable sad *adj*
mistaken wrong *adj.*
mix *v.*
modern new *adj.*

moist wet *adj.*
most very *adv.*
multiply grow *v.*

nasty **nice** *adj.*
naughty wrong *adj.*
navy blue *adj.*
near *adj.*
nearly almost *adv.*
neighboring near *adj.*
new *adj.*
nice *adj.*
noisy loud *adj.*
normal usual *adj.*

occupation work *n.*
occur happen *v.*
odor smell *n.*
old **new** *adj.*
open **fasten** *v.*
orange *adj.*
order *n.*
ordinary usual *adj.*
outdated **new** *adj.*
outstanding **usual** *adj.*
overweight **thin** *adj.*
owl bird *n.*

P

parched **wet** adj.
parrot bird n.
patter knock v.
pattern order n.
peach orange adj.
peacock bird n.
peculiar **usual** adj.
penguin bird n.
phony **real** adj.
place put v.
plain **pretty** adj.
pleasant nice adj.
plump **thin** adj.
poach cook v.
pounce grab v.
pound knock v.
powerful strong adj.
practical useful adj.
precious valuable adj.
pretty adj.
priceless valuable adj.
profession work n.
purple adj.
put v.

quick adj.
quiet **loud** adj.
quit end v.

R

rap knock v.
rare **usual** adj.
real adj.
recover save v.
red adj.
reduce **grow** v.
release **grab** v.
rescue save v.
reserve keep v.
retain keep v.
right **wrong** adj.
road n.
roar laugh v.
roaring loud adj.
roast cook v.
rough **even** adj.
roughly almost adv.
ruby red adj.
rush hurry v.

sad adj.
sad **happy** adj.
sample try v.
save v.
save keep v.
say v.
scamper hurry v.
scarcely **very** adv.
scare frighten v.
scent smell n.
scold talk v.

scrawny **thin** adj.
scream yell v.
screech yell v.
scribble draw v.
sea gull bird n.
seal fasten v.
seize grab v.
separate **join** v.
separate **mix** v.
sequence order n.
shriek yell v.
shrink **grow** v.
sick ill adj.
sickly ill adj.
silent **loud** adj.
simmer cook v.
simple **hard** adj.
sketch draw v.
skinny thin adj.
slender thin adj.
slice cut v.
slight thin adj.
slim thin adj.
slow **quick** adj.
small **large** adj.
smell n.
smooth even adj.
snatch grab v.
snicker laugh v.
snip cut v.
sob **laugh** v.
soft adj.
soft **loud** adj.
soggy wet adj.
soiled dirty adj.
solid **soft** adj.
soothe **frighten** v.

261

sopping wet *adj.*
sorrowful sad *adj.*
speedy quick *adj.*
splendid pretty *adj.*
spotless **dirty** *adj.*
spread grow *v.*
spring jump *v.*
stale **new** *adj.*
start **end** *v.*
state say *v.*
steam cook *v.*
stew cook *v.*
stir mix *v.*
stop end *v.*
strange **usual** *adj.*
street road *n.*
stride walk *v.*
strong *adj.*
stuff *n.*
stunning pretty *adj.*
sturdy **soft** *adj.*
swell grow *v.*

T

take place happen *v.*
talk *v.*
tall large *adj.*
tap knock *v.*
task job *n.*
tender soft *adj.*
terrify frighten *v.*
test try *v.*

thin *adj.*
thump knock *v.*
tie fasten *v.*
tiny **large** *adj.*
toast cook *v.*
toddler child *n.*
tot child *n.*
tough hard *adj.*
tough **soft** *adj.*
trace draw *v.*
trade work *n.*
true real *adj.*
try *v.*
turnpike road *n.*

U

ugly **pretty** *adj.*
undertaking job *n.*
underweight thin *adj.*
unexpected **usual** *adj.*
unfair wrong *adj.*
unhappy sad *adj.*
unhealthy ill *adj.*
unite join *v.*
unjust wrong *adj.*
unlawful wrong *adj.*
unpleasant **nice** *adj.*
unwell ill *adj.*
upgrade improve *v.*
useful *adj.*
useless **useful** *adj.*
usual *adj.*

V

valuable *adj.*
very *adv.*
violet purple *adj.*

W

walk *v.*
weak **strong** *adj.*
weep **laugh** *v.*
well **ill** *adj.*
wet *adj.*
wicked wrong *adj.*
withhold keep *v.*
woodpecker bird *n.*
work *n.*
worsen **improve** *v.*
worthless **useful** *adj.*
worthless **valuable** *adj.*
wrong *adj.*

Y

yell *v.*
yellow *adj.*
youngster child *n.*

almost *adv.* just short of. *Loren is* **almost** *as old as Carrie.*

about nearly; almost. *It takes Ann* **about** *ten minutes to walk to school.*

approximately almost exactly. *That basket will hold* **approximately** *thirty apples.*

nearly almost but not quite. *Joey* **nearly** *caught the fish, but it got away.*

roughly about. *Both bedrooms are* **roughly** *the same size.*

bird *n.* a warm-blooded animal that lays eggs. A bird has two wings and a body covered with feathers. *Did you ever wish you could fly like a* **bird***?*

owl a bird that has a large head, large eyes, and a short hooked bill. Owls usually fly and hunt at night. *An* **owl** *was sitting on the tree branch in the moonlight.*

parrot a colorful bird that is popular as a pet and that can be trained to repeat words. *My pet* **parrot** *can say "Pretty bird."*

peacock a very large male peafowl that has shiny blue and green feathers and a tail that can be spread out like a large fan. *The* **peacock** *spread its tail and walked along the lake.*

penguin a sea bird that cannot fly, lives in or near Antarctica, and has white feathers on its front and black feathers on its back. *The* **penguin** *dived into the icy water to catch fish.*

sea gull a bird that lives on coasts and has long wings. It usually has gray and white feathers and webbed feet. *A* **sea gull** *circled high above the sailboat.*

woodpecker a bird with a hard, pointed bill. The woodpecker drills into the bark of trees to get insects. *That tapping noise is the sound of a* **woodpecker** *drilling for its dinner.*

blue *adj.* having the color of a clear sky. *On a sunny day, the* **blue** *boat matched the sky.*

aqua light greenish-blue. *The water near the shore has a lovely* **aqua** *color.*

navy dark blue. *The highway police wear* **navy** *uniforms.*

brown *adj.* of the color of wood or soil. *The leaves on the ground had all turned* **brown***.*

beige light yellowish-brown. *The* **beige** *rug will blend with the green and brown furniture in the living room.*

chestnut reddish-brown. *I stroked the pony's* **chestnut** *mane.*

child n. a young boy or girl. *Every man, woman, and* **child** *needs exercise to stay fit.*

baby a very young child; infant. *The* **baby** *crawled happily around the playpen and then began shaking its rattle.*

infant a child from the earliest period of life up to about two years of age. *She laid the* **infant** *in a crib.*

toddler a child who has learned to walk but is still unsteady on his or her feet. *The* **toddler** *walked a few steps and then fell down.*

tot a small child. *The clown leaned down and handed the* **tot** *a balloon.*

youngster a young person or child. *"When I was a* **youngster,** *there was no TV," Grandma said.*

antonyms: adult, grownup

Word Bank

cook v. to prepare food for eating by using heat.

bake	fry	steam
barbecue	poach	stew
boil	roast	toast
broil	simmer	

cut v. to form, separate, or divide by using a sharp instrument. *Please* **cut** *the rope into six pieces.*

chop to cut up into small pieces. *Dad* **chopped** *a carrot and some potatoes and put them in the soup.*

clip to cut the surface growth of. *Barb* **clipped** *the bushes to make them look neat.*

hack to cut with heavy blows. *Andy* **hacked** *his way through the thick jungle.*

slice to cut into thin, flat pieces. *I* **sliced** *two pieces of bread from the loaf.*

snip to cut with short, quick strokes. *Liza used scissors to* **snip** *the ribbons in half before she made the bows.*

dirty adj. full of or covered with dirt; not clean. *Don loaded the* **dirty** *laundry into the washing machine.*

filthy extremely dirty. *The walls were so* **filthy** *that you could not tell what color they were.*

grimy covered with heavy dirt. *He scrubbed the grease and soot from his* **grimy** *hands.*

grubby dirty and messy. *We fed the stray dog and washed his* **grubby** *coat.*

messy untidy. *I swept out the* **messy** *closet and put everything in order.*

soiled having become or been made dirty. *The tablecloth was* **soiled** *where someone had spilled gravy.*

antonyms: clean adj., spotless

draw v. to make a picture with lines. *Mandy* **drew** *a picture of her apartment building.*

doodle to scribble while thinking about something else. *Molly doodled on a notepad while she listened to the story.*

scribble to draw carelessly. *I scribbled some lines with each crayon to try out the different colors.*

sketch to make a rough drawing. *Daniel quickly sketched the bird before it flew away.*

trace to copy by following lines seen through a sheet of transparent paper. *Louis carefully traced the sailboat picture in the magazine.*

end *v.* to bring to a close. *The president ended the meeting.*

complete to make or do entirely. *I completed the work in a day.*

finish to reach the end of. *He finished the book.*

quit to stop doing. *You will never win if you quit trying.*

stop to cut off an action. *The fence stopped me from going farther.*

antonyms: begin, continue, start

even *adj.* without bumps, gaps, or rough parts. *The table wiggled because the floor was not even.*

flat having a smooth, even surface. *I need something flat to write on.*

level having a flat, even surface. *It is easier to walk along level ground than to walk up and down hills.*

smooth having a surface that is not rough or uneven. *She likes to roller-skate where the sidewalk is smooth.*

antonyms: bumpy, rough

fasten *v.* to attach firmly. *She fastened the tag to her skirt.*

bind to hold together. *Birds bind their nests with mud.*

button to fasten or close a garment by slipping small disks through holes. *Button your coat, or you will be cold.*

close to shut. *The lid of the trunk would not close.*

knot to fasten by tying together one or more pieces of string, rope, or twine. *She knotted the two pieces of rope together.*

seal to close tightly with glue, wax, or other hardening material. *He sealed the letter shut so that no one would read it.*

tie to fasten with a cord or rope. *She tied the box shut with cord.*

antonyms: loosen, open *v.*

frighten *v.* to make or become afraid. *The thunder and lightning frightened us.*

alarm to make suddenly very worried. *News of the accident alarmed the family.*

scare to startle or shock. *A loud noise scared the sleeping cat.*

(continued)

265

frighten (continued)

terrify to frighten greatly. *The spreading forest fire **terrified** the animals.*

antonyms: calm *v.*, soothe

grab *v.* to take hold of suddenly. *I **grabbed** the railing to stop myself from falling.*

grasp to take hold of firmly with the hand. *I **grasped** a branch and pulled myself up.*

pounce to seize by swooping. *The cat **pounced** on the rubber mouse.*

seize to take hold of suddenly and by force. *The thief **seized** the package and ran.*

snatch to grasp quickly. *Gabriel **snatched** the ball before his teammate could reach it.*

antonyms: drop *v.*, free *v.*, release

grow *v.* to become larger in size. *My little sister **grew** too big for me to pick up.*

expand to make or become large in size, volume, or amount. *The balloon **expanded** until it popped.*

extend to make longer; lengthen. *We plan to **extend** our visit from a week to ten days.*

multiply to make or become more in number. *The number of students in this school has **multiplied** in the past ten years.*

spread to stretch over a wider area. *As water continued dripping, the puddle **spread.***

swell to become larger in size or volume as a result of pressure from the inside. *The sponge **swelled** as it soaked up water.*

antonyms: contract *v.*, decrease, reduce, shrink

happen *v.* to take place, occur. *When did the earthquake **happen**?*

occur to come to pass. *How did the accident **occur**?*

take place to come about. *The wedding will **take place** on board the ship.*

happy *adj.* very satisfied. *I was **happy** to hear the good news.*

cheerful merry, lively. *The **cheerful** song helps him forget his worries.*

glad pleased. *"I would be **glad** to help," said Victor.*

jolly full of fun. *The **jolly** waitress liked making us laugh.*

joyful showing, feeling, or causing great joy or happiness. *The puppy galloped toward its owner with a **joyful** bark.*

antonyms: gloomy, miserable, sad

hard *adj.* difficult to solve, understand, or express. *This book is too **hard** for a first grader.*

difficult hard to make, do, or understand. *Denise practiced the **difficult** dance steps over and over.*

tough difficult to do. *Fixing the rusty old car was going to be a **tough** job.*

antonyms: easy, simple

---

hold *v.* to have or keep in the arms or hands. *Please **hold** this package for me so that I can unlock the door.*

clasp to hold or hug tightly. *The little girl **clasped** the wriggling puppy.*

clutch to hold tightly with the hands. *She **clutched** the handlebars of her bike as she rode down the busy street.*

cradle to hold as if in a small bed for a baby. *I **cradled** the kitten in my arms until it fell asleep.*

hug to put one's arms around and hold closely. *The two friends **hugged** each other when they said good-bye.*

---

hurry *v.* to act or move quickly. *We will miss the bus unless we **hurry**.*

rush to act or move too quickly. *You are likely to make mistakes if you **rush** through your work.*

scamper to run or go hurriedly. *The squirrels **scampered** away when the cat suddenly appeared.*

---

ill *adj.* not healthy. *She stayed home from school because she was **ill**.*

ailing feeling ill or having pain. *My **ailing** uncle will stay with us until he is better.*

sick suffering from an illness. *The vet gave us medicine for our **sick** cat.*

sickly tending to become sick. *My **sickly** brother usually has the flu at least five times every winter.*

unhealthy harmful to one's health. *They often eat **unhealthy** foods, such as candy.*

unwell not well; sick. *"I am sorry to hear that you have been **unwell**," he said.*

antonyms: fit *adj.*, healthy, well *adj.*

---

improve *v.* to make or become more excellent. *Bonita can **improve** her grades by studying harder.*

amend to change so as to improve. *The law was **amended** to make it more fair.*

better to improve. *The new library will **better** the lives of those who use it.*

help to aid the progress of. *Hard practice has **helped** her piano playing.*

upgrade to raise to a higher rank or level of excellence. *The factory **upgraded** its products by using better materials.*

antonyms: harm, hurt, worsen

---

job *n.* a piece of work. *Building a house is a big **job**.*

(continued)

job (continued)

assignment a job that has been given to someone. *Katie's **assignment** was to sweep the floors and halls.*

chore a small job, usually done on a regular schedule. *His least favorite **chore** was to put out the garbage every Monday.*

task a piece of work to be done. *Moving that dresser is a **task** for two people.*

undertaking a task that one accepts or attempts. *Fixing a roof can be a dangerous **undertaking**.*

join *v.* to bring or come together. *Let's **join** hands in a circle.*

connect to serve as a way of joining things. *A wire **connects** the lamp with the plug.*

unite to join in action for a certain purpose. *Neighbors from near and far **united** to repair the flood damage.*

antonyms: divide, separate *v.*

jump *v.* to rise up or move through the air by using the leg muscles. *Tom **jumped** as he threw the basketball.*

hop to move with light, quick leaps. *A robin **hopped** along the ground looking for worms.*

hurdle to jump over. *Debby **hurdled** a low stone wall and kept running.*

leap to jump quickly or suddenly. *I **leaped** to the left when I saw the bicycle coming.*

spring to move upward or forward in one quick motion. *The deer easily **sprang** across the brook.*

keep *v.* to have and not give up. *Did Rob give you that watch to **keep**?*

reserve to set aside for a special purpose. *I **reserve** my warmest and most comfortable boots for winter hiking.*

retain to continue to have. *The company moved, but it **retained** most of its long-time employees.*

save to keep from wasting or spending. *She will **save** her money this week.*

withhold to refuse to give. *The boss **withheld** their paychecks until the job was completely finished.*

Word Bank

knock *v.* to make a noise by hitting a hard surface.

bang	patter	tap
drum	pound	thump
hammer	rap	

large *adj.* bigger than average in size or amount. *Elephants and hippos are **large** animals.*

big of great size. *We bought a **big** watermelon for the picnic.*

deep extending down far below the surface. *I dropped the bucket into the **deep** well.*

enormous gigantic in overall size. *The **enormous** tree was bigger than a house.*

heavy weighing a lot. *The box was too **heavy** to lift.*

huge very big, giant-sized. *We realized that the **huge** funnel cloud was a tornado.*

immense of great size or extent; of a size that is or seems too great to measure. *The **immense** desert went on for as far as I could see.*

tall having greater than ordinary height. *A **tall** boy got our ball out of the tree.*

antonyms: little, small, tiny *adj.*

---

laugh *v.* to smile and make sounds to show amusement or scorn. *That funny TV program always makes me **laugh**.*

chuckle to laugh quietly. *She **chuckled** to herself as she read the comic strip.*

giggle to laugh nervously or as if tickled or amused. *We **giggled** with excitement as Mom opened the gift.*

roar to laugh very loudly. *The audience **roared** when the clown picked up the strong man.*

snicker to laugh in a mean or sly way. *It is unkind to **snicker** when a classmate gives the wrong answer.*

antonyms: bawl, cry *v.*, sob *v.*, weep

like *v.* to be fond of. *He **likes** to hike in the mountains.*

admire to look at with great pleasure. *Everyone **admired** her beautiful hair.*

appreciate to know the worth or quality of. *She **appreciated** the careful drawings.*

enjoy to get pleasure from. *We **enjoyed** the cool weather.*

love to have strong, warm feelings for. *Eddy **loves** his new puppy.*

antonyms: dislike *v.*, hate *v.*

---

loud *adj.* having a large amount of sound. *The window slammed shut with a **loud** bang.*

noisy making or filled with a loud or unpleasant sound. *They had to shout to be heard in the **noisy** factory.*

roaring making a loud, deep sound. *The **roaring** engine drowned out the radio.*

antonyms: quiet *adj.*, silent, soft

---

mix *v.* to combine or blend. ***Mix** the peanuts and raisins in a bowl.*

blend to combine completely. *To make the color orange, **blend** red and yellow.*

stir to mix by using repeated circular motions. ***Stir** the soup as you heat it.*

antonyms: divide *v.*, separate *v.*

near

near *adj.* close in distance or time. *We will choose a winner in the **near** future.*

close near in space, time, or relationship. *Yoko is a **close** friend of mine.*

neighboring living near or located close by; bordering. *People from all the **neighboring** towns came to Greenville for the circus.*

antonyms: distant, far

new *adj.* having lately come into being. *A **new** supermarket has just opened near us.*

fresh just made, grown, or gathered. *I enjoy eating **fresh** vegetables.*

modern up-to-date. *The office replaced the old computers with a more **modern** kind.*

antonyms: old, outdated, stale

nice *adj.* kind, pleasant, agreeable. *The boy in the picture has a **nice** smile.*

friendly showing friendship. *Some **friendly** children asked her to join their game.*

helpful providing aid. *The police officer was **helpful** when we got lost.*

pleasant giving pleasure; agreeable. *We enjoyed the **pleasant** scent of the pine trees.*

antonyms: disagreeable, nasty, unpleasant

orange *adj.* of a reddish-yellow color. *The **orange** curtains made the room look like a bright sunset.*

carrot of a bright orange color named for the vegetable. *He has **carrot**-red hair.*

peach of a yellowish-pink color named for the fruit. *Her **peach** dress matched the glow in her cheeks.*

order *n.* a group of things one after another. *The students' names were called in ABC **order**.*

arrangement the way things are placed in relation to each other. *We planned the seating **arrangement** for the dinner party.*

formation a particular arrangement. *Wild geese fly in a V-shaped **formation**.*

pattern a group of things or events that forms a regular arrangement. *He did not like to change the **pattern** of his daily duties.*

sequence the following of one thing after another in a regular, fixed way. *The seasons always follow each other in the same **sequence**.*

pretty *adj.* pleasing to the eye or ear.

adorable	enchanting	handsome
attractive	fair	lovely
beautiful	good-looking	magnificent
cute	gorgeous	splendid
dainty	graceful	stunning

antonyms: homely, plain, ugly

purple *adj.* of a color between blue and red. *The king wore a robe of **purple** velvet.*

lavender light purple. *The flower had pale **lavender** blossoms.*

violet bluish-purple. ***Violet** clouds streaked the sky at sunset.*

put *v.* to cause to be in a certain place. ***Put** the spoons in the drawer.*

lay to put or set down. *He **lays** his coat on the bed.*

place to put in a particular place or order. *She **placed** a bowl of fruit in the center of the table.*

quick *adj.* very fast; rapid. *The frog disappeared into the pond with one **quick** leap.*

hasty done too quickly to be correct or wise; rash. *Manuel is careful and never makes a **hasty** decision.*

speedy moving or happening quickly. *The **speedy** horse soon galloped out of sight.*

antonyms: leisurely, slow

real *adj.* not artificial or made up. *Those silk flowers look **real**.*

actual really existing or happening. *The water looked cold, but the **actual** temperature was warm.*

authentic worthy of belief; true. *The book gave an **authentic** picture of life in the Wild West.*

genuine not false; real or pure. *He examined the pearls carefully to make sure that they were **genuine**.*

true being in agreement with fact or reality. *Is it **true** that bees make honey?*

antonyms: fake, false, phony

red *adj.* having the color of strawberries. *Stop signs are usually **red**.*

crimson bright red. *The American flag has **crimson** and white stripes.*

ruby deep red. *The **ruby**-colored flowers were beautiful in the sunlight.*

road *n.* an open way for vehicles, persons, or animals to pass along or through. *This **road** will take you to the next town.*

(continued)

Thesaurus

sad

road (continued)

boulevard a broad street, often with trees and grass planted in the center or along the sides. *Shoppers enjoyed strolling along the shady* **boulevard**.

highway a main public road. *Which* **highway** *is the fastest route between St. Paul and Minneapolis?*

lane a narrow path or road between fences, hedges, or walls. *We walked along the* **lane** *between the corn field and the wheat field.*

street a road in a city or town. *The post office and the town hall are on this* **street**.

turnpike a wide highway that drivers pay a toll to use. *Cars on the* **turnpike** *slowed as they neared the toll booths.*

sad *adj.* feeling or causing sorrow. *The teacher's illness was* **sad** *news for the class.*

depressed feeling down, lonely, and hopeless. *I was* **depressed** *for days after my best friend moved away.*

disappointed let down after having hoped for or expected something. *Mei was* **disappointed** *when the field trip was cancelled.*

gloomy sad and discouraged. *The losing team felt* **gloomy**.

miserable suffering or uncomfortable. *The rain and mosquitoes made the campers* **miserable**.

sorrowful grieving or feeling heartache after a loss or injury. *He was* **sorrowful** *after his dog died.*

unhappy without joy or pleasure. *She tried to forget the* **unhappy** *summer.*

antonyms: cheerful, glad, happy

---

save *v.* to keep from danger or harm. *She grabbed the railing and* **saved** *herself from falling on the ice.*

recover to get something back; to regain. *The police* **recovered** *the lost truck.*

rescue to remove from a dangerous place. *I* **rescued** *my cat from the tree.*

antonyms: endanger, lose

---

say *v.* to make known or put across in words. *What did your brother* **say** *in the letter?*

exclaim to cry out or say suddenly. *"That's mine!"* **exclaimed** *the child.*

state to say in a very clear, exact way. *The rule* **states** *that the pool closes at 5:00 P.M.*

---

smell *n.* what the nose senses. *The* **smell** *of smoke warns us of fire.*

aroma a pleasant smell. *The* **aroma** *of Aunt Carrie's cooking made us hungry.*

odor a strong smell. *The* **odor** *of mothballs clung to the coat.*

scent a light smell. *The woman had left, but the* **scent** *of her perfume remained.*

---

soft *adj.* not hard or firm. *The* **soft** *cheese spread smoothly.*

delicate very easily broken or torn. *A slight tug will snap the* **delicate** *chain.*

fluffy having hair, feathers, or material that stands up in a soft pile. *I want a warm **fluffy** bathrobe for winter.*

tender easily bruised or hurt. *Her **tender** hands were sore from weeding.*

antonyms: solid, sturdy, tough

strong *adj.* having much power, energy, or strength. *A **strong** wind made the treetops sway.*

mighty having or showing great power, strength, or force. *All the animals in the forest feared the **mighty** mountain lion.*

powerful having power, authority, or influence. *The **powerful** king ruled over every city, town, and village in the land.*

antonyms: feeble, weak

stuff *n.* things that people need, use, or keep. *I have too much **stuff** in my backpack.*

belongings a person's possessions. *Please keep your personal **belongings** in your desk or in the classroom closet.*

equipment the things that are needed for a job, activity, or project. *The players loaded all of their soccer **equipment** into the van.*

goods things that can be bought and sold. *The clothing store sells **goods** such as shirts.*

ingredients parts that make up a mixture or recipe. *Do we have all the **ingredients** we need to make brownies?*

junk things that are kept or stored even though they are old, broken, or no longer used. *It's fun to look through the old **junk** in the attic.*

material anything that can be used to make something else. *The police vests are made of bulletproof **material**.*

talk *v.* to say words. *Carmen and I **talked** on the phone last night.*

answer to say, write, or do something in reply or in reply to. *"Yes, I will come to your party," Terry **answered**.*

argue to disagree. *Jane and Michael **argued** about which movie to see.*

gossip to repeat talk that is often not true. *That silly boy likes to **gossip** about people he does not even know.*

scold to speak angrily to for doing something bad. *I **scolded** my cat for scratching the chair.*

Shades of Meaning

How thin is thin?

thin *adj.* having little fat on the body.

1. **thin**:
   lanky   lean   slender   slim
2. **thinner**:
   slight   underweight
3. **very thin**:
   bony   scrawny   skinny

antonyms: chubby, fat, plump

Thesaurus

try *v.* to put to use for the purpose of judging. *If you like apples, **try** these.*

attempt to make an effort. *The student pilot **attempted** his first solo landing today.*

experiment to do a number of tests to learn or prove something. *She **experimented** to find out which colors looked best in her design.*

sample to test by trying a small part. ***Sample** a dish before you serve it to guests.*

test to use in order to discover any problems. ***Test** the brakes and the horn to be sure that they work.*

U

useful *adj.* being of use or service; helpful. *The car and the telephone have turned out to be very **useful** inventions.*

convenient suited to one's needs or purpose. *It is **convenient** to have a supermarket nearby.*

handy useful, convenient, serving many purposes. *The rope that I took on the camping trip was very **handy**.*

helpful providing what is needed or useful. *A map can be very **helpful** when you are lost.*

practical having or serving a useful purpose. *Would you rather receive a **practical** gift or one that is just for fun?*

antonyms: impractical, useless, worthless

usual *adj.* happening regularly or all of the time. *Her **usual** breakfast is toast and orange juice.*

common found or occurring often. *Squirrels are **common** in many parts of the United States.*

familiar well-known. *Jason played several **familiar** songs, and everyone sang along.*

normal of the usual or regular kind. *We had the **normal** amount of rain this spring.*

ordinary not unusual in any way. *A visit from my aunt turns an **ordinary** day into a special event.*

antonyms: extraordinary, outstanding, peculiar, rare, strange, unexpected

V

valuable *adj.* worth a lot of money. *Land that contains oil is very **valuable**.*

costly of high price or value. *The queen wore a **costly** diamond necklace and earrings.*

expensive having a high price. *Nina has been saving her money for a year to buy an **expensive** bike.*

precious having very great value. *The crown contained diamonds, rubies, and other **precious** gems.*

priceless too valuable to be given a price. *A museum guard watched over the **priceless** paintings.*

antonyms: cheap, inexpensive, worthless

very *adv.* to a high degree. *We were **very** tired after a hard day's work.*

especially more than usually. *All my friends are nice, but Ginny is **especially** kind.*

extra unusually; especially. *Last week the weather was **extra** hot, even for summer.*

extremely to a very high degree. *Some dinosaurs were **extremely** large animals.*

greatly very much; to a large degree. *That artist's work has been **greatly** admired for centuries.*

most to a high degree. *"This has been a **most** delightful evening," said the guest.*

antonyms: barely, hardly, scarcely

walk *v.* to move on foot at an easy and steady pace. *I had to **walk** home when my bike broke.*

march to walk to an even beat. *The soldiers **marched** in the parade.*

stride to walk with long steps. *John **strode** to the chalkboard, sure of his answer.*

wet *adj.* being covered or soaked with water. *I wiped the table with a **wet** cloth.*

damp slightly wet. *His feet left footprints in the **damp** sand.*

drenched wet through and through. *Take this umbrella, or you will get **drenched**!*

dripping being so wet that drops fall. *I wiped my **dripping** forehead after running in the hot sun.*

moist slightly wet. *In the morning the grass is **moist** with dew.*

soggy soaked with moisture. *Her sneakers were **soggy** from walking in the rain.*

sopping thoroughly soaked. *He pulled his **sopping** hat from the puddle and squeezed out the water.*

antonyms: arid, dry, parched

work *n.* a way by which a person earns money. *Michael is looking for gardening **work**.*

business a person's occupation, trade, or work. *Mrs. Roth is in the **business** of selling houses.*

career a profession that a person follows as a life's work. *My father began his **career** as a firefighter when he was twenty.*

occupation a profession, business, or job. *Working as an airline pilot is an interesting **occupation**.*

profession a job that requires training and special study. *Her college courses will prepare her for the teaching **profession**.*

trade an occupation, especially one requiring special skill with the hands. *My aunt chose carpentry as her **trade** because she likes working with wood.*

wrong

Shades of Meaning

wrong *adj.*

1. **not correct:**
   false   incorrect
   faulty   inexact
   inaccurate   mistaken

2. **bad:**
   criminal   unfair
   evil   unjust
   illegal   unlawful
   naughty   wicked

antonyms: 1. accurate, correct, right **2.** fair, good, just, lawful

yell *v.* to cry out loudly. ***Yell*** *for help.*

bellow to shout in a deep, loud voice. *"Who goes there?" the giant* ***bellowed.***

howl to make a long, wailing cry. *He* ***howled*** *with pain when he stubbed his toe.*

scream to make a long, loud, piercing cry or sound. *The child* ***screamed*** *when the dog ran away with his ball.*

screech to make a high, harsh cry or sound. *"Pretty Polly," the parrot* ***screeched***.

shriek to make a loud, shrill sound. *She* ***shrieked*** *in fright when the window suddenly slammed shut.*

yellow *adj.* having the color of the sun. ***Yellow*** *tulips lined the sidewalk in front of the apartment building.*

gold having a deep yellow color. *Wheat turns a* ***gold*** *color when it is ripe.*

lemon having the color of ripe lemons. *The* ***lemon***-*yellow walls seemed to fill the room with sunshine.*

Spelling-Meaning Index

able ability, abler, ablest, ably, disable, unable

age aged, ageless, ages, aging

air aired, airing, airless, airplane, airplanes

apple apples

art artful, artist, artistic, artists, arts

baby babied, babies, babyhood, babying, babyish

balloon ballooned, ballooning, balloons

bare bareback, bared, barefoot, barehanded, bareheaded, barely, bareness, barer, bares, barest, baring

basket basketful, basketry, baskets

bear bear hug, bearish, bearishly, bears, bearskin, grizzly bear, polar bear

begin beginner, beginning, begins

bird birdbath, birdcage, birdcall, birder, birds, bird's-eye, bird watcher

birthday birthdays

blow blower, blowing, blown, blows

blue blueness, bluer, blues, bluest

boil boiled, boiler, boiling, boils

boot booted, bootie, boots

bow¹ bows

bow² bowed, bowing, bows

boy boyhood, boyish, boys

bright brighten, brightener, brighter, brightest, brightly, brightness

butter buttered, buttering, butter, buttery, unbuttered

button buttoned, buttoning, buttons, unbutton

care cared, careful, carefully, careless, carelessly, cares, caring

carry carriage, carried, carrier, carries, carrying

center centered, centering, centers, central

certain certainly, certainty

chair chairs

chew chewable, chewed, chewi, chews, chewy

child childhood, childish, ch shly, childishness, childless, childless, childlike, children

chop chopped, chopr chopping, chops

circle circled, circl rcling

circus circuses

city cities

class class ays

clay clay

clear clearer, clearest, rly, clearness, clears, clearin

uncl othed, clothes, clothing, cloths

clouded, cloudiness, clouding, s, cloudy

wn clowned, clowning, clowns

oach coached, coaches, coaching

coin coins

color colored, colorful, colorfully, coloring, colorless, colors

Spelling-Meaning Index

come become, comes, coming, incoming

cook cooked, cooker, cookery, cookie, cooking, cooks, overcooked, precooked, uncooked, undercooked

cost costing, costly, costs

cough coughed, coughing, coughs

count account, countable, counted, counter, counting, countless, counts, miscount, recount, uncounted

rack cracked, cracker, cracking, cks

cr..d crowded, crowding, crowds

cro.. crowned, crowning, crowns

cry ..d, cries, crying

cube ..es, cubic

dance da.. dances, dan..ble, danced, dancer,

dark darken, ..er, darkest, darkly, darkness

daughter daugh..

day daybreak, da.. daylight, days, today..daydream, ..rday

die died, dies, dying

dirt dirtily, dirtiness, d..

do doer, does, doing, re..

dollar dollars

door doors

drop dropped, dropper, dropping, droplet, drops

drum drummed, drummer, drumming, drums

dry dried, drier, driest, dryer, drying, dryness

ear earful, ears

eight eighteen, eighth, eightieth, eights, eighty

face faced, faceless, faces, facing

fair¹ fairer, fairest, fairly, fairness, unfair, unfairly, unfairness

fair² fairs

farm farmed, farmer, farming, farms

feel feeler, feeling, feels, unfeeling

fight fighter, fighting, fights

fix fixable, fixed, fixer, fixes, fixing

float floatable, floated, floating, floats

fly¹ flier, flies, flying

fly² flies

foil¹ foiled, foiler, foiling, foils

foil² foils

follow followed, follower, following, follows

forget forgetful, forgetfully, forgetfulness, forgets, forgettable, forgetting, unforgettable

four fours, fourteen, fourth

friend befriend, friendless, friendliness, friendly, friends, unfriendly

front front, frontier, fronting, fronts

garden gardened, gardener, gardening, gardens

giraffe giraffes

Spelling-Meaning Index

girl   girlhood, girlish, girlishly, girls

grade   graded, grader, grades, grading

grandfather   grandfatherly, grandfathers

grandmother   grandmotherly, grandmothers

grin   grinned, grinning, grins

ground   grounded, grounding, grounds

hair   hairless, hairs, hairy

happen   happened, happening, happens

happy   happier, happiest, happily, happiness, unhappy

head   headed, heading, headless, heads

hear   heard, hearer, hearing, hears

hello   helloed, helloes, helloing

help   helped, helper, helpful, helpfully, helpfulness, helping, helpless, helplessly, helplessness

her   hers, herself

him   himself

hold   holder, holding, holds

hope   hoped, hopeful, hopefully, hopefulness, hopeless, hopelessly, hopelessness, hopes, hoping

hour   hourly, hours

huge   hugely, hugeness, huger, hugest

hunt   hunted, hunter, hunting, hunts

hurry   hurried, hurriedly, hurriedness, hurries, hurrying, unhurried

hurt   hurtful, hurting, hurts, unhurt

ice   iced, ices, icier, iciest, iciness, icing, icy

inside   insider, insides

invite   invitation, invited, invites, inviting

it   its

jar   jarful, jars

join   joined, joiner, joining, joins, joint, rejoin

joke   joked, joker, jokes, joking, jokingly

joy   enjoy, enjoyable, enjoyably, enjoyment, joyful, joyfully, joyfulness, joyless, joylessly, joylessness, joyous, joyously, joyousness, joys

judge   judged, judges, judgeship, judging, judgment

jump   jumped, jumper, jumping, jumps, jumpy

kind   kinder, kindest, kindliness, kindly, kindness, unkind

knee   kneel, knees

knife   knives

knock   knocked, knocker, knocking, knocks

knot   knots, knotted, knotting, knotty

know   knowable, knowing, knowingly, knowledge, known, knows, unknown

large   enlarge, enlargement, largely, largeness, larger, largest

last   lastly

late   lately, lateness, later, latest

Spelling-Meaning Index

laugh laughable, laughably, laughed, laughing, laughingly, laughs, laughter

law lawful, lawfully, lawfulness, lawless, lawlessly, lawlessness, laws, lawyer, outlaw, outlawed, unlawful, unlawfully

lawn lawns

lay layer, layered, layering, lays

leave leaves, leaving

lie lies, lying

life lifeless, lifelike, lives

like liken, likeness, likewise, unlike

little littler, littlest

loud aloud, louder, loudest, loudly, loudness

love lovable, lovableness, lovably, loved, loveless, loveliness, lovely, lover, loves, loving, lovingly

luck luckily, luckiness, luckless, lucky, unlucky

lunch lunched, lunches, lunching, lunchroom, lunchtime

---

make maker, makes, making, remake

market marketed, marketing, markets

match¹ matchable, matched, matcher, matches, matching, matchless

match² matches

milk milked, milker, milkiness, milking, milks, milky

mind mindful, mindfully, mindfulness, mindless, mindlessly, mindlessness, minds, remind, reminder, unmindful

mine mined, miner, mines, mining

mix mixable, mixed, mixer, mixes, mixing, mixture, unmixed

most mostly

mouth mouthed, mouthful, mouthing, mouths

---

napkin napkins

near neared, nearer, nearest, nearing, nearly, nearness, nears

need needed, needful, needing, needless, needs, needy

neighbor neighbored, neighborhood, neighboring, neighborly, neighbors

new anew, newer, newest, newly, newness, renew

nice nicely, niceness, nicer, nicest

noise noiseless, noises, noisily, noisiness, noisy

north northerly, northern, northerner

note noted, notes, noting

nothing nothingness

---

oil oiled, oiliness, oiling, oils, oily

orange orangeade, oranges

order disorder, ordered, ordering, orderly, orders, reorder

our ours, ourselves

outside outsider

own owned, owner, ownership, owning, owns

---

page paged, pages, paging

paint painted, painter, painting, paints, repaint

pair   paired, pairing, pairs

park   parked, parking, parks

party   partied, parties, partying

pat   pats, patted, patting

patch   patchable, patched, patches, patching, patchy

pay   payable, payer, paying, payment, pays, repay, repayment

peace   peaceable, peaceably, peaceful, peacefully, peacefulness

pear   pears

pencil   penciled, penciling, pencils

penny   pennies, penniless, pennilessness

picnic   picnicked, picnicker, picnicking, picnics

pie   pies

place   displace, misplace, misplaced, placed, placement, places, placing, replace

point   pointed, pointer, pointing, points, pointy

pond   ponds

pony   ponies

pretty   prettier, prettiest, prettily, prettiness

puppy   puppies

purple   purpled, purples, purpling, purplish

quart   quarter, quartered, quartering, quarterly, quartet, quarts

queen   queenlike, queenly, queens

quick   quicken, quicker, quickest, quickly, quickness

quit   quits, quitter, quitting

rabbit   rabbits

raw   rawer, rawest, rawness

read   readable, reading, reads

round   around, rounded, rounder, roundest, rounding, roundness, rounds

row   rowed, rower, rowing, rows

rub   rubbed, rubbing, rubs

sad   sadden, sadder, saddest, sadly, sadness

save   saved, saver, saves, saving, savings

scare   scared, scares, scaring, scary

school   preschool, preschooler, schooled, schooling, schools, unschooled

scratch   scratched, scratches, scratching, scratchy

scream   screamed, screaming, screams

screen   screened, screening, screens

second[1]   seconds

second[2]   secondary, seconded, seconding, secondly, seconds

seem   seemed, seeming, seemingly, seems

send   sender, sending, sends, sent

serve   servant, served, server, serves, service, serving

sew   sewed, sewing, sewn, sews

Spelling-Meaning Index

share   shared, sharer, shares, sharing

shoe   shoeing, shoeless, shoes

shut   shuts, shutter, shutting

sick   homesick, seasick, sicker, sickest, sickly, sickness

sight   sighted, sighting, sightless, sights

sing   singable, singer, singing, sings

skin   skinned, skinning, skinny, skins

smart   smarten, smarter, smartest, smartly, smartness

smell   smelled, smelling, smells, smelly

smile   smiled, smiles, smiling

smoke   smoked, smokeless, smokes, smokiness, smoking, smoky

soap   soaped, soaping, soaps, soapy

sock   socks

soft   soften, softer, softest, softly, softness

soil   soils

sold   resold, unsold

son   grandson, son-in-law, sons, stepson

sound   sounded, sounding, soundless, soundlessly, soundproof, sounds

space   spaced, spaces, spacing

speak   speakable, speaker, speaking, speaks

spoil   spoiled, spoiling, spoils, unspoiled

spoon   spooned, spoonful, spooning, spoons

spray   sprayed, sprayer, spraying, sprays

spread   spreadable, spreading, spreads

spring   springlike, springs

squeeze   squeezable, squeezed, squeezer, squeezes, squeezing

stage   staged, stages, staging

star   starless, starlet, starred, starring, starry, stars

stick   sticker, stickers, stickier, stickiest, stickily, stickiness, sticking, sticks, sticky, unstick

storm   stormed, storming, storms, stormy

story   stories

straight   straighten, straightener, straighter, straightest

straw   straws

stream   streams

street   streets

string   restring, stringing, strings, stringy

strong   stronger, strongest, strongly

sudden   suddenly, suddenness

summer   summers, summery

sun   sunbeam, sunburn, sunburst, sundial, sundown, sunflower, sunglasses, sunless, sunlight, sunnier, sunniest, sunny, sunrise, sunset, sunshine, suntan

talk   talkative, talked, talker, talking, talks

tap   tapped, tapper, tapping, taps

teach   reteach, teacher, teaches, teaching

tell   retell, teller, telling, tells

thank thanked, thankful, thankfully, thankfulness, thanking, thankless, thanks

their theirs

thick thicken, thickener, thickening, thicker, thickest, thicket, thickly, thickness

thin thinly, thinned, thinner, thinness, thinnest, thinning, thins

third thirdly, thirds

thought rethought, thoughtful, thoughtfully, thoughtfulness, thoughtless, thoughtlessly, thoughtlessness

three threefold, threes, threesome

throw thrower, throwing, thrown, throws

tie retie, tied, ties, tying, untie

tight tighten, tighter, tightest, tightly, tightness

tooth toothed, toothing, toothless, toothy

toy toys

trace retrace, traceable, traced, traceless, tracer, traces, tracing

travel traveled, traveler, traveling, travelogue, travels

try trial, tried, tries, trying, untried

turn turned, turning, turns, unturned

use misuse, reuse, reusable, usable, usage, used, useful, usefully, usefulness, useless, uselessly, uselessness, user, uses, using

walk walked, walker, walking, walks

wall walled, walling, walls

watch watchdog, watched, watcher, watches, watchful, watchfulness, watching, watchtower

weak weaken, weaker, weakest, weakling, weakly, weakness

week biweekly, weekday, weekend, weekender, weekly, weeknight, weeks

weigh weighed, weigher, weighing, weighs, weight, weights

wide widely, widen, wideness, wider, widest, width

wild wilder, wildest, wildness

window windows

winter winters, wintry

word reword, worded, wordiness, wording, wordless, words, wordy

work rework, workable, worked, worker, working, works

wrap wrapped, wrapper, wrapping, wraps, unwrap

write rewrite, writer, writes, writing, written

wrong wronged, wrongful, wronging, wrongs

yellow yellowed, yellowing, yellowish, yellows, yellowy

Spelling Dictionary

Spelling Table

This Spelling Table shows many of the letter combinations that spell the same sounds in different words. Use this table for help in looking up words that you do not know how to spell.

Sounds	Spellings	Sample Words
/ă/	a, ave, au	bat, have, laugh
/ā/	a, ai, ay, ea, eigh, ey	tale, later, rain, pay, great, eight, they
/âr/	air, are, ear, eir, ere	fair, care, bear, their, where
/ä/	a, al	father, calm
/är/	ar	art
/b/	b, bb	bus, rabbit
/ch/	ch, tch	chin, match
/d/	d, dd	dark, sudden
/ĕ/	a, ai, e, ea, ie	any, said, went, head, friend
/ē/	e, ea, ee, ey, y	these, we, beast, tree, honey, lady
/f/	f, ff, gh	funny, off, enough
/g/	g, gg	get, egg

Sounds	Spellings	Sample Words
/h/	h, wh	hat, who
/hw/	wh	whoop
/ĭ/	e, ee, i, ui, y	before, been, mix, give, build, gym
/ī/	i, ie, igh, uy, y	time, mind, pie, fight, buy, try
/îr/	ear, ere	near, here
/j/	dge, g, ge, j	judge, gym, age, jet
/k/	c, ch, ck, k	picnic, school, stick, keep
/kw/	qu	quick
/l/	l, ll	last, all
/m/	m, mm	mop, summer
/n/	kn, n, nn	knee, nine, penny
/ng/	n, ng	think, ring
/ŏ/	a, o	was, pond

Spelling Dictionary

Sounds	Spellings	Sample Words
/ō/	ew, o, oa, oe, ough, ow	sew, most, hope, float, toe, though, row
/ô/	a, al, au, augh, aw, o, ough	wall, talk, pause, taught, lawn, soft, brought
/ôr/	oor, or, ore	door, storm, store
/oi/	oi, oy	join, toy
/ou/	ou, ow	loud, now
/o͝o/	oo, ou	good, could
/o͞o/	ew, o, oe, oo, ou, ough, ue	flew, do, shoe, spoon, you, through, blue
/p/	p, pp	paint, happen
/r/	r, wr	rub, write
/s/	c, s, ss	city, same, grass
/sh/	s, sh	sure, sheep

Sounds	Spellings	Sample Words
/t/	ed, t, tt	fixed, tall, kitten
/th/	th	they
/th/	th	thin, teeth
/ŭ/	o, oe, ou, u	front, come, does, tough, sun
/yo͞o/	u	use
/ûr/	ear, er, ir, or, ur	learn, herd, girl, word, turn
/v/	f, v	of, very
/w/	o, w, wh	one, way, whale
/y/	y	yes
/z/	s, z	please, zoo
/zh/	s	usual
/ə/	a, e, i, o, u	about, silent, pencil, lemon, circus

Spelling Dictionary

How to Use a Dictionary

Finding an Entry Word

Guide Words

The word you want to find in a dictionary is listed in ABC order. To find it quickly, turn to the part of the dictionary that has words with the same first letter. Use the guide words at the top of each page for help. Guide words name the first entry word and the last entry word on each page.

Base Words

To find a word ending in **-ed** or **-ing**, you usually must look up its base word. To find **saved** or **saving**, for example, look up the base word **save**.

Reading an Entry

Read the dictionary entry below. Look carefully at each part of the entry.

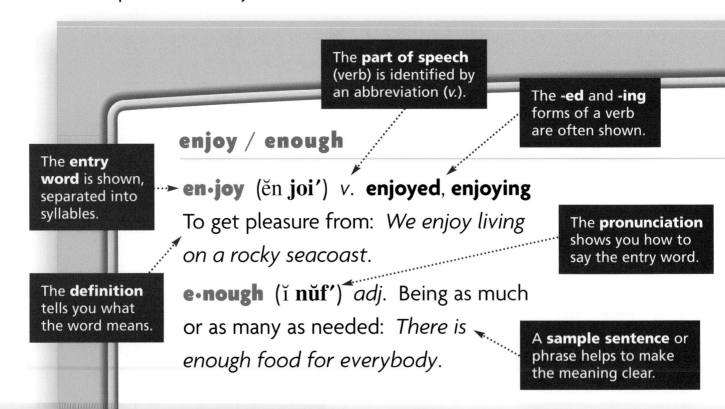

The **part of speech** (verb) is identified by an abbreviation (*v.*).

The **-ed** and **-ing** forms of a verb are often shown.

The **entry word** is shown, separated into syllables.

enjoy / enough

en·joy (ĕn joi′) *v.* **enjoyed**, **enjoying**
To get pleasure from: *We enjoy living on a rocky seacoast.*

The **pronunciation** shows you how to say the entry word.

The **definition** tells you what the word means.

e·nough (ĭ nŭf′) *adj.* Being as much or as many as needed: *There is enough food for everybody.*

A **sample sentence** or phrase helps to make the meaning clear.

a·bout (ə **bout′**) *prep.* **1.** Close in time to: *It is about midnight.* **2.** Concerned with: *That book is about pets.*

a·bove (ə **bŭv′**) *prep.* Over or directly over but not touching: *The sun is above us.*

ache (āk) *v.* **ached, aching** To feel a dull steady pain: *I ache all over.*

a·corn (ā′ kôrn′) *n., pl.* **acorns** The nut of an oak tree.

af·ter (ăf′ tər) *prep.* Behind in place or order: *The clowns came after the elephants in the parade.*

af·ter·noon (ăf′ tər **noon′**) *n., pl.* **afternoons** The part of the day from noon until sunset.

a·gain (ə **gĕn′**) *adv.* Once more: *If you do not win this time, try again.*

age (āj) *n., pl.* **ages** The length of time someone or something has been alive: *Julia's age is eight.*

a·go (ə **gō′**) *adj. and adv.* Before the present time: *They moved to Chicago five years ago.*

air (âr) *n., pl.* **airs** The colorless, odorless, tasteless mixture of gases that surrounds the earth: *We breathe air.*

air·plane (âr′ plān′) *n., pl.* **airplanes** A vehicle with wings that can fly through the air: *Airplanes are driven by propellers or jet engines.*

Pronunciation Key					
ă	pat	ŏ	pot	ûr	fur
ā	pay	ō	go	*th*	the
âr	care	ô	paw	th	thin
ä	father	ôr	for	hw	whoop
är	farm	oi	oil	zh	usual
ĕ	pet	o͝o	book	ə	ago, item,
ē	be	o͞o	boot		pencil,
ĭ	pit	yo͞o	cute		atom,
ī	ice	ou	out		circus
îr	near	ŭ	cut	ər	butter

Abbreviation Key			
n.	noun	*prep.*	preposition
v.	verb	*interj.*	interjection
adj.	adjective	*sing.*	singular
adv.	adverb	*pl.*	plural
pron.	pronoun	*p.*	past
conj.	conjunction	*p. part.*	past participle

a·live (ə **līv′**) *adj.* Living: *My old dog is dead, but my puppy is still alive.*

al·most (ôl′ mōst′) *adv.* Nearly; just short of: *The muffins are almost done.*

a·lone (ə **lōn′**) *adj.* Without anyone or anything else: *I get scared if I'm alone in the house.*

al·so (ôl′ sō) *adv.* Besides; too: *My watch tells time and also gives the date.*

al·ways (ôl′ wāz) *adv.* At all times; every single time: *I always leave at six o'clock.*

an·y·one (ĕn′ ē wŭn′) *pron.* Any person; anybody: *I don't want to see anyone right now.*

ap·plause (ə **plôz′**) *n.* Enjoyment or approval expressed, especially by the clapping of hands: *The actor enjoyed the audience's applause.*

Spelling Dictionary

ap·ple (ăp′ əl) *n., pl.* **apples** A red-skinned fruit.

A·pril (ā′ prəl) *n.* The fourth month of the year. April has 30 days: *It's hot and rainy in April.*

aq·ua (ăk′ wə) *n.* A light bluish-green color: *The boat was painted aqua to match the sea.*

are (är) *v.* **1.** Second person singular present tense of **be**: *You are my friend.* **2.** First, second, and third person plural present tense of **be**: *They are my grandparents.*

aren't (ärnt) Contraction of "are not": *They aren't here yet.*

a·round (ə round′) *prep.* In a circle surrounding: *I wore a belt around my waist.*

ar·row (ăr′ ō) *n., pl.* **arrows** A straight thin shaft that is shot from a bow. An arrow has a pointed head at one end and feathers at the other.

ar·tist (är′ tĭst) *n., pl.* **artists** A person who practices an art, such as painting, sculpture, or music: *The artist painted the picture.*

artist

as·sist (ə sĭst′) *v.* **assisted**, **assisting** To give help; aid: *Please assist me with this difficult job.*

as·tron·o·mer (ə strŏn′ ə mər) *n., pl.* **astronomers** An expert in the study of stars, planets, comets, and galaxies: *The astronomer looked through her telescope to see the stars.*

astronomer

at·tend (ə tĕnd′) *v.* **attended**, **attending** To be present at: *All our friends attended the party.*

a·ward (ə wôrd′) *n., pl.* **awards** Something given for outstanding performance or quality: *She won an award for her singing.*

a·way (ə wā′) *adv.* At or to a distance: *The lake is two miles away.*

aw·ful (ô′ fəl) *adj.* Very bad; terrible: *That movie was awful.*

a·while (ə hwīl′) *adv.* For a short time: *Let's wait awhile.*

288

ba·by (bā′ bē) *n., pl.* **babies** A very young child; infant: *A baby grows up to be an adult.*

back (băk) *n., pl.* **backs** The part of something that is away from the main or front part; the opposite of front: *The delivery entrance is at the back of the building.*

bait (bāt) *n.* Food placed on a hook or in a trap to attract and catch fish, birds, or other animals: *We used worms as bait to catch fish.*

ball (bôl) *n., pl.* **balls** Something that is round or nearly round: *Wind the string into a ball.*

bal·loon (bə lōōn′) *n., pl.* **balloons** A small, bright-colored rubber bag that floats when filled with air or another gas.

bar·ber (bär′ bər) *n., pl.* **barbers** A person whose work is cutting hair and shaving or trimming beards.

barber

bare (bâr) *adj.* **barer**, **barest** Without clothing or covering; naked: *The sand tickled my bare feet.*
♦ *These sound alike* **bare**, **bear**.

bare·back ri·der (bâr′ băk′ rī′ dər) *n., pl.* **bareback riders** A person who rides an animal, usually a horse, without using a saddle: *The bareback rider performed at the rodeo.*

bark[1] (bärk) *n., pl.* **barks** The short, gruff sound made by a dog and certain other animals.

bark[2] (bärk) *n., pl.* **barks** The outer covering of the trunks, branches, and roots of trees.

base·ment (bās′ mənt) *n., pl.* **basements** The lowest floor of a building, usually below ground level; cellar.

bas·ket (băs′ kĭt) *n., pl.* **baskets** A container often made of woven grasses or strips of wood used to carry, collect, or contain things.

be (bē) *v.* **are**, **was**, **were** **1.** To have a quality: *Jake and Pablo are always truthful.* **2.** To occupy a certain place or position: *All my friends were at the party.*

bear (bâr) *n., pl.* **bears** A large animal with a shaggy coat and a very short tail: *Bears eat mainly fruit and insects.*
♦ *These sound alike* **bear**, **bare**.

Spelling Dictionary

be·cause (bǐ kôz′) *conj.* For the reason that: *I left because I was sick.*

bed·spread (bĕd′ sprĕd′) *n., pl.* **bedspreads** A top cover for a bed.

be·fore (bǐ fôr′) *prep.* Ahead of; earlier than: *The dog got home before I did.*

be·gin (bǐ gǐn′) *v.* **began**, **begun**, **beginning 1.** To start to do: *I began taking piano lessons last year.* **2.** To have as a starting point: *Proper nouns begin with capital letters.*

be·hind (bǐ hīnd′) *prep.* To or at the back of: *The apple trees are behind the barn.* *adv.* In the place or situation of being left: *My friends stayed behind.*

beige (bāzh) *n.* A light yellowish-brown color: *My carpet is beige.*

be·long (bǐ lông′) *v.* **belonged**, **belonging** To be owned by: *That sweater belongs to Maria.*

be·low (bǐ lō′) *prep.* At or to a lower place, level, or position than: *Your bunk is below mine. It is two degrees below zero.*

bet·ter (bĕt′ ər) *adj.* Comparative of **good**: *This car is better than that one.* *adv.* Comparative of **well**: *My dog behaves better than Carla's does.*

be·tween (bǐ twēn′) *prep.* In the space separating: *A few trees stand between the house and the road.*

be·yond (bǐ yŏnd′) *prep.* On or to the far side of: *The forest is beyond the lake.*

bird (bûrd) *n., pl.* **birds** A warm-blooded animal that lays eggs: *A bird has two wings and a body covered with feathers.*

bird·bath (bûrd′ băth) *n., pl.* **birdbaths** An outdoor bowl or basin, usually in a garden, with water for birds to bathe in.

birdbath

bird·cage (bûrd′ kāj) *n., pl.* **birdcages** A cage, usually made of wire or cane, for keeping pet birds.

bird·call (bûrd′ kôl) *n., pl.* **birdcalls** The natural song, chirp, or other sound a bird makes.

bird watch·er (bûrd′ wŏch′ ər) *n., pl.* **bird watchers** A person who spends time observing wild birds in their natural habitat.

birth·day (bûrth′ dā′) *n., pl.* **birthdays** The day or anniversary of a person's birth.

black (blăk) *n.* The darkest of all colors; the opposite of white. *adj.* Being of the color black.

blew (bloo) *v.* Past tense of **blow**: *A breeze blew the leaves all over the yard.* ◆ *These sound alike* **blew**, **blue**.

blind (blīnd) *adj.* **blinder**, **blindest** Unable to see; sightless.

blis·ter (blĭs′ tər) *n., pl.* **blisters** A thin, fluid-filled sac that forms on the skin as a result of a burn or an irritation: *My tight shoe rubbed a blister on my heel.*

bliz·zard (blĭz′ ərd) *n., pl.* **blizzards** A very long, heavy snowstorm with strong winds: *The blizzard blocked the roads with snow.*

blouse (blous) *n., pl.* **blouses** A shirtlike outer garment for women and girls that covers the body from the neck to the waist.

blow (blō) *v.* **blew, blown, blowing** To shape by pushing air into: *Can you blow a bubble?*

blue (blōo) *adj.* **1.** Having the color of a clear sky. **2.** Having a gray or purplish color, as from cold or a bruise. **3.** Sad and gloomy.
◆ *These sound alike* **blue, blew.**

bod·y (bŏd′ ē) *n., pl.* **bodies** The main part of something: *The body of a letter is made up of paragraphs.*

boil (boil) *v.* **boiled, boiling** To cook in a very hot liquid: *Mom boiled the potatoes for twenty minutes.*

boom (bōom) *n., pl.* **booms** A loud, deep, hollow sound like the sound of thunder.

both (bōth) *adj.* The two; the one as well as the other: *Both sides of the valley are steep.*

bot·tom (bŏt′ əm) *n., pl.* **bottoms** **1.** The lowest part of something: *I found my socks in the bottom of my drawer.* **2.** The land under a body of water.

bought (bôt) *v.* Past tense and past participle of **buy**: *My sister bought a new bicycle.*

bounce (bouns) *v.* **bounced, bouncing** To spring back after hitting a surface: *The ball bounced off the wall.*

bow¹ (bō) *n., pl.* **bows** A weapon for shooting arrows.

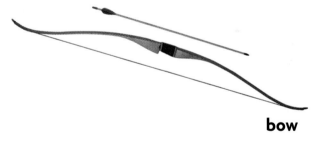

bow

bow² (bou) *v.* **bowed, bowing** To bend the body, head, or knee to show agreement or respect: *He bowed when he met the king. n., pl.* **bows** A bending of the body or head to show respect or thanks: *The jugglers took a bow at the end of the act.*

bow³ (bou) *n., pl.* **bows** The front part of a ship or a boat.

boy (boi) *n., pl.* **boys** A young male person: *The boy helped his father carry a large box.*

Spelling Dictionary

break (brāk) v. **broke**, **breaking** To separate into two or more pieces as the result of force; crack or split: *We pulled until the rope broke.*

breath·less (brĕth′ lĭs) adj. Out of breath; panting: *We were breathless after running up the stairs.*

breeze (brēz) n., pl. **breezes** A light wind: *The breeze cooled us on the hot day.*

bright (brīt) adj. **brighter**, **brightest** Giving off or filled with a lot of light; shining: *The bright sun lit up the meadow.*

bright·ness (brīt′ nĭs) n. The quality of being bright: *The brightness of the headlights shone through the night.*

bring (brĭng) v. **brought**, **bringing** To take with oneself: *Bring the books home.*

broke (brōk) v. Past tense of **break**: *I broke the vase yesterday.*

brought (brôt) v. Past tense and past participle of **bring**: *She brought her homework with her.*

but·ter (bŭt′ ər) n., pl. **butters** A soft, yellowish fatty food that is made from milk or cream.

butter

but·ton (bŭt′ n) n., pl. **buttons** A disk used to fasten together parts of a piece of clothing.

buy (bī) v. **bought**, **buying** To get by paying for: *We bought the car that Mickey was selling.*

buzz (bŭz) v. **buzzed**, **buzzing** To make a low, humming sound like that of a bee: *The alarm clock buzzed.*

cal·a·mine lo·tion (kăl′ ə mĭn lō′ shən) n. A soothing liquid used to relieve itching skin: *I put calamine lotion on my insect bites.*

calamine lotion

cal·en·dar (kăl′ ən dər) n., pl. **calendars** A chart that shows the months, weeks, and days of the year: *I wrote my schedule on the calendar.*

calm·ly (käm′ lē) adv. Not excitedly; without being nervous.

can (kăn) helping v. **could** To have the ability to: *You can skate well. I can name all fifty states.*

can·not (kăn′ ŏt) or (kă nŏt′) v. Not able to: *Sue has lost her money and cannot find it.*

can't (kănt) Contraction of "cannot": *I can't untie this knot.*

care (kâr) *n., pl.* **cares** The responsibility of keeping well and safe: *Are you in the doctor's care?* *v.* **cared, caring** To keep well and safe: *I care for my garden.*

care·ful (kâr' fəl) *adj.* Taking the necessary care; not careless: *She is careful when she crosses the street.*

care·less (kâr' lĭs) *adj.* **1.** Not taking the necessary care: *Careless writers often make spelling mistakes.* **2.** Done or made without care: *Careless work merits a low grade.*

car·pet (kär' pĭt) *n., pl.* **carpets** A heavy woven fabric used as a covering for a floor.

car·ry (kăr' ē) *v.* **carried, carrying** To take from one place to another: *Dad carried the groceries into the house.*

cast (kăst) *n., pl.* **casts** The actors in a play or a movie: *The cast took a bow at the end of the play.*

catch (kăch) *v.* **caught, catching** **1.** To get hold of or grasp something that is moving: *I'll throw the ball, and you catch it.* **2.** To come upon suddenly; surprise; capture: *The wolf caught the deer in a small meadow.*

caught (kôt) *v.* Past tense and past participle of **catch**: *She caught the ball that he threw.*

cell (sĕl) *n., pl.* **cells** The smallest and most basic part of a plant or animal.
♦ *These sound alike* **cell, sell**.

cen·ter (sĕn' tər) *n., pl.* **centers** The middle position, part, or place: *Put the vase of flowers in the center of the table.*

Pronunciation Key

ă	pat	ŏ	pot	ûr	fur
ā	pay	ō	go	*th*	**the**
âr	care	ô	paw	th	thin
ä	father	ôr	for	hw	whoop
är	farm	oi	oil	zh	usual
ĕ	pet	ŏŏ	book	ə	ago, item,
ē	be	ōō	boot		pencil,
ĭ	pit	yōō	cute		atom,
ī	ice	ou	out		circus
îr	near	ŭ	cut	ər	butter

chain (chān) *n., pl.* **chains** **1.** A row of links, usually metal, joined together: *My bicycle chain broke.* **2.** A series of things that are related or connected as if linked together: *They operate a chain of supermarkets in Florida.*

chain

chair (châr) *n., pl.* **chairs** A piece of furniture made for sitting on. A chair has a seat, a back, and usually four legs. Some chairs have arms.

chalk (chôk) *n.* A piece of a soft mineral that is used for writing on a blackboard or other surface.

chal·lenge (chăl' ənj) *n., pl.* **challenges** A call to take part in a contest or fight to see who is better, faster, or stronger: *The Red Team will meet the challenge of the Blue Team.*

change (chānj) *v.* **changed, changing** To make or become different: *You have changed since last year.*

Spelling Dictionary

char·ac·ter (kăr' ĭk tər) *n., pl.* **characters** A person or figure in a story, book, play, or movie: *The wolf is a character in many fairy tales.*

check (chĕk) *v.* **checked**, **checking** To test or examine to make sure something is correct or as it should be; review: *Check your answers after doing the math problems.*

cheese (chēz) *n., pl.* **cheeses** A food made from the pressed curds of milk: *I love cheese and crackers.*

cheese

cher·ry (chĕr' ē) *n., pl.* **cherries** A small, rounded red or yellow fruit with a hard seed.

chew (choo) *v.* **chewed**, **chewing** To crush or wear away with the teeth: *Always chew your food well.*

chill (chĭl) *n., pl.* **chills** A feeling of coldness, usually with shivering: *Chills and sneezing are signs of a cold.*

choice (chois) *n., pl.* **choices** The act of choosing: *May I help you with your choice of books?*

cir·cle (sûr' kəl) *n., pl.* **circles** Something that is more or less round: *There is a circle of children around the clown.*

cir·cus (sûr' kəs) *n., pl.* **circuses** A colorful traveling show with acrobats, clowns, and trained animals: *Acrobats performed at the circus.*

cit·y (sĭt' ē) *n., pl.* **cities** A place where many people live close to one another. Cities are larger than towns.

clear (klîr) *adj.* **clearer**, **clearest** **1.** Free from clouds, mist, or dust: *Today the sky was clear.* **2.** Easy to see, hear, or understand; obvious: *The teacher gave a clear explanation.*

clock (klŏk) *n., pl.* **clocks** An instrument for measuring and indicating time, often having a numbered dial with moving hands.

close (klōs) *adj.* **closer**, **closest** Near in space, time, or relationship: *The playground is close to school.*

close·ly (klōs' lē) *adv.* With careful attention; in a thorough way: *Watch the baby closely so he will not get hurt.*

clo·sing (klō' zĭng) *n., pl.* **closings** In a letter, the ending word or phrase that appears before the sender's signature. *Sincerely, Best regards,* and *Yours truly* are all common closings for a letter: *He wrote his name after the closing.*

cloth (klôth) *n., pl.* **cloths** Material made by weaving together threads of cotton, wool, silk, linen, or manmade fibers: *This shirt is made out of silk cloth.*

clothes (klōz) *or* (klōthz) *pl. n.* Coverings, as shirts or dresses, worn on the human body; garments.

cloud (kloud) *n., pl.* **clouds** A white or gray object in the sky made up of tiny drops of water or ice floating high in the air: *A rain cloud drifted toward us.*

clown (kloun) *n., pl.* **clowns** A performer in a circus who does tricks or funny stunts.

coach (kōch) *n., pl.* **coaches** A person who trains or teaches athletes, teams, or performers: *The baseball coach showed Tammy how to hold the bat.*

coin (koin) *n., pl.* **coins** A piece of metal issued by a government for use as money.

cold (kōld) *adj.* **colder**, **coldest** **1.** Being at a low temperature: *The water was cold.* **2.** Chilly: *I was cold without my coat.*

col·lar (kŏl' ər) *n., pl.* **collars** A leather or metal band for the neck of an animal: *Attach the dog's leash to its collar.*

col·or (kŭl' ər) *n., pl.* **colors** A tint other than black or white: *This picture includes all the colors of the rainbow.*

comb (kōm) *v.* **combed**, **combing** To smooth or arrange with a comb: *I comb my hair to make it straight.*

come (kŭm) *v.* **came**, **come**, **coming** To move toward the speaker or toward a place: *The children came home quickly when they were called for dinner.*

com·e·dy (kŏm' ĭ dē) *n., pl.* **comedies** A play, movie, or other work that is meant to make people laugh and that ends happily: *The comedy was full of jokes.*

Pronunciation Key

ă	pat	ŏ	pot	ûr	fur
ā	pay	ō	go	*th*	**the**
âr	care	ô	paw	th	**thin**
ä	father	ôr	for	hw	**wh**oop
är	farm	oi	**oil**	zh	usual
ĕ	pet	ōō	book	ə	ago, item,
ē	be	ōō	boot		pencil,
ĭ	pit	yōō	cute		atom,
ī	ice	ou	**out**		circus
îr	near	ŭ	cut	ər	butter

com·pare (kəm pâr') *v.* **compared**, **comparing** To study in order to see how things are the same or different: *We compared bees and spiders.*

com·pass rose (kŭm' pəs rōz) *n., pl.* **compass roses** A symbol on a map with points that show the directions in the map: *The compass rose shows which way is north.*

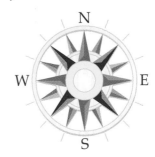

compass rose

com·put·er room (kəm pyōō' tər rōōm) *n., pl.* **computer rooms** A room, especially in a school, where computers and computer equipment are available for people to use: *I did my research in the computer room.*

con·cert hall (kŏn' sûrt hôl) *n., pl.* **concert halls** A large building or room where people can attend musical performances: *The band played at the concert hall.*

cone (kōn) *n., pl.* **cones** A solid object that has a flat, round base and tapers to a point at the opposite end: *I put the ice cream in a cone.*

con·stel·la·tion (kŏn′ stə lā′ shən) *n., pl.* **constellations** A star group that is shaped like and named after an animal, person, or object: *The constellation Orion looks like a man.*

constellation

con·tact (kŏn′ tăkt) *n., pl.* **contacts** A touching or coming together of persons or objects: *I came in contact with the ball when I caught it.*

cook·ie (kŏŏk′ ē) *n., pl.* **cookies** A small, sweet cake.

cor·rect (kə rĕkt′) *adj.* Free from error: *Your addition is correct.*

cost (kôst) *n., pl.* **costs** The amount paid for something; price: *The cost of the tickets was $15.00. v.* **cost, costing** To have as a price: *The tickets cost $15.00 each.*

cot·ton (kŏt′ n) *n.* A plant grown for the fluffy white fibers that surround its seeds: *That cloth is made from cotton.*

cotton

couch (kouch) *n., pl.* **couches** A sofa.

cough (kôf) *v.* **coughed, coughing** To force air from the lungs with a sudden sharp noise: *The smoky campfire made Jan cough.*

could (kŏŏd) *or* (kəd) *v.* Past tense of **can**: *He could watch the baseball game.*

could·n't (kŏŏd′ nt) Contraction of "could not": *They couldn't find their boots.*

count (kount) *v.* **counted, counting** To find the total of; add up: *Count your change.*

coun·try (kŭn′ trē) *n., pl.* **countries** A land in which people live under a single government: *We studied several foreign countries.*

cov·er (kŭv′ ər) *v.* **covered, covering** To put something over or on: *I covered my ears with my hands.*

cow·ard (kou′ ərd) *n., pl.* **cowards** A person who has no courage: *The coward was afraid to swim in the shallow lake.*

coy·o·te (kī ō′ tē) *or* (kī′ ōt) *n., pl.* **coyotes** An animal similar to a wolf that lives in western North America.

crack (krăk) *v.* **cracked**, **cracking** To break with a sudden sharp sound: *We cracked the ice. n., pl.* **cracks** A partial split or break: *There is a crack in the mirror.*

crawl (krôl) *v.* **crawled**, **crawling** To move slowly on the hands and knees; creep: *The baby crawled across the room.*

croc·o·dile (krŏk′ ə dīl′) *n., pl.* **crocodiles** A large reptile with thick skin, sharp teeth, and long, narrow jaws: *The crocodile caught a snake in its big jaws.*

crocodile

crop (krŏp) *n., pl.* **crops** A plant that is grown and harvested: *Corn and wheat are important food crops.*

cross (krôs) *v.* **crossed**, **crossing** To go to the other side of: *Let's cross the street.*

crowd (kroud) *n., pl.* **crowds** A large number of people gathered together: *A crowd waited for the train.*

Pronunciation Key					
ă	pat	ŏ	pot	ûr	fur
ā	pay	ō	go	*th*	**the**
âr	care	ô	paw	th	**thin**
ä	father	ôr	for	hw	**wh**oop
är	farm	oi	oil	zh	usual
ě	pet	ŏŏ	book	ə	ago, item,
ē	be	ōō	boot		pencil,
ĭ	pit	yōō	cute		atom,
ī	ice	ou	out		circus
îr	near	ŭ	cut	ər	butter

crown (kroun) *n., pl.* **crowns** A head covering, often made of gold and jewels. A crown is worn by a king or queen.

crown

cry (krī) *v.* **cried**, **crying 1.** To shed tears; weep: *We cried at the end of the sad story.* **2.** To make a special sound or call, as an animal does.

cube (kyōōb) *n., pl.* **cubes** A solid shape that has six square faces of equal size: *Put the ice cubes in your water.*

curl·y (kûr′ lē) *adj.* **curlier, curliest** Having curls or tending to curl.

cus·tom (kŭs′ təm) *n., pl.* **customs** Something that the members of a group usually do: *Shaking hands when meeting someone is a custom.*

dair·y (dâr′ ē) *n., pl.* **dairies** A farm that produces milk: *The workers at the dairy milk cows.*

dance (dăns) *v.* **danced**, **dancing** To move in time to music.

dark·ness (därk′ nĭs) *n.* Partial or total absence of light.

daugh·ter (dô′ tər) *n., pl.* **daughters** A female child: *Mrs. Harris has two daughters and one son.*

day·break (dā′ brāk) *n.* Dawn: *The farmer started work at daybreak.*

daybreak

day·care (dā′ kâr) *n.* Daytime care for children: *The toddler goes to daycare while her mother and father work.*

day·dream (dā′ drēm) *v.* **daydreamed**, **daydreaming** To imagine or think in a dreamy way.

day·light (dā′ līt) *n.* The light of day: *We will work as long as we have daylight.*

De·cem·ber (dĭ sĕm′ bər) *n.* The twelfth month of the year. December has 31 days: *Christmas is in December.*

de·cide (dĭ sīd′) *v.* **decided**, **deciding** To make up one's mind; make a choice: *I decided to leave.*

dec·i·mal (dĕs′ ə məl) *n., pl.* **decimals** A fraction in which the denominator is 10 or 10 multiplied by itself a number of times. Decimals are written with a decimal point separating the fraction from the whole number: *The decimal .3 = 3/10.*

deer (dîr) *n., pl.* **deer** An animal that has hoofs, chews its cud, and often lives in wooded areas. The males usually have antlers: *The deer stamped its hooves.*

des·sert (dĭ zûrt′) *n., pl.* **desserts** Food, such as fruit, served last at lunch or dinner: *Finish your dinner before you get your dessert.*

de·stroy (dĭ stroi′) *v.* **destroyed**, **destroying** To ruin completely: *The fire destroyed several homes.*

die (dī) *v.* **died**, **dying** To stop living; become dead: *The flowers died in the spring snowstorm.*

dig·it (dĭj′ ĭt) *n., pl.* **digits** One of the Arabic numerals, 1, 2, 3, 4, 5, 6, 7, 8, 9, and sometimes 0: *There are three digits in the number 524.*

dirt (dûrt) *n.* **1.** Earth or soil. **2.** Something filthy, such as mud.

dirt·y (dûr′ tē) *adj.* **dirtier**, **dirtiest** Full of or covered with dirt; not clean; filthy.

dis·tant (dĭs′ tənt) *adj.* Far away in space or time: *Do you see that distant peak on the horizon?*

do (dо̄о) *v.* **did**, **done**, **doing**, **does** To carry out an action: *I will do my homework now.*

does·n't (dŭz' nt) Contraction of "does not": *He doesn't know me.*

dol·lar (dŏl' ər) *n., pl.* **dollars** A unit of money equal to 100 cents.

done (dŭn) *v.* Past participle of **do**: *I have done my job.*

down·stream (doun' strēm') *adj.* and *adv.* In the direction of the current of a stream: *The fish swam downstream.*

drag·on (drăg' ən) *n., pl.* **dragons** An imaginary fire-breathing monster that is usually pictured as a giant lizard or reptile with wings and claws: *The dragon breathed fire as it flew into the air.*

dragon

draw (drô) *v.* **drew**, **drawn**, **drawing** To make a picture with lines: *I will draw that tree.*

dream (drēm) *n., pl.* **dreams** A series of pictures, thoughts, or emotions occurring during sleep. *v.* **dreamed**, **dreaming** To have a dream or daydream: *What did you dream about last night?*

Pronunciation Key					
ă	pat	ŏ	pot	ûr	fur
ā	pay	ō	go	*th*	**the**
âr	care	ô	paw	th	**thin**
ä	father	ôr	for	hw	**whoop**
är	farm	oi	oil	zh	usual
ĕ	pet	о̄о	book	ə	ago, item,
ē	be	о̄о	boot		pencil,
ĭ	pit	yо̄о	cute		atom,
ī	ice	ou	out		circus
îr	near	ŭ	cut	ər	butter

drew (drо̄о) *v.* Past tense of **draw**: *She drew a picture of her family.*

drop (drŏp) *v.* **dropped**, **dropping** **1.** To fall or let fall in drops. **2.** To fall or let fall: *I dropped a dish on the floor.*

dry (drī) *v.* **dried**, **drying** To make or become free from water or moisture: *Jill dried the wet puppy with a towel.*

each (ēch) *adj.* Being one of two or more persons or things thought of separately; every: *Did you speak to each child?*

ea·ger·ness (ē' gər nĭs) *n.* A feeling of being eager; hopefulness about something yet to happen.

ear (îr) *n., pl.* **ears** The part of the body with which people and animals hear.

eas·y (ē' zē) *adj.* **easier**, **easiest** Needing little effort; not hard: *The homework was easy.*

Spelling Dictionary

eight (āt) *n., pl.* **eights** A number, written 8, that is equal to the sum of 7 + 1: *Count to eight.* *adj.* Being one more than seven: *I earned eight dollars.*

el·bow (ĕl′ bō) *n., pl.* **elbows** The joint or bend between the lower and upper arm.

e·mer·gen·cy (ĭ mûr′ jən sē) *n., pl.* **emergencies** A situation that develops suddenly and unexpectedly and calls for immediate action: *Whom should we call in case of an emergency?*

en·joy (ĕn joi′) *v.* **enjoyed, enjoying** To get pleasure from: *We enjoy living on a rocky seacoast.*

e·nough (ĭ nŭf′) *adj.* Being as much or as many as needed: *There is enough food for everybody.*

-er A suffix that forms nouns. The suffix -er means "a person who": *teacher.*

e·rase (ĭ rās′) *v.* **erased, erasing** To remove by rubbing or wiping: *I erased the misspelled word and wrote it correctly.*

e·ven (ē′ vən) *adj.* Capable of being divided by 2 without having anything left over: *We know that 6, 18, and 100 are even numbers.*

e·vent (ĭ vĕnt′) *n., pl.* **events** Something that happens: *The town newspaper reports events such as accidents, marriages, and births.*

eve·ry·bod·y (ĕv′ rē bŏd′ ē) *pron.* Every person; everyone: *Everybody makes a mistake sometime.*

eve·ry·thing (ĕv′ rē thĭng′) *pron.* All things: *Everything in the store is for sale.*

ex·am (ĭg zăm′) *n., pl.* **exams** A shortened form of the word **examination**: *I got an A on my spelling exam.*

ex·am·i·na·tion (ĭg zăm′ ə nā′ shən) *n., pl.* **examinations** **1.** The act of looking at carefully; inspection: *A close examination of the jewel showed that it was a fake.* **2.** A set of questions designed to test knowledge or skills.

ex·ci·ted (ĭk sīt′ əd) *adj.* Stirred up: *The children got excited when they saw the clown.*

ex·cuse (ĭk skyōōz′) *v.* **excused, excusing** To forgive: *Please excuse me for being late.*

ex·pect (ĭk spĕkt′) *v.* **expected, expecting** To look for as likely to happen or appear: *The farmers expect an early frost this year.*

ex·plain (ĭk splān′) *v.* **explained, explaining** To make clear or understandable: *The teacher explained why leaves change color.*

ex·plore (ĭk splôr′) *v.* **explored, exploring** To go into or travel through an unknown or unfamiliar place for the purpose of discovery: *United States astronauts have explored the moon.*

explore

ex·pres·sion (ĭk sprĕsh′ ən) *n., pl.* **expression** A show of emotion or strong feeling: *He had an angry expression on his face.*

eye (ī) *n., pl.* **eyes** The organ of sight in people and animals: *I wear glasses because my left eye is weak.*
♦ *These sound alike* **eye, I.**

fair (fâr) *n., pl.* **fairs** A showing of farm and home products, often together with entertainment.

fan·tas·tic (făn tăs′ tĭk) *adj.* Very remarkable: *You did a fantastic job.*

far·a·way (fär′ ə wā′) *adj.* Very distant: *The prince lived in a faraway kingdom.*

farm·er (fär′ mər) *n., pl.* **farmers** A person who raises crops or animals on a farm: *The farmer fed his chickens.*

fast (făst) *adv.* **faster, fastest** With speed; quickly: *You are driving too fast.*

fear (fîr) *n., pl.* **fears** A feeling caused by a sense of danger or the expectation that something harmful may happen. *v.* **feared, fearing** To be afraid of: *You have nothing to fear.*

fear·ful (fîr′ fəl) *adj.* Feeling fear: *I was fearful of losing my way in the forest.*

fear·less (fîr′ lĭs) *adj.* Having no fear; afraid of nothing.

feast (fēst) *n., pl.* **feasts** A fancy meal: *We prepared a feast for the wedding.*

feast

fe·ver (fē′ vər) *n., pl.* **fevers** A body temperature that is higher than normal: *His forehead felt hot because he had a fever.*

fic·tion (fĭk′ shən) *n.* Written works that tell about made-up events and characters: *I like fiction stories about dragons and fairies.*

fight (fīt) *v.* **fought, fighting 1.** To use the body or weapons to try to hurt or gain power over someone: *The army will fight the enemy forces.* **2.** To quarrel or argue: *They often fight over who will sit in the front seat.*

Spelling Dictionary

fight·er (fīt′ ər) *n., pl.* **fighters** An animal or person who uses force to hurt or gain power over others or to defend against an enemy or opponent.

find (fīnd) *v.* **found, finding** To look for and discover: *Please help me find my pen.*

first (fûrst) *adj.* Coming before all others: *The first house on the block is nicer than the last one.*

fish·ing rod (fĭsh′ ĭng rŏd) *n., pl.* **fishing rods** A long, slender rod or stick with a hook, a line, and often a reel, used for catching fish: *I caught two fish with my fishing rod.*

fishing rod

fix (fĭks) *v.* **fixed, fixing** To repair.

flake (flāk) *n., pl.* **flakes** A small, thin piece of something.

flame (flām) *n., pl.* **flames** The hot visible and often bright gases given off by a fire.

flew (flōō) *v.* Past tense of **fly¹**: *The bird flew through the air.*

flow·er (flou′ ər) *n., pl.* **flowers** A plant that usually has colorful petals: *Roses and daisies are flowers.*

flu (flōō) *n.* A short name for influenza, which is a disease of the respiratory system caused by viruses. It is usually like a very bad cold, with headache, fever, cough, and pain in the muscles: *I had to stay in bed when I had the flu.*

fly¹ (flī) *v.* **flew, flies, flown, flying** **1.** To move through the air with wings: *Most birds can fly.* **2.** To operate or pilot an aircraft or spacecraft: *I want to learn to fly a plane.*

fly² (flī) *n., pl.* **flies** An insect, such as the common housefly, that has a single pair of thin, clear wings.

foam (fōm) *n.* A mass of very small bubbles.

fol·low (fŏl′ ō) *v.* **followed, following** **1.** To go or come after: *The ducklings followed their mother to the pond.* **2.** To take the same path as: *I followed the trail for a mile.* **3.** To come after in order or time: *Night follows day.*

foot (fŏŏt) *n., pl.* **feet** The part of the leg of a person or an animal on which it stands or walks.

for·est (fôr′ ĭst) *n., pl.* **forests** A large growth of trees: *Many wild animals live in the forest.*

for·get (fər gĕt′) *v.* **forgot, forgotten** or **forgot, forgetting** To be unable to remember: *I forgot my friend's new address.*

for·tune (fôr′ chən) *n., pl.* **fortunes** A large amount of money or property: *Our neighbor has a fortune in antique furniture.*

fought (fôt) *v.* Past tense and past participle of **fight**: *My dog was hurt when it fought with another dog.*

found (found) *v.* Past tense and past participle of **find**.

fourth (fôrth) *adj.* Coming after the third: *Tuesday is the third day of the week, and Wednesday is the fourth day.*

frac·tion (frăk′ shən) *n., pl.* **fractions** Two numbers with a line between them that express a part of a whole. The fraction 7/10 means that the whole is divided into 10 equal amounts, and 7 of them make up the part expressed by the fraction. The 10 is called the denominator and the 7 is called the numerator of the fraction: *The fraction 1/2 means one half.*

freeze (frēz) *v.* **froze, frozen, freezing** To change from a liquid to a solid by loss of heat; the opposite of melt: *The pond froze over during the cold night.*

freeze

freight (frāt) *n.* Goods carried by a train, ship, truck, or other vehicle: *The train carried a freight of coal.*

Fri·day (frī′ dē) *or* (frī′ dā) *n., pl.* **Fridays** The sixth day of the week.

friend (frĕnd) *n., pl.* **friends** A person one knows, likes, and enjoys being with.

friend·ly (frĕnd′ lē) *adj.* **friendlier, friendliest 1.** Showing friendship; not unfriendly: *My new neighbor gave me a friendly smile.* **2.** Liking to meet and to talk with others: *A friendly guide asked us if we needed more directions.*

fright·en·ing (frīt′ n ĭng) *adj.* Causing fear; scary: *The dragon mask he wore was frightening.*

front (frŭnt) *n., pl.* **fronts** The area directly ahead of the forward part: *The front of the theater is on Main Street.* *adj.* In or facing the forward part: *The front door is locked.*

frown (froun) *v.* **frowned, frowning** To wrinkle the forehead to show that one is unhappy or puzzled; the opposite of smile: *Mom frowned at the mess.*

fruit (fro͞ot) *n., pl.* **fruits** A seed-bearing plant part that is fleshy or juicy, eaten as food. Apples, oranges, grapes, melons, and bananas are fruits: *I bit the juicy fruit.*

Spelling Dictionary

fry·ing pan (**frī'** ĭng păn) *n., pl.*
frying pans A shallow pan with a long
handle, used for frying foods; skillet.

-ful A suffix that forms adjectives. The
suffix *-ful* means "full of" or "having":
beautiful.

full (fŏŏl) *adj.* **fuller, fullest** Holding
as much as possible; filled; the
opposite of empty: *Water ran down
the side of the full bucket.*

fun·ny (**fŭn'** ē) *adj.* **funnier, funniest**
Causing amusement or laughter.

gar·den (**gär'** dn) *n., pl.* **gardens** A
piece of land where flowers,
vegetables, or fruit are grown.

gas (găs) *n.* A shortened form of
the word **gasoline**.

gas·o·line (**găs'** ə lēn') *or* (găs' ə
lēn') *n.* A liquid made from
petroleum. Gasoline burns easily and
is used as a fuel to make engines run.

gi·ant (**jī'** ənt) *adj.* Extremely large;
huge.

gift (gĭft) *n., pl.* **gifts** Something
given; present.

gi·gan·tic (jī **găn'** tĭk) *adj.* Being
like a giant in size, strength, or power:
*Some of the dinosaurs were gigantic
creatures.*

gi·raffe (jĭ **răf'**) *n., pl.* **giraffes** A
tall African animal with short horns,
very long neck and legs, and a tan
coat with brown spots.

girl (gûrl) *n., pl.* **girls** A young female
person: *The girl greeted her friends.*

glad (glăd) *adj.* **gladder, gladdest**
1. Bringing happiness or pleasure: *The
letter brought glad news.* **2.** Pleased;
happy: *We were glad to be home again.*

glad·ly (**glăd'** lē) *adv.* In a glad or
willing way: *I will gladly loan you the
money you need.*

glow (glō) *v.* **glowed, glowing** To
shine without giving off heat: *Some
insects glow in the dark.*

gog·gles (**gŏg'** əlz) *pl. n.* A pair of
glasses worn to protect the eyes
against water, dust, wind, or sparks:
*The welder wore goggles when he
used a blowtorch.*

gold·fish (**gōld'** fĭsh') *n., pl.* **goldfish**
or **goldfishes** A small golden-orange
or reddish freshwater fish often kept in
home aquariums.

good (gŏŏd) *adj.* **better, best**
1. Suitable for a particular use:
Crayons are good for drawing. **2.** Not
weakened or damaged: *The old dog's
hearing is still good.*

grain (grān) *n., pl.* **grains 1.** The
small, hard, edible seed of cereal
plants, especially of wheat, corn, or
rice. **2.** Cereal plants, as wheat or rye:
We grow grain to make bread.

grain

grand·fa·ther (grănd′ fä′ *th*ər)
n., pl. **grandfathers** The father of
one's father or mother.

grand·moth·er (grănd′ mŭ*th*′ ər)
n., pl. **grandmothers** The mother of
one's father or mother.

greet·ing (grēt′ ĭng) *n., pl.*
greetings In a letter, the opening
phrase that addresses the person to
whom the letter is written: *The
letter began with a friendly greeting.*

grin (grĭn) *v.* **grinned, grinning** To
smile: *The child grinned with delight
at the birthday present.*

gui·tar (gĭ tär′) *n., pl.* **guitars** A
musical instrument with a long neck
attached to a sound box that is usually
shaped like a pear with a flat back and
front. Musicians play the guitar by
plucking its strings with their fingers or a
pick: *He tuned the strings on his guitar.*

guitar

gym (jĭm) *n., pl.* **gyms** A shortened
form of the word **gymnasium**.

gym·na·si·um (jĭm nā′ zē əm) *n., pl.*
gymnasiums A room for indoor
sports and exercise: *I play basketball
in the gymnasium.*

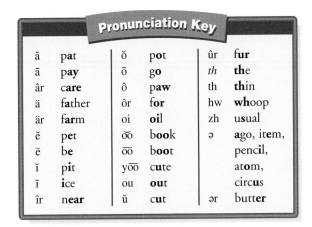

Pronunciation Key					
ă	pat	ŏ	pot	ûr	fur
ā	pay	ō	go	*th*	the
âr	care	ô	paw	th	thin
ä	father	ôr	for	hw	whoop
är	farm	oi	oil	zh	usual
ě	pet	oo	book	ə	ago, item,
ē	be	ōo	boot		pencil,
ĭ	pit	yōo	cute		atom,
ī	ice	ou	out		circus
îr	near	ŭ	cut	ər	butter

hair (hâr) *n., pl.* **hairs** A covering of
fine, thin strands that grow from the
skin: *Lou has curly red hair.*
◆ *These sound alike* **hair, hare.**

hair·cut (hâr′ kŭt) *n., pl.* **haircuts**
The act of cutting hair or the style in
which it is cut.

ham·bur·ger (hăm′ bûr′ gər) *n., pl.*
hamburgers A patty of fried or
broiled ground beef, usually served in
a roll or bun: *Dad cooked
hamburgers for dinner.*

ham·mer (hăm′ ər) *n., pl.* **hammers**
A hand tool with a metal head and a
long handle. Hammers are used
especially for driving nails.

hap·pen (hăp′ ən) *v.* **happened,
happening** To take place; occur: *Tell
me everything that happened today.*

305

Spelling Dictionary

hare (hâr) *n., pl.* **hares** An animal that is related to and looks like a rabbit. A hare has longer ears and larger hind feet than a rabbit: *The hare's ears stood up straight.*
♦ These sound alike **hare**, **hair**.

harm·ful (härm′ fəl) *adj.* Causing or able to cause damage: *Pollution can be harmful to one's health.*

har·vest (här′ vĭst) *v.* **harvested**, **harvesting** To gather a crop: *We harvested the corn.*

has·n't (hăz′ nt) Contraction of "has not": *She hasn't called yet.*

have·n't (hăv′ nt) Contraction of "have not": *We haven't told anyone.*

hawk (hôk) *n., pl.* **hawks** A large bird with a short, hooked bill, strong claws, and keen eyesight. Hawks catch small birds and animals for food: *The hawk soared through the air.*

hawk

head (hĕd) *n., pl.* **heads** The top part of the body, containing the brain, eyes, ears, nose, mouth, and jaws.

head·ing (hĕd′ ĭng) *n., pl.* **headings** Something, such as a title, that is put at the head of a page, letter, or chapter: *Look at the heading to find the date of the letter.*

heal·thy (hĕl′ thē) *adj.* **healthier**, **healthiest** In good health; not sick.

hear (hîr) *v.* **heard**, **hearing** **1.** To take in sounds through the ear: *We hear a dog barking.* **2.** To receive information: *I hear that a storm is on the way.*
♦ These sound alike **hear**, **here**.

heart (härt) *n., pl.* **hearts** **1.** The muscular organ that pushes blood through the system of blood vessels in the body. In human beings and other animals that have backbones, the heart has four chambers and is located in the chest. **2.** Something that is shaped like a heart.

hel·i·cop·ter (hĕl′ ĭ kŏp′ tər) *n., pl.* **helicopters** An aircraft that is kept in the air by a horizontal propeller that rotates above the craft: *The helicopter hovered above the ground.*

helicopter

hel·lo (hĕ lō′) *or* (hə lo′) *interj.* A word used as a greeting.

hel·met (hĕl′ mĭt) *n., pl.* **helmets** A head covering made of a hard material such as metal. A helmet is worn to protect the head, as in some sports.

help·less (hĕlp′ lĭs) *adj.* Not able to take care of or defend oneself: *The townspeople were helpless in the violent blizzard.*

her (hûr) *pron.* The objective case of **she**: *Do you see her? adj.* Relating or belonging to her: *Where did she put her hat?*

here (hîr) *adv.* At or in this place: *Put the package here.*
◆ *These sound alike* **here**, **hear**.

her·self (hər sĕlf′) *pron.* Her own self: *She blamed herself.*

he's (hēz) Contraction of "he is" or "he has": *He's my best friend.*

him·self (hĭm sĕlf′) *pron.* His own self: *He found himself in a strange place.*

hole (hōl) *n., pl.* **holes** An opening into or through something: *I tore a hole in my shirt.*
◆ *These sound alike* **hole**, **whole**.

hol·i·day (hŏl′ ĭ dā) *n., pl.* **holidays** A day or period of time set aside to honor someone or to celebrate a special event: *Thanksgiving Day is my favorite holiday.*

home·sick (hōm′ sĭk′) *adj.* Unhappy and longing for home and family: *I was homesick for the first few days of camp.*

home·work (hōm′ wûrk) *n., pl.* School assignments to be done at home.

hon·or (ŏn′ ər) *n., pl.* **honors** Special respect or high regard: *We display the flag to show honor to the United States. v.* **honored**, **honoring** To show special respect for.

hope·ful (hōp′ fəl) *adj.* Feeling or showing hope.

hope·less (hōp′ lĭs) *adj.* **1.** Having no hope: *The lost hikers felt hopeless.* **2.** Offering no hope: *The search for the lost wallet proved hopeless.*

hor·net (hôr′ nĭt) *n., pl.* **hornets** Any of several large stinging wasps that often build large, papery nests.

hornet

horse (hôrs) *n., pl.* **horses** The large hoofed animal that has four legs and a long mane and tail. Horses are used for riding, pulling vehicles, and carrying loads.

hos·pi·tal (hŏs′ pĭ təl) *n., pl.* **hospitals** A medical institution that treats sick and injured people.

hour (our) *n., pl.* **hours** A unit of time that is equal to 60 minutes: *There are 24 hours in a day.*
◆ *These sound alike* **hour**, **our**.

house (hous) *n., pl.* **houses** A building people live in: *We moved into our new house.*

hug (hŭg) *v.* **hugged**, **hugging** To put one's arms around and hold closely, especially to show love; embrace: *The old friends hugged when they met.* *n., pl.* **hugs** A tight clasp with the arms, especially to show love; an embrace: *Give me a hug.*

huge (hyo͞oj) *adj.* **huger**, **hugest** Very big; enormous.

hu·mid (**hyo͞o′** mĭd) *adj.* Having a large amount of water or water vapor in the air; damp: *Water from the humid air clung to us.*

hur·ri·cane (**hûr′** ĭ kān′) *n., pl.* **hurricanes** A very powerful storm with extremely strong winds over 75 miles per hour and heavy rains: *The hurricane flooded the town.*

hurricane

hur·ry (**hûr′** ē) *v.* **hurried**, **hurrying** To act or move quickly; rush: *Do not hurry through your work.*

hurt (hûrt) *v.* **hurt**, **hurting** To have a feeling of pain: *Does your ankle still hurt?*

I (ī) *pron.* The person who is the speaker or writer: *"I am tired today." "I am writing to you from our beach house."*
♦ These sound alike **I**, **eye**.

I'd (īd) Contraction of "I had," "I would," or "I should": *I'd rather leave now, not later.*

i·mag·i·na·tion (ĭ măj′ ə **nā′** shən) *n.* The mind's ability to be creative: *Use your imagination to write an interesting story.*

in·ter·state (**ĭn′** tər stāt′) *adj.* Of, existing between, or connecting two or more states: *The interstate sign told us when we crossed the state line.*

in·vite (ĭn **vīt′**) *v.* **invited**, **inviting** To ask someone to come somewhere to do something: *How many guests did you invite to the party?*

ir·ri·tate (**ĭr′** ĭ tāt′) *v.* **irritated**, **irritating** To cause to become sore or sensitive: *The smoke irritated my eyes.*

is·n't (**ĭz′**ənt) Contraction of "is not": *That isn't my dog.*

itch (ĭch) *v.* **itched**, **itching** To have or cause to have a tickling feeling in the skin.

its (ĭts) *adj.* Belonging to it: *Everything was in its place.*
♦ These sound alike **its**, **it's**.

it's (ĭts) Contraction of "it is" or "it has": *It's raining.*
♦ These sound alike **it's**, **its**.

jack·et (jăk′ ĭt) *n., pl.* **jackets** A short coat or parka.

Jan·u·ar·y (jăn′ yōō ĕr′ ē) *n.* The first month of the year. January has 31 days: *It often snows in January.*

jeans (jēnz) *pl., n.* Pants usually made of a strong blue cloth.

jel·ly (jĕl′ ē) *n., pl.* **jellies** A soft, semisolid food. One kind of jelly is made by boiling sugar and fruit juice with a substance that hardens the liquid.

jew·el (jōō′ əl) *n., pl.* **jewels** A precious stone; gem.

jewel

join (join) *v.* **joined, joining** **1.** To enter into the company of: *Please join us for lunch.* **2.** To become a member of: *I would like to join the club.*

joint (joint) *n., pl.* **joints** A place where two or more bones come together. There are joints at the elbows and knees.

Pronunciation Key

ă	pat	ŏ	pot	ûr	fur
ā	pay	ō	go	*th*	the
âr	care	ô	paw	th	thin
ä	father	ôr	for	hw	whoop
är	farm	oi	oil	zh	usual
ĕ	pet	ŏŏ	book	ə	ago, item,
ē	be	ōō	boot		pencil,
ĭ	pit	yōō	cute		atom,
ī	ice	ou	out		circus
îr	near	ŭ	cut	ər	butter

joke (jōk) *v.* **joked, joking** To say or do something funny: *I was only joking when I said that.*

joy (joi) *n., pl.* **joys** A feeling of great happiness or delight: *We felt joy at being with our family again.*

joy·ful (joi′ fəl) *adj.* Feeling, showing, or causing joy: *Grandpa's birthday was a joyful family event.*

judge (jŭj) *n., pl.* **judges** A person who decides the winner of a contest or race: *The judge carefully watched the contestants.*

jug·gler (jŭg′ lər) *n., pl.* **jugglers** A person who tosses things into the air and catches them to entertain people: *The juggler tossed four balls and a plate into the air.*

Ju·pi·ter (jōō′ pĭ tər) *n.* The planet that is fifth in distance from the sun. Jupiter is the largest planet in our solar system: *The planet Jupiter orbits our sun.*

just (jŭst) *adj.* Following what is right or fair: *Is this law just?*

kind (kīnd) *adj.* **kinder, kindest**
Helpful, considerate, and gentle.

kind·ness (kīnd′ nĭs) *n., pl.*
kindnesses The quality or condition
of being kind: *The teacher's kindness
made her popular with her students.*

knee (nē) *n., pl.* **knees** The place
where the thigh bone and lower leg
bone come together: *The dancer
bent his knee and then straightened
his leg.*

knew (nōō) *or* (nyōō) *v.* Past tense of
know: *I knew how to solve the
problem.*
♦ These sound alike **knew, new**.

knife (nīf) *n., pl.* **knives** A sharp
blade attached to a handle. A knife is
used for cutting or carving.

knock (nŏk) *v.* **knocked, knocking**
To make a loud noise by hitting a hard
surface: *I knocked and knocked, but
nobody came to the door.*

knot (nŏt) *n., pl.* **knots** A fastening
made by tying together pieces of
string, rope, or twine.

knot

know (nō) *v.* **knew, knowing** To
understand or have the facts about:
Do you know what causes thunder?
♦ These sound alike **know, no**.

knuck·le (nŭk′ əl) *n., pl.* **knuckles**
The place where the bones of the
finger or thumb come together.

lad·der (lăd′ ər) *n., pl.* **ladders** A
device for climbing, made of two
long side pieces joined by short rods
used as steps: *We climbed up the
ladder to the attic.*

large (lärj) *adj.* **larger, largest**
Bigger than average in size or
amount: *The zoo has large animals,
such as hippos and giraffes.*

last (lăst) *adj.* Coming, being, or
placed after all others; final: *We won
the last game of the season. We
had won a game at last.*

late (lāt) *adj.* **later, latest** Coming
after the expected, usual, or proper
time: *We were late for school. adv.*
After the usual, expected, or proper
time: *The train arrived late.*

laugh (lăf) *v.* **laughed, laughing,
laughs** To smile and make sounds to
show amusement or scorn. *n., pl.*
laughs The act or sound of laughing.

laugh·a·ble (lăf′ ə bəl) *adj.* Likely
to cause laughter or amusement:
*The sack race was a laughable
event.*

laugh·ing·ly (**lăf′** ĭng lē′) *adv.* Jokingly: *Paula laughingly said that I swim like a stone fish.*

laugh·ter (**lăf′** tər) *n.* The act or sound of laughing: *The baby's laughter told us that he was happy.*

law (lô) *n., pl.* **laws** A rule that tells people what they must or must not do: *It is against the law to drive without a license.*

lawn (lôn) *n., pl.* **lawns** A piece of ground, often near a house or in a park, planted with grass.

lawn

lay (lā) *v.* **laid, laying** To put or set down: *You can lay your books on my desk.*

leash (lēsh) *n., pl.* **leashes** A cord, chain, or strap attached to a collar or harness and used to hold or lead an animal: *Put your dog on a leash before you take him for a walk.*

leave (lēv) *v.* **left, leaving 1.** To go away from; go: *Are you leaving this afternoon?* **2.** To let stay behind: *Did you leave your book on the desk?*

-less A suffix that forms adjectives. The suffix *-less* means "not having" or "without": *harmless.*

les·son (**lĕs′** ən) *n., pl.* **lessons** Something to be learned or taught: *Janet goes to her skating lesson every Saturday.*

let's (lĕts) Contraction of "let us": *Let's play this game.*

let·ter (**lĕt′** ər) *n., pl.* **letters** A written message to someone that is usually sent by mail in an envelope.

li·brar·i·an (lī **brĕr′** ē ən) *n., pl.* **librarians** A person who works in or is in charge of a library: *The librarian helped us find the book.*

li·brar·y (**lī′** brĕr′ ē) *n., pl.* **libraries** A place where books, magazines, records, and other reference materials are kept for reading and borrowing: *I checked out a book from the library.*

lie (lī) *n., pl.* **lies** A statement that is not the truth.

life (līf) *n., pl.* **lives** The fact of being alive or staying alive: *I risked my life to save the drowning child.*

life·guard (**līf′** gärd′) *n., pl.* **lifeguards** A person who is hired to look out for the safety of swimmers: *The lifeguard carefully watched the swimmers.*

light (līt) *adj.* **lighter**, **lightest** Not dark; bright.

light·ing (lī′ tĭng) *n.* Light or lights supplied: *Good lighting is important in the classroom.*

like (līk) *v.* **liked**, **liking** To be fond of; enjoy: *I like playing the drums.*

lis·ten·er (lĭs′ ən ər) *n., pl.* **listeners** Someone who listens.

lit·tle (lĭt′ l) *adj.* **littler** or **less**, **littlest** or **least** Small: *Dolls look like little people.*

live·stock (līv′ stŏk) *n.* Animals that are raised on a farm or ranch: *Pigs are a kind of livestock.*

load (lōd) *n., pl.* **loads** Something that is carried, lifted, or supported; burden: *The ox carried a heavy load.*

loose (lōōs) *adj.* **looser**, **loosest** Not tight: *I put on a loose sweater.*

loud·ly (loud′ lē) *adv.* In a loud way.

love (lŭv) *v.* **loved**, **loving** To have warm feelings for; lacking hate: *The mother loved her baby.*

lum·ber (lŭm′ bər) *n.* Timber that is sawed into boards and planks.

lunch (lŭnch) *n., pl.* **lunches** A meal eaten at midday. *v.* **lunched**, **lunching** To eat a midday meal.

lunch·room (lŭnch′ rōōm) *n., pl.* **lunchrooms** A room with tables where students eat lunch while at school.

lunch·time (lŭnch′ tīm) *n., pl.* **lunchtimes** The time set aside for eating a meal at midday.

-ly A suffix that forms adverbs. The suffix *-ly* means "in a way that is": *quickly.*

ma·chine (mə shēn′) *n., pl.* **machines** A combination of mechanical parts that work together to perform a certain task: *Vacuum cleaners are machines that make housework easier.*

machine

make (māk) *v.* **made**, **making** To form, shape, or put together: *I made a paper snowflake.*

make·up (māk′ ŭp′) *n., pl.* **makeups** Materials put on the face or body for a play: *The makeup made the boy look like an old man.*

March (märch) *n.* The third month of the year. March has 31 days: *Spring begins in March.*

mark (märk) *n., pl.* **marks 1.** A visible trace, such as a scratch, on a surface: *The car had a mark on it.* **2.** A written symbol: *The sentence needs an exclamation mark.* **3.** Something, as a line, that shows position: *The orange cone is the halfway mark in the race.*

mar·ket (**mär′** kĭt) *n., pl.* **markets** A store that sells food: *I bought lamb chops at the meat market.*

market

match (măch) *v.* **matched**, **matching** To be alike: *The two colors match exactly.*

math (măth) *n.* A shortened form of the term **mathematics**.

math·e·mat·ics (măth′ ə **măt′** ĭks) *n.* The study of numbers, shapes, and measurements.

may (mā) *helping v., past tense* **might** Used to show possibility or express a request for permission: *May I take a swim?*

May (mā) *n.* The fifth month of the year. May has 31 days: *Does your school end in May?*

me·di·a cen·ter (**mē′** dē ə **sĕn′** tər) *n., pl.* **media centers** A room or part of a room in which films, movies, CDs, and other communication items are made available for people to use or borrow: *Let's watch a movie in the media center.*

med·i·cine (**mĕd′** ĭ sĭn) *n., pl.* **medicines** A substance used to treat a disease or relieve pain: *I take medicine when I'm sick.*

mel·o·dy (**mĕl′** ə dē) *n., pl.* **melodies** A pleasing series of musical tones: *She played a soft melody on the piano.*

men·u (**mĕn′** yo͞o) *n., pl.* **menus** A list of foods and drinks available for a meal: *Pasta was on the menu.*

might (mīt) *v.* Past tense of **may**: *I might have gone hiking, but it rained.*

mild (mīld) *adj.* **milder**, **mildest** Gentle or moderate in action or effect: *We had a mild winter.*

mile (mīl) *n., pl.* **miles** A unit of length equal to 5,280 feet or 1,760 yards.

mind (mīnd) *n., pl.* **minds** The part of a human being that thinks, feels, understands, and remembers: *You use your mind to do math.*

mir·ror (mĭr′ ər) *n., pl.* **mirrors** A surface, as of glass, that reflects the image of an object placed in front of it.

Mon·day (mŭn′ dē) *or* (mŭn′ dā) *n., pl.* **Mondays** The second day of the week.

mon·key (mŭng′ kē) *n., pl.* **monkeys** Any of a group of animals that have long arms and legs, and hands and feet that are adapted for climbing and grasping objects. Monkeys, especially the smaller ones, have long tails: *The monkey climbed up the tree.*

most (mōst) *adv.* In the greatest degree or size: *The roller coaster is the most exciting ride.*

moth (môth) *n., pl.* **moths** A flying insect that is usually active at night and has feathery antennas. A moth looks like a butterfly but usually has a stouter body. The larvae of some moths damage cloth and fur.

mo·tion (mō′ shən) *n., pl.* **motions** The act or process of moving; movement or gesture: *She made a waving motion with her hand.*

moun·tain (moun′ tən) *n., pl.* **mountains** An area of land that rises to a great height.

move (mōōv) *v.* **moved**, **moving** To change or cause to change position: *Move your chair closer to the window.*

mu·si·cian (myōō zĭsh′ ən) *n., pl.* **musicians** A person who is skilled in music, especially as a professional composer or performer: *The musician sang and played the piano.*

musician

nap·kin (năp′ kĭn) *n., pl.* **napkins** A piece of cloth or soft paper used while eating to protect the clothes or to wipe the mouth and fingers.

nar·row (năr′ ō) *adj.* **narrower**, **narrowest** Small or slender in width; not wide.

naugh·ty (nô′ tē) *adj.* **naughtier**, **naughtiest** Behaving in a disobedient way; bad: *Brian was naughty because he stayed at the park too long.*

neigh·bor (nā′ bər) *n., pl.* **neighbors** A person who lives next door to or near another.

-ness A suffix that forms nouns. The suffix *-ness* means "condition" or "quality": *kindness.*

new (nōō) *or* (nyōō) *adj.* **newer,**
newest Having lately come into being;
not old: *The new supermarket just*
opened.
◆ *These sound alike* **new, knew.**

news·pa·per (nōōz′ pā′ pər) *or*
(nyōōz′ pā′ pər) *n., pl.* **newspapers** A
printed paper that is usually issued
every day and contains news, articles,
and advertisements: *I read the*
newspaper in order to learn about
current events.

next (nĕkst) *adj.* Coming right before
or after, as in space or time: *The next*
day was sunny. adv. In the time,
position, or order that is closest or
that follows right after: *What comes*
next?

nib·ble (nĭb′ əl) *v.* **nibbled, nibbling**
To bite at gently: *The puppy nibbled*
my toes.

nice (nīs) *adj.* **nicer, nicest** Pleasing;
agreeable: *It was a nice party. You*
look nice in that outfit.

night (nīt) *n., pl.* **nights** The time
between sunset and sunrise, especially
the hours of darkness: *I sleep at night.*

night

Pronunciation Key

ă	pat	ŏ	pot	ûr	fur
ā	pay	ō	go	*th*	the
âr	care	ô	paw	th	thin
ä	father	ôr	for	hw	whoop
är	farm	oi	oil	zh	usual
ĕ	pet	ŏŏ	book	ə	ago, item,
ē	be	ōō	boot		pencil,
ĭ	pit	yōō	cute		atom,
ī	ice	ou	out		circus
îr	near	ŭ	cut	ər	butter

night·mare (nīt′ mâr′) *n., pl.*
nightmares A bad dream: *The*
nightmare woke me up.

no (nō) *adv.* Not so: *No, I'm not*
going. adj. Not any.
◆ *These sound alike* **no, know.**

no·bod·y (nō′ bŏd′ ē) *pron.* No
person; no one: *Nobody was looking.*

noise (noiz) *n., pl.* **noises** A loud or
unpleasant sound.

none (nŭn) *pron.* **1.** Not any: *None*
of the books are here. **2.** Not one:
None wanted to go.

non·fic·tion (nŏn fĭk′ shən) *adj.*
Writings that are not fiction,
especially books that discuss facts and
give general information. The story of
a person's life, called a biography, is
an example of nonfiction: *This*
nonfiction book has a lot of facts
about animals.

north (nôrth) *n.* The direction to the
right of a person who faces the
sunset: *Geese fly north for the*
summer.

nostril | open

nos·tril (nŏs′ trəl) *n., pl.* **nostrils**
Either of the outer openings of the nose.

No·vem·ber (nō věm′ bər) *n.* The eleventh month of the year. November has 30 days.

num·ber (nŭm′ bər) *n., pl.* **numbers**
1. A symbol or word used in counting: *What number follows six?* **2.** A numeral given to something to identify it: *What is your house number?*

nurse (nûrs) *n., pl.* **nurses** A person who cares for or is trained to care for sick people: *The nurse took my temperature.* *v.* **nursed, nursing**
1. To be a nurse for, as for a sick patient: *We nursed the patient back to health.* **2.** To take special care of: *I brought the plants indoors and nursed them through the long winter.*

ob·serve (əb zûrv′) *v.* **observed, observing** To see and pay attention to: *They observed a bird on the ledge.*

o'·clock (ə klŏk′) *adv.* Of or according to the clock: *When the bell rings, it will be 11 o'clock.*

Oc·to·ber (ŏk tō′ bər) *n.* The tenth month of the year. October has 31 days: *Columbus Day is in October.*

oc·to·pus (ŏk′ tə pəs) *n., pl.*
octopuses A sea animal that has a large head, a soft, rounded body, and eight long arms. The undersides of the arms have sucking disks used for holding.

octopus

odd (ŏd) *adj.* **odder, oddest** Leaving a remainder of one when divided by two: *Five and nine are odd numbers.*

of·ten (ô′ fən) *adv.* Many times: *I often read before going to sleep.*

oil (oil) *n., pl.* **oils** A greasy, usually liquid substance that burns easily and does not mix with water. Oils are used as fuel and food. They help parts of machines move easily: *Mom added a quart of oil to the truck engine.*

ol·ive green (ŏl′ ĭv grēn) *n.* A grayish-green color similar to that of an unripe olive: *The soldier's uniform was olive green.*

once (wŭns) *adv.* One time only: *We feed our dog once a day.* *conj.* As soon as: *You can leave once you've done your chores.*

o·pen (ō′ pən) *adj.* Not shut, closed, fastened, or sealed: *An open book lay on the desk. The door is open.*

or·ange (ôr′ ĭnj) *n., pl.* **oranges 1.** A round, juicy fruit with a reddish-yellow skin. Oranges grow in warm places. **2.** A reddish-yellow color: *Carrots are orange.*

or·bit (ôr′ bĭt) *v.* **orbited**, **orbiting** To move in a path, or orbit, around a larger body: *The moon orbits Earth.*

or·der (ôr′ dər) *n., pl.* **orders 1.** A grouping of things, one after another. **2.** A request for items to be sent: *The teacher placed an order for 20 arithmetic books. v.* **ordered**, **ordering** To place a request for: *We ordered a new washing machine.*

ought (ôt) *helping v.* Used to show: **1.** Duty: *We ought to try to help them.* **2.** What is likely: *Dinner ought to be ready by this time.*

our (our) *adj.* Belonging to us: *Our car is being repaired.*
◆ *These sound alike* **our**, **hour**.

out·doors (out dôrz′) *adv.* In or into the open air; outside. *n.* The open air.

ox (ŏks) *n., pl.* **oxen** A type of large, horned animal related to domestic cattle. Farmers in many countries keep oxen and use them for work, such as pulling heavy loads: *The oxen pulled the plow on the farm.*

oxen

Pronunciation Key

ă	pat	ŏ	pot	ûr	fur
ā	pay	ō	go	*th*	**the**
âr	care	ô	paw	th	thin
ä	father	ôr	for	hw	whoop
är	farm	oi	oil	zh	usual
ĕ	pet	ŏŏ	book	ə	ago, item,
ē	be	ōō	boot		pencil,
ĭ	pit	yōō	cute		atom,
ī	ice	ou	out		circus
îr	near	ŭ	cut	ər	butter

pack (păk) *v.* **packed**, **packing** To fill with things; load: *We packed all our suitcases into the trunk.*

page (pāj) *n., pl.* **pages** One side of a printed or written paper, as in a book or newspaper.

paid (pād) *v.* Past tense of **pay**: *I paid the bill before I left.*

pain·less (pān′ lĭs) *adj.* Without hurting.

paint (pānt) *n., pl.* **paints** Coloring matter put on surfaces to protect or decorate them: *We need another bucket of paint.*

pair (pâr) *n., pl.* **pairs** Two matched things that are usually used together: *I lost a pair of running shoes.*
◆ *These sound alike* **pair**, **pear**.

pan·cake (păn′ kāk′) *n., pl.* **pancakes** A thin flat cake of batter cooked on a hot griddle or in a skillet. A pancake is sometimes called a flapjack.

panda | perfect

pan·da (păn′ də) *n., pl.* **pandas** An animal of China that looks like a bear and has thick fur with black and white markings.

pants (pănts) *pl. n.* Trousers or slacks.

par·rot (păr′ ət) *n., pl.* **parrots** A tropical bird with a hooked bill and brightly colored feathers. Parrots can be taught to imitate spoken words: *She taught her parrot to say her name.*

par·tner (pärt′ nər) *n., pl.* **partners** Either of a pair of persons dancing, competing, or working together: *The partners danced quickly across the floor.*

par·ty (pär′ tē) *n., pl.* **parties** A gathering of people for fun: *We went to a birthday party.*

pas·sen·ger (păs′ ən jər) *n., pl.* **passengers** A person riding in a vehicle, as a car or airplane: *The passenger got on the plane.*

pas·ture (păs′ chər) *n., pl.* **pastures** Ground where animals graze: *The horses ate the grass in the pasture.*

patch (păch) *n., pl.* **patches** A piece of material used to mend a hole, a rip, or a worn place.

pa·tient (pā′ shənt) *n., pl.* **patients** A person who is receiving medical treatment: *The doctor examined the patient.*

pause (pôz) *v.* **paused**, **pausing** To stop briefly: *Pause after the comma when you read.*

paw (pô) *n., pl.* **paws** The foot of a four-footed animal that has claws.

pay (pā) *v.* **paid**, **paying** To give or spend money for things bought or for work done: *I paid for my ticket.*

peace (pēs) *n.* The absence of war or fighting.
♦ *These sound alike* **peace**, **piece**.

pea·nut (pē′ nŭt′) *n., pl.* **peanuts** An oily, edible nutlike seed that ripens underground in pods.

peanut

pear (pâr) *n., pl.* **pears** A yellow or brown fruit that has a round bottom and is narrow at the top. Pears grow on trees.
♦ *These sound alike* **pear**, **pair**.

pen·cil (pĕn′ səl) *n., pl.* **pencils** A thin stick of black or colored material used for writing or drawing.

pen·ny (pĕn′ ē) *n., pl.* **pennies** A coin used in the United States and Canada; cent. One hundred pennies equal one dollar.

peo·ple (pē′ pəl) *n., pl.* **people** Human beings; persons: *Many people came to the football game.*

per·fect (pûr′ fĭkt) *adj.* Without any mistakes: *My drawing is a perfect copy of yours.*

per·son (pûr′ sən) *n., pl.* **persons** A human being; individual: *Any person who wants to can come.*

phone (fōn) *n.* or *v.* A shortened form of the word **telephone**.

pic·nic (pĭk′ nĭk) *n., pl.* **picnics** A party in which those taking part carry their food with them and eat it outdoors.

pie (pī) *n., pl.* **pies** A food made of a filling, such as of fruit or meat, baked in a crust.

piece (pēs) *n., pl.* **pieces** A part that has been broken, taken, or cut from a whole, a set, or a collection: *Put a piece of pie on my plate.*
♦ *These sound alike* **piece**, **peace**.

pil·low (pĭl′ ō) *n., pl.* **pillows** A case filled with soft material, as down, and used to cushion a person's head during rest or sleep.

pi·lot (pī′ lət) *n., pl.* **pilots** A person who operates an aircraft.

pi·o·neer (pī′ ə nîr′) *n., pl.* **pioneers** A person who is first to settle in a region: *The pioneers explored the new land.*

plan (plăn) *n., pl.* **plans** A way of doing something that has been thought out ahead of time: *What are your plans for the day?* *v.* **planned**, **planning** To decide on a plan of or for: *I will plan what to eat on the camping trip.*

plane (plān) *n., pl.* **planes** A shortened form of the word **airplane**.

	Pronunciation Key				
ă	pat	ŏ	pot	ûr	fur
ā	pay	ō	go	*th*	**the**
âr	care	ô	paw	th	thin
ä	father	ôr	for	hw	whoop
är	farm	oi	oil	zh	usual
ĕ	pet	ŏŏ	book	ə	ago, item,
ē	be	ōō	boot		pencil,
ĭ	pit	yōō	cute		atom,
ī	ice	ou	out		circus
îr	near	ŭ	cut	ər	butter

plan·et (plăn′ ĭt) *n., pl.* **planets** A heavenly body that moves in an orbit around a star, such as the sun: *The planet Mars is smaller than Earth.*

planet

plat·form (plăt′ fôrm) *n., pl.* **platforms** A raised floor or surface, as for a speaker or performer: *I stepped up on the platform to give my speech.*

play·er (plā′ ər) *n., pl.* **players** A person who takes part in a game or sport.

please (plēz) *v.* **pleased**, **pleasing** To be willing to: *Please tell us a story.*

point (point) *v.* **pointed**, **pointing** To call attention to something with the finger: *The librarian pointed to the sign that said "Quiet."*

Spelling Dictionary

poi·son (poi′ zən) *n., pl.* **poisons** A substance that, when swallowed or breathed, causes injury, sickness, or death, especially by chemical means.

po·ny (pō′ nē) *n., pl.* **ponies** A kind of horse that remains small when grown.

poo·dle (po͞od′ l) *n., pl.* **poodles** A breed of dog that has thick, curly hair: *She carefully brushed and styled the poodle's fur.*

poodle

pop·corn (pŏp′ kôrn′) *n.* Corn that bursts and becomes white and puffy when heated.

po·ta·to (pə tā′ tō) *n., pl.* **potatoes** A starchy vegetable that has firm white flesh. Potatoes grow underground and are the thick, rounded tubers that grow on the stems of a leafy plant.

pow·der (pou′ dər) *n., pl.* **powders** A dry substance consisting of many very small particles.

pow·er (pou′ ər) *n., pl.* **powers** The ability or authority to control others: *The President has power over the armed forces.*

pow·er·ful (pou′ ər fəl) *adj.* Having power, authority, or influence: *The speaker made a powerful speech.*

pret·ty (prĭt′ ē) *adj.* **prettier**, **prettiest** Pleasing to the eye or ear.

price (prīs) *n., pl.* **prices** The amount of money asked or paid for something.

prob·lem (prŏb′ ləm) *n., pl.* **problems** A question or difficulty that must be solved or thought about: *There were 12 problems on the math test. Is there a problem with the car?*

pro·ces·sion (prə sĕsh′ ən) *n., pl.* **processions** A group of persons, vehicles, or objects moving along in an ordered way: *We watched the wedding procession march down the aisle.*

pro·duce (prō do͞os′) *v.* **produced**, **producing** To make by working with raw materials; manufacture: *The factory produces tractors.*

pro·gram (prō′ grăm′) *n., pl.* **programs** A performance or show, especially before an audience: *Which television programs do you like?*

pump·kin (pŭmp′ kĭn) *n., pl.* **pumpkins** A large, round fruit with a thick, orange rind and many seeds.

pumpkin

pup·py (pŭp′ ē) *n., pl.* **puppies** A young dog.

pur·ple (pûr′ pəl) *adj.* Of a color between blue and red: *Grape juice is purple.*

320

quack (kwăk) *n., pl.* **quacks** The sound made by a duck. *v.* **quacked, quacking** To make a quack.

quart (kwôrt) *n., pl.* **quarts** A measurement equal to two pints.

queen (kwēn) *n., pl.* **queens** A woman who is the ruler of a country.

ques·tion (kwĕs′ chən) *n., pl.* **questions** Something that is asked: *I don't understand your question.*

quick (kwĭk) *adj.* **quicker, quickest** Very fast; not slow: *I turned on the light with a quick movement of my hand.*

quick·ly (kwĭk′ lē) *adv.* In a quick way; not slowly: *Come here quickly!*

quit (kwĭt) *v.* **quit, quitting** To stop doing: *I quit work at five o'clock.*

rab·bit (răb′ ĭt) *n., pl.* **rabbits** A burrowing animal with long ears, soft fur, and a short, furry tail: *The rabbit hopped across the lawn.*

rain·coat (rān′ kōt′) *n., pl.* **raincoats** A waterproof coat worn to protect against rain.

rain for·est (rān′ fôr′ ĭst) *n., pl.* **rain forests** A thick evergreen forest in a tropical region with high annual rainfall: *The thick trees shaded the ground in the rain forest.*

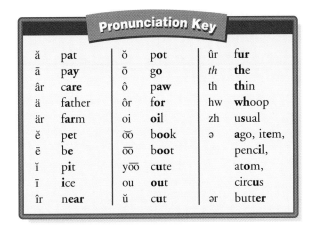

rainforest

raw (rô) *adj.* **rawer, rawest** Uncooked: *I made a salad of raw vegetables.*

re- A prefix that means "again": *refill.*

real (rēl) *adj.* Not imaginary or made up; actual: *This story is about real people.*

re·check (rē chĕk′) *v.* **rechecked, rechecking** To check again.

re·cit·al (rĭ sīt′ əl) *n., pl.* **recitals** A public performance, as of music: *She sang at the recital.*

re·fresh·ment (rĭ frĕsh′ mənt) *n., pl.* **refreshments** **1.** The act of refreshing or condition of being refreshed. **2. refreshments** Food and drink: *They served refreshments of punch and cookies after the recital.*

re·hearse (rĭ hûrs′) *v.* **rehearsed, rehearsing** To practice in preparation for a public performance: *They rehearse the play before they perform.*

re·heat (rē hēt′) *v.* **reheated, reheating** To heat again.

re·join (rē join′) *v.* **rejoined, rejoining** To join again.

re·lay (rē′ lā) *adj.* Performed by a group or team of people that work in turns: *I ran first for my team in the relay race.*

re·peat (rĭ pēt′) *v.* **repeated, repeating** To say or do again: *Please repeat your last question.*

re·play (rē plā′) *v.* **replayed, replaying** To play again.

re·read (rē rēd′) *v.* **reread, rereading** To read again.

res·tau·rant (rĕs′ tər ənt) *n., pl.* **restaurants** A place where meals are served to the public: *The Italian restaurant serves pasta.*

re·use (rē yōoz′) *v.* **reused, reusing** To use again.

re·ward (rĭ wôrd′) *n., pl.* **rewards** Something that is given in return for a worthy act or service: *You deserve a medal as a reward for your bravery.*

re·write (rē rīt′) *v.* **rewrote, rewritten, rewriting** To write again: *She rewrote her messy paper.*

ride (rīd) *v.* **rode, ridden, riding** **1.** To sit on and cause to move: *I ride my bicycle to school.* **2.** To be carried in a vehicle or on the back of an animal: *I'll ride on the scooter.*

right (rīt) *adj.* In accordance with fact, reason, or truth; correct: *I tried to think of the right answer.*

ring·mas·ter (rĭng′ măs′ tər) *n., pl.* **ringmasters** A person who directs a circus performance: *The ringmaster came to the center of the tent to begin the show.*

ringmaster

ripe (rīp) *adj.* **riper, ripest** Fully grown and developed: *A ripe peach is sweeter than a green one.*

riv·er (rĭv′ ər) *n., pl.* **rivers** A large stream of water that is often fed by smaller streams flowing into it: *We like to fish in the river.*

road (rōd) *n., pl.* **roads** An open way for vehicles, persons, or animals to pass along or through.
♦ *These sound alike* **road, rode**.

roar (rôr) *n., pl.* **roars** A loud, deep cry or sound, such as a lion makes: *We heard the roar of a huge tiger.* *v.* **roared, roaring 1.** To utter or make a roar. **2.** To laugh very loudly.

rob·in (rŏb′ ĭn) *n., pl.* **robins** A North American songbird with a rust-red breast and a dark gray back. Robins eat insects, worms, and fruit: *The robin made a nest in the tree.*

robin

rode (rōd) *v.* Past tense of **ride**: *I rode the bus to school this morning.* ◆ *These sound alike* **rode, road**.

rough (rŭf) *adj.* **rougher, roughest** Bumpy or uneven; not smooth: *Hickory trees have rough bark.*

round (round) *adj.* **rounder, roundest** Shaped like a ball or circle: *An orange is round.*

route (rout) *n., pl.* **routes** A road or lane of travel between two places: *We take the easiest route to get there.*

rug (rŭg) *n., pl.* **rugs** A piece of thick, heavy fabric used as a floor covering; a carpet.

Pronunciation Key

ă	pat	ŏ	pot	ûr	fur	
ā	pay	ō	go	*th*	**the**	
âr	care	ô	paw	th	**thin**	
ä	father	ôr	**for**	hw	**whoop**	
är	farm	oi	**oil**	zh	usual	
ĕ	pet	ŏŏ	**book**	ə	ago, item,	
ē	be	ōō	**boot**		pencil,	
ĭ	pit	yōō	cute		atom,	
ī	ice	ou	**out**		circus	
îr	**near**	ŭ	cut	ər	butter	

sad·ness (săd′ nĭs) *n.* The quality or condition of not being happy; the opposite of joy.

safe·ly (sāf′ lē) *adv.* In a safe manner.

salt (sôlt) *n., pl.* **salts** A white substance that is found in deposits in the earth and in sea water and is used to season and preserve food.

san·dal (săn′ dl) *n., pl.* **sandals** A shoe made of a sole and straps used to fasten it to the foot.

sat·el·lite (săt′ l īt′) *n., pl.* **satellites** An object launched by a rocket in order to orbit and often study Earth or another heavenly body: *Television signals are often sent through a satellite.*

satellite

Spelling Dictionary

sauce (sôs) *n., pl.* **sauces** A liquid dressing or relish served with food.

save (sāv) *v.* **saved**, **saving** **1.** To rescue from danger. **2.** To keep from wasting or spending.

save

scale of miles (skāl′ ŭv mīlz′) *n., pl.* **scales of miles** A reference showing the relationship of the spaces between places on a map and the actual distances between the real places represented on the map: *On this scale of miles, one inch equals one mile.*

scar (skär) *v.* **scarred**, **scarring** To mark with or form a scar.

scare (skâr) *v.* **scared**, **scaring** To frighten or become frightened.

scar·let (skär′ lĭt) *n.* A bright red color: *The scarlet cherries looked delicious.*

school (skool) *n., pl.* **schools** A place for teaching and learning.

score·board (skôr′ bôrd) *n., pl.* **scoreboards** A large board for showing the score of a game: *The winners' names were shown on the scoreboard.*

score·keep·er (skôr′ kē′ pər) *n., pl.* **scorekeepers** A person who keeps track of or tallies the score in a game or competition.

scout (skout) *n., pl.* **scouts** Someone who goes out from a group to gather information: *The scout went ahead to search for the path.*

scram·ble (skrăm′ bəl) *v.* **scrambled**, **scrambling** To mix together in a confused mass.

scrap (skrăp) *n.* **1.** A fragment or particle: *We picked up every scrap of paper.* **2. scraps** Leftover bits of food or other material: *My dog loves table scraps.*

scrape (skrāp) *v.* **scraped**, **scraping** **1.** To rub in order to clean, smooth, or shape: *Scrape the mud off of your shoes.* **2.** To injure the surface of by rubbing against something sharp or rough: *I scraped my knee.*

scratch (skrăch) *n., pl.* **scratches** A thin, shallow cut or mark made with or as if with a sharp tool: *The thorns of the rose bush made a scratch on my arm.* *v.* **scratched**, **scratching** To dig, scrape, damage, or wound with nails, claws, or something sharp or rough: *I fell on the cement and scratched my knee.*

scream (skrēm) *v.* **screamed**, **screaming** To make a long, loud cry or sound; yell. *n., pl.* **screams** A long, loud piercing cry.

sea·sick (sē′ sĭk′) *adj.* Dizzy and sick from the motion of a ship.

sec·ond¹ (sĕk′ ənd) *n., pl.* **seconds** A unit of time equal to 1/60 of a minute: *I will be ready in one second.*

sec·ond² (sĕk′ ənd) *adj.* **1.** Coming after the first: *Elena won second prize.* **2.** Another: *May I have a second chance?*

see (sē) *v.* **saw, seen, seeing** To take in with the eyes; look at: *I see my socks under the bed.*

seek (sēk) *v.* **sought, seeking** To try to find or get; look for: *We are seeking directions.*

seem (sēm) *v.* **seemed, seeming** To appear to be: *You seem worried.*

sell (sĕl) *v.* **sold, selling** To exchange something for money: *I sold my bike for $50.00.*
♦ These sound alike **sell, cell**.

Sep·tem·ber (sĕp tĕm′ bər) *n.* The ninth month of the year. September has 30 days: *The weather gets cooler in September.*

serve (sûrv) *v.* **served, serving** To present or offer food for others to eat: *Dad served dinner to the family.*

sew (sō) *v.* **sewed, sewing** To make, repair, or fasten a thing with stitches using a needle and a thread.

sew

sha·dow (shăd′ ō) *n., pl.* **shadows** A shaded area made when light is blocked.

Pronunciation Key

ă	pat	ŏ	pot	ûr	fur	
ā	pay	ō	go	*th*	*the*	
âr	care	ô	paw	th	thin	
ä	father	ôr	for	hw	whoop	
är	farm	oi	oil	zh	usual	
ĕ	pet	o͝o	book	ə	ago, item,	
ē	be	o͞o	boot		pencil,	
ĭ	pit	yo͞o	cute		atom,	
ī	ice	ou	out		circus	
îr	near	ŭ	cut	ər	butter	

shake (shāk) *v.* **shook, shaken, shaking** To move back and forth or up and down with short, quick movements: *Shake the orange juice to mix it up.*

share (shâr) *v.* **shared, sharing** To have, use, or do together with another or others: *Let's share this last orange.* *n., pl.* **shares** A part; portion: *Everyone has an equal share of the pizza.*

shark (shärk) *n., pl.* **sharks** A large, fierce ocean animal that has a big mouth and sharp teeth.

she (shē) *pron.* The female one mentioned earlier.

shell (shĕl) *n., pl.* **shells** The hard outer covering of certain animals or plants. Crabs, snails, turtles, eggs, and nuts all have shells.

shell

Spelling Dictionary

she's (shēz) Contraction of "she is" or "she has": *She's my sister.*

shin·y (shī′ nē) *adj.* **shinier, shiniest** Bright: *We polished the car until it was shiny.*

shirt (shûrt) *n., pl.* **shirts** A garment for the upper part of the body. A shirt usually has a collar, sleeves, and an opening in the front.

shoe (sho͞o) *n., pl.* **shoes** An outer covering for the foot: *His left shoe hurts his big toe.*

shoe·lace (sho͞o′ lās′) *n., pl.* **shoelaces** A string used for lacing and fastening a shoe.

shook (sho͝ok) *v.* Past tense of **shake**: *I shook my opponent's hand.*

shrink (shrĭngk) *v.* **shrank** or **shrunk, shrinking** To make or become smaller; the opposite of grow: *If you wash the wool sweater in hot water, it will shrink.*

shut (shŭt) *v.* **shut, shutting** To close: *Shut the window. adj.* To be closed: *The door is shut.*

sick (sĭk) *adj.* **sicker, sickest** Suffering from an illness.

sick·ly (sĭk′ lē) *adj.* Tending to become sick; frail: *One puppy was sickly and kept apart.*

sick·ness (sĭk′ nĭs) *n., pl.* **sicknesses** The condition of being sick; illness: *The sickness kept me in bed for a week.*

sight (sīt) *n., pl.* **sights** Something seen or worth seeing: *The baby whale was a wonderful sight.*

sig·na·ture (sĭg′ nə chər) *n., pl.* **signatures** A person's name written in that person's own handwriting: *I wrote my signature on my paper.*

si·lent (sī′ lənt) *adj.* Making or having no sound; quiet: *The room was silent during the test.*

sing·er (sĭng′ ər) *n., pl.* **singers** Someone who performs a song.

sink (sĭngk) *n., pl.* **sinks** A basin with a drain and faucets for turning on and off a water supply.

siz·zle (sĭz′ əl) *v.* **sizzled, sizzling** To make the hissing sound of frying fat.

skate (skāt) *n., pl.* **skates 1.** A boot or shoe having a metal blade used for gliding on ice. **2.** A roller skate. *v.* **skated, skating** To move along on skates.

skate

sleep (slēp) *v.* **slept, sleeping** To be or fall asleep; the opposite of wake.

slurp (slûrp) *v.* **slurped, slurping** To eat or drink noisily.

small (smôl) *adj.* **smaller, smallest** Little; tiny.

smart (smärt) *adj.* **smarter, smartest** Having a quick mind; bright.

smell (smĕl) *v.* **smelled**, **smelling** To use the nose to notice an odor. *n., pl.* **smells** Odor; scent: *The smell of roses filled the garden.*

smooth (smōōth) *adj.* **smoother**, **smoothest** Having a surface that is not rough or uneven.

snow·flake (snō′ flāk′) *n., pl.* **snowflakes** A single crystal of snow.

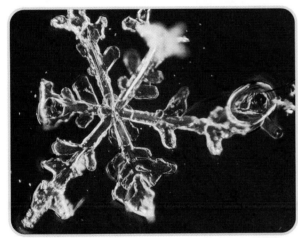

snowflake

soak (sōk) *v.* **soaked**, **soaking** To make or become completely wet: *The rain soaked our clothes and hair.*

soc·cer (sŏk′ ər) *n.* A game played on a field by two teams, each of which tries to kick a ball into the opposing team's goal.

sock (sŏk) *n., pl.* **socks** A short covering for the foot that reaches above the ankle and ends below the knee.

so·da (sō′ də) *n., pl.* **sodas** A soft drink containing carbonated water. Soda is sometimes called pop.

soft (sôft) *adj.* **softer**, **softest** Not hard or firm: *The pillow is soft.*

Pronunciation Key

ă	pat	ŏ	pot	ûr	fur
ā	pay	ō	go	*th*	**the**
âr	care	ô	paw	th	thin
ä	father	ôr	for	hw	whoop
är	farm	oi	oil	zh	usual
ĕ	pet	ŏŏ	book	ə	ago, item,
ē	be	ōō	boot		pencil,
ĭ	pit	yōō	cute		atom,
ī	ice	ou	out		circus
îr	near	ŭ	cut	ər	butter

soft·ness (sôft′ nĭs) *n.* The quality of being soft; smoothness or fineness in feel or look: *The little girl loved the softness of the kitten's fur.*

soil (soil) *n., pl.* **soils** The loose top layer of the earth's surface in which plants can grow; dirt: *We planted seeds in the soil.*

sold (sōld) *v.* Past tense of **sell**: *He sold the flowers last week.*

some (sŭm) *adj.* Being a number or quantity that is not specified or that is not known: *We bought some apples.*

some·one (sŭm′ wŭn′) *pron.* Some person; somebody: *Is someone at the door?*

some·thing (sŭm′ thĭng) *pron.* A thing that is not named: *Something is wrong.*

some·times (sŭm′ tīmz′) *adv.* Now and then; at times: *I see them sometimes but not often.*

sought (sôt) *v.* Past tense and past participle of **seek**: *We sought a way to make our sick cat feel better.*

sound (sound) *n., pl.* **sounds**
Something that is heard: *The sound of the drum was very loud.*

sound·less (**sound'** lĭs) *adj.* Without sound: *The diver enjoyed the soundless underwater world.*

space (spās) *n., pl.* **spaces** **1.** The area without limits where the stars, planets, comets, and galaxies are. **2.** The open area between objects: *Leave a space for my chair.*

spa·ghet·ti (spə gĕt' ē) *n.* A food made of a mixture of flour and water that is shaped into long strings and is cooked by boiling.

spaghetti

speak (spēk) *v.* **spoke, spoken, speaking** To say words; talk: *Please speak louder so the class can hear you.*

speak·er (spē' kər) *n., pl.* **speakers** A person who speaks: *The speaker told our class about his trip to Chicago.*

speech (spēch) *n., pl.* **speeches** A public address or talk: *The President's speech was broadcast on television.*

speed lim·it (spēd' lĭm' ĭt) *n., pl.* **speed limits** The highest speed a driver can legally drive on a certain part of a road. Speed limits are posted on signs along the roadway: *Going above the speed limit means you're going too fast.*

spend (spĕnd) *v.* **spent, spending** **1.** To pay out: *I spent $5 for the used book.* **2.** To use: *Spend your time wisely.*

spent (spĕnt) *v.* Past tense of **spend**: *I spent $10 at the movies.*

splash (splăsh) *n., pl.* **splashes** The act or sound of splashing.

spoil (spoil) *v.* **spoiled** or **spoilt, spoiling** To become unfit for use; ruin: *The meat spoiled.*

spoke (spōk) *v.* Past tense of **speak**: *Mom spoke to the doctor about my fever.*

spoon (spo͞on) *n., pl.* **spoons** A piece of silverware with a shallow bowl at the end of its handle. Spoons are used for measuring, serving, or eating food: *I need a spoon to eat my soup.*

spray (sprā) *v.* **sprayed, spraying** To make water or another liquid come out of a container in many small drops: *We sprayed the garden with water from the hose.*

spray

spring (sprĭng) *n., pl.* **springs** The season of the year between winter and summer when plants begin to grow.

squeak (skwēk) *n., pl.* **squeaks** A high, thin cry or sound such as a mouse makes. *v.* **squeaked, squeaking** To make a squeak.

squeeze (skwēz) *v.* **squeezed, squeezing 1.** To press together with force: *The baby squeezed the rubber toy.* **2.** To force by pressing: *We squeezed through the door.*

stair (stâr) *n., pl.* **stairs 1.** A series or flight of steps. **2.** One of a flight of steps.
◆ *These sound alike* **stair, stare.**

stand (stănd) *v.* **stood, standing** To take or stay in an upright position on one's feet: *Let's stand in the shade to cool off.*

stare (stâr) *v.* **stared, staring** To look with a steady, often wide-eyed gaze.
◆ *These sound alike* **stare, stair.**

start·er (stärt′ ər) *n., pl.* **starters** A person who gives a signal to start a race: *The runners waited for the starter to shoot the starting gun.*

stead·y (stĕd′ ē) *adj.* **steadier, steadiest** Not changing in rate or pace: *A steady rain is falling.*

stick·y (stĭk′ ē) *adj.* **stickier, stickiest** Tending to stick: *Glue is sticky.*

stom·ach (stŭm′ ək) *n., pl.* **stomachs** In human beings and other animals that have backbones, the large muscular pouch into which food passes when it leaves the mouth and esophagus: *My stomach was full after I ate the big meal.*

stood (sto͝od) *v.* Past tense of **stand**: *I stood next to the door.*

Pronunciation Key

ă	pat	ŏ	pot	ûr	fur
ā	pay	ō	go	*th*	the
âr	care	ô	paw	th	thin
ä	father	ôr	for	hw	whoop
är	farm	oi	oil	zh	usual
ĕ	pet	o͝o	book	ə	ago, item,
ē	be	o͞o	boot		pencil,
ĭ	pit	yo͞o	cute		atom,
ī	ice	ou	out		circus
îr	near	ŭ	cut	ər	butter

stop (stŏp) *v.* **stopped, stopping 1.** To end moving, acting, or operating: *Dad stopped at the red light.* **2.** To bring or to come to an end: *The rain finally stopped.*

storm (stôrm) *n., pl.* **storms** A strong wind with rain, hail, sleet, or snow.

sto·ry (stôr′ ē) *n., pl.* **stories** A tale made up to entertain people: *I have just read an adventure story.*

straight (strāt) *adj.* **straighter, straightest** Not curving, curling, or bending; not crooked: *I have straight hair.*

strange (strānj) *adj.* **stranger, strangest** Not ordinary; unusual: *I heard a strange sound.*

straw·ber·ry (strô′ bĕr′ ē) *n., pl.* **strawberries** A small red fruit that has many tiny seed-containing growths on its surface.

strawberry

Spelling Dictionary

stream (strēm) *n., pl.* **streams** A small body of flowing water: *That stream flows into the river by our house.*

street (strēt) *n., pl.* **streets** A road in a city or town: *I live on this street.*

stretch (strěch) *v.* **stretched**, **stretching** To draw out to a greater length or width: *I stretched the rubber band.*

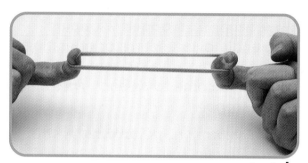

stretch

string (strǐng) *n., pl.* **strings** A cord for fastening or tying: *Tie the pile of newspapers with string.*

strong (strông) *adj.* **stronger**, **strongest** Having much power, energy, or strength: *A strong horse pulled the heavy cart.*

stub·born (stǔb' ərn) *adj.* Not willing to change in spite of requests from others: *The stubborn child refused to wear boots.*

stuff (stǔf) *n.* **1.** Belongings, goods, or equipment: *Leave your football stuff at school.* **2.** Useless material; junk: *Get rid of that stuff in the garage.*

sub·ject (sǔb' jǐkt) *n., pl.* **subjects** Something that is thought about, discussed, or represented; topic: *Horses were the subject of the story.*

sud·den (sǔd' n) *adj.* **1.** Happening without warning: *We were caught in a sudden snowstorm.* **2.** Rapid; quick: *With a sudden movement, I caught the falling vase.*

sum·mer (sǔm' ər) *n., pl.* **summers** The hottest season of the year. Summer is between spring and autumn.

Sun·day (sǔn' dē) *or* (sǔn' dā) *n., pl.* **Sundays** The first day of the week.

sun·shine (sǔn' shīn') *n.* Sunlight.

surf (sûrf) *n.* The waves of the sea as they break on a shore or reef: *I like to swim in the surf.*

surf

sur·prise (sər prīz') *n., pl.* **surprises** Something unexpected.

sweet (swēt) *adj.* **sweeter**, **sweetest** Having a pleasing taste like that of sugar.

swim (swǐm) *v.* **swam**, **swimming** To move through the water by moving the arms, legs, or fins: *Who taught you how to swim?*

tag (tăg) *n., pl.* **tags** A small strip, label, or tab attached to something else, especially to identify the item or to give its price: *The price tag on the jacket says $20.*

tale (tāl) *n., pl.* **tales** A story, usually an imaginary or made-up one: *I like the tale of Paul Bunyan.*

talk (tôk) *v.* **talked, talking 1.** To say words; speak. **2.** To have a conversation. *n., pl.* **talks** An informal speech: *The speaker gave a talk on the Pilgrims.*

tap (tăp) *v.* **tapped, tapping** To strike gently: *I tapped my friend on the shoulder.*

tape (tāp) *v.* **taped, taping** To record on tape: *I taped the TV program so I could watch it again.*

taught (tôt) *v.* Past tense and past participle of **teach**: *The teacher taught us a new song that she had learned.*

teach (tēch) *v.* **taught, teaching** To give lessons in: *Our teacher taught the class another dance.*

teach·er (tē' chər) *n., pl.* **teachers** A person who teaches or gives instruction.

tel·e·phone (tĕl' ə fōn') *v.* **telephoned, telephoning** To call or talk with by telephone.

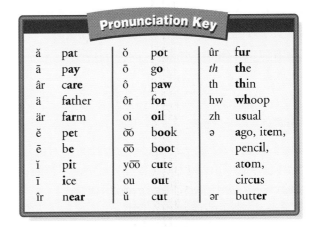

Pronunciation Key					
ă	pat	ŏ	pot	ûr	fur
ā	pay	ō	go	*th*	the
âr	care	ô	paw	th	thin
ä	father	ôr	for	hw	whoop
är	farm	oi	oil	zh	usual
ě	pet	ŏŏ	book	ə	ago, item,
ē	be	ōō	boot		pencil,
ĭ	pit	yōō	cute		atom,
ī	ice	ou	out		circus
îr	near	ŭ	cut	ər	butter

tel·e·scope (tĕl' ĭ skōp') *n., pl.* **telescopes** A device that uses an arrangement of lenses or mirrors in a long tube to make distant objects appear closer: *I can see the star better if I look through the telescope.*

telescope

tell (tĕl) *v.* **told, telling 1.** To express in words: *I'm not going to tell a lie.* **2.** To repeat a tale or give an account of: *Please tell me a story.*

thank (thăngk) *v.* **thanked, thanking** To say that one is grateful: *I thanked them for their help.*

thank·less (thăngk′ lĭs) *adj.* Not appreciated or not likely to receive thanks.

that (thăt) *adj., pl.* **those 1.** Being the one farther away or at a distance: *That desk is yours and this one is mine.* **2.** Being the one indicated or just mentioned: *Did you see that lightning? pron., pl.* **those 1.** Being the one farther away or at a distance: *This is a pigeon and that is a sparrow.* **2.** Being the one indicated or just mentioned: *What does that mean?*

their (thâr) *pron.* Belonging to them: *They put their boots in the closet.*
♦ These sound alike **their, there, they're**.

there (thâr) *adv.* **1.** At or in that place: *Set the package there on the table.* **2.** To or toward that place: *I bicycled there and back.*
♦ These sound alike **there, their, they're**.

there's (thârz) Contraction of "there is": *There's a full moon tonight.*

these (thēz) *adj.* and *pron.* Plural of **this**: *These houses are very old. Are these your gloves?*

they (thā) *pron.* The persons, animals, or things last talked about; those ones: *Elephants are large, but they move quickly.*

they're (thâr) Contraction of "they are."
♦ These sound alike **they're, their, there**.

thick (thĭk) *adj.* **thicker, thickest** Having much space between opposite sides; not thin: *A thick board does not break very easily.*

thick

thick·ness (thĭk′ nĭs) *n., pl.* **thicknesses** The quality of having much space between opposite sides.

thin (thĭn) *adj.* **thinner, thinnest** Having little space between opposite surfaces or sides; not thick.

thin

thing (thĭng) *n., pl.* **things** An object, creature, or matter that is not named: *What is that thing on the table?*

think (thĭngk) *v.* **thought, thinking 1.** To use one's mind to form ideas and make decisions: *I think that I should leave now.* **2.** To believe: *Pam thinks that it is too cold to go swimming.*

third (thûrd) *adj.* Coming after the second: *They picked the first two TV shows to watch, and I picked the third one.*

this (thĭs) *adj., pl.* **these 1.** Being the one present, nearby, or just mentioned: *I like this book.* **2.** Being the one that is nearer than another: *This car is smaller than that one. pron., pl.* **these 1.** Being the one present, nearby, or just mentioned: *This is my house.* **2.** Being the one that is nearer than another: *These are oak trees, and those are pines.*

thorn (thôrn) *n., pl.* **thorns** A sharp point growing on a branch or stem of a plant.

thorn

those (thōz) *adj. and pron.* Plural of **that**: *Those socks don't match.*

though (thō) *adv.* However; nevertheless: *The shirt is pretty; it doesn't fit, though.*

thought (thôt) *v.* Past tense and past participle of **think**: *I thought about what you said.*

thou·sand (thou′ zənd) *n., pl.* **thousands** The number written 1,000 that is equal to the product of 10 x 100: *Can you count by thousands? adj.* Being ten times one hundred: *There were a thousand people in the stadium.*

three (thrē) *adj.* Being one more than two: *I had to wait for three hours.*

threw (thro͞o) *v.* Past tense of **throw**: *I threw the ball into the air.*
♦ *These sound alike* **threw, through**.

thrill (thrĭl) *v.* **thrilled, thrilling** To feel or cause to feel a sudden sensation of joy, fear, or excitement: *The acrobat thrilled the spectators. n., pl.* **thrills** A sudden, exciting sensation.

through (thro͞o) *prep.* In one side and out the other side of: *We walked through the park to the bus stop.*
♦ *These sound alike* **through, threw**.

throw (thrō) *v.* **threw, throwing** To send through the air by moving the arm quickly: *I will catch the towel if you throw it to me.*

tie (tī) *v.* **tied, tying** To fasten with a cord or rope: *Wrap the package and tie it with a string. n., pl.* **ties** A narrow band of cloth worn around the neck and tied in front; necktie.

tight (tīt) *adj.* **tighter, tightest** Held firmly in place; not loose: *I tied a tight knot.*

333

Spelling Dictionary

tight·rope (tīt′ rōp′) *n., pl.* **tightropes** A rope or wire stretched high above the ground. Acrobats and circus performers walk and balance on a tightrope: *The performer put out his arms to balance on the tightrope.*

tip (tĭp) *n., pl.* **tips** A small extra sum of money given to someone who has provided a service: *He paid the bill and then left a tip for the waiter.*

toast (tōst) *n.* Sliced bread heated and browned: *Please put jam on my toast.*

toast

to·day (tə dā′) *n.* The present day: *Today is my birthday.* *adv.* During or on the present day: *We're having a party today.*

to·geth·er (tə gĕ*th*′ ər) *adv.* In or into a single group or place; with each other: *We were in the car together.*

told (tōld) *v.* Past tense of **tell**: *I told a story.*

to·mor·row (tə môr′ ō) *n.* The day after today. *adv.* On or for the day after today: *I will return your book tomorrow.*

tooth (tōōth) *n., pl.* **teeth** One of the hard, bony parts in the mouth that is used to chew and bite: *I broke a tooth when I bit into some taffy.*

tor·na·do (tôr nā′ dō) *n., pl.* **tornadoes** *or* **tornados** A twisting, dangerous storm. A tornado has a funnel-shaped cloud that comes down from a thundercloud: *The tornado tore down the house.*

tor·toise (tôr′ təs) *n., pl.* **tortoises** A turtle, especially one that lives only on land: *The tortoise walked slowly across the sand.*

tornado

tough (tŭf) *adj.* **tougher**, **toughest** **1.** Strong; not likely to break or tear. **2.** Difficult: *We had a tough time getting to the top of the mountain.*

toy (toi) *n., pl.* **toys** Something that children play with.

trac·tor (trăk′ tər) *n., pl.* **tractors** A vehicle driven by an engine and equipped with large tires that have deep treads. A tractor is used for pulling farm machinery.

trail (trāl) *n., pl.* **trails** A path or track, especially through the woods.

train·ing (trā′ nĭng) *n.* The act, process, or routine of instructing or directing or of being trained: *She went through training to become a lifeguard.*

trans·por·ta·tion (trăns′ pər tā′ shən) *n.* A means of transporting people or goods: *Planes are fast transportation.*

tra·peze (tră pēz′) *n., pl.* **trapezes** A short, horizontal bar hung from two parallel ropes used for acrobatics: *The acrobat jumped onto the swinging trapeze.*

trav·el (trăv′ əl) *v.* **traveled**, **traveling** To go from one place to another: *The whole family traveled around the world.*

treat (trēt) *n., pl.* **treats** Something such as food or entertainment that is given by one person to another: *Our teacher let us each choose a treat from her candy jar.*

trout (trout) *n., pl.* **trout** A freshwater fish that often has a spotted body and is related to the salmon: *Trout live in the river.*

trout

true (trōo) *adj.* **truer**, **truest** Being in agreement with fact or reality.

try (trī) *v.* **tried**, **trying** To make an effort: *She tried to win the prize.*

turn (tûrn) *v.* **turned**, **turning** To move or cause to move around a center; rotate; spin: *I heard the key turn in the lock. n., pl.* **turns** A chance or time to do something: *It is my turn to drive the boat.*

un- A prefix that means: **1.** Not: *unhappy.* **2.** Opposite of: *untie.*

un·buck·le (ŭn bŭk′ əl) *v.* **unbuckled**, **unbuckling** To open or unfasten a buckle: *Don't unbuckle your safety belt until the car stops.*

un·cle (ŭng′ kəl) *n., pl.* **uncles** The brother of one's mother or father or the husband of one's aunt.

un·clear (ŭn klîr′) *adj.* Not clear; not well organized: *The report is unclear.*

un·der (ŭn′ dər) *prep.* **1.** Below: *A boat passed under the bridge.* **2.** Less, smaller, or lower than: *Children under five years of age are admitted free.*

un·der·tow (ŭn′ dər tō′) *n., pl.* **undertows** A current beneath the surface of a body of water running in a direction opposite to that of the current at the surface: *The pull of the undertow can be dangerous to swimmers.*

Spelling Dictionary

un·fair (ŭn fâr') *adj.* **unfairer, unfairest** Not fair; not right: *We think the decision is unfair.*

un·fold (ŭn fōld') *v.* **unfolded, unfolding** To open the folds of and spread out: *I unfolded the letter and read it.*

un·hurt (ŭn hûrt') *adj.* Not hurt; not injured: *The driver was unhurt in the accident.*

un·known (ŭn nōn') *adj.* Not known or familiar; strange: *We bought a beautiful drawing by an unknown artist.*

un·luck·y (ŭn lŭk' ē) *adj.* Having or bringing bad luck.

un·safe (ŭn sāf') *adj.* Dangerous or risky; not safe: *It is unsafe to swim alone.*

un·sure (ŭn shŏŏr') *adj.* Lacking confidence; uncertain.

un·tie (ŭn tī') *v.* **untied, untying 1.** To loosen or undo: *I could not untie the knots in my shoelace.* **2.** The opposite of tie.

un·til (ŭn tĭl') *prep.* Up to the time of: *They studied until dinner.*

un·wrap (ŭn răp') *v.* **unwrapped, unwrapping** To open by removing the wrapper from; to open a present: *May I unwrap my gifts, or must I wait until tomorrow?*

use·ful (yōōs' fəl) *adj.* Being of use or service; helpful; not useless: *Our map of Chicago was useful when we visited there.*

veg·e·ta·ble (vĕj' ĭ tə bəl) *n., pl.* **vegetables** A plant whose roots, leaves, stems, flowers, or other parts are used as food: *Carrots are my favorite vegetable.*

ver·y (vĕr' ē) *adv.* **1.** To a high degree; extremely: *I am a very happy person today.* **2.** Exactly: *I said the very same thing.*

vi·o·let (vī' ə lĭt) *n.* A reddish-blue color: *The vase was violet and pink.*

violet

voice (vois) *n., pl.* **voices** Sound produced by using the mouth and vocal cords in speaking, singing, or shouting: *I recognized your voice on the telephone.*

wag·on train (wăg′ ən trān′) *n., pl.*
wagon trains A line or train of wagons
traveling cross-country: *The settlers
took a wagon train to Oregon.*

wagon train

wait·er (wā′ tər) *n., pl.* **waiters** A
person who serves food and drink to
customers, as in a restaurant: *The
waiter brought us our food.*

wall (wôl) *n., pl.* **walls** A solid
structure that forms a side of a
building or room.

want (wŏnt) *v.* **wanted**, **wanting** To
wish or desire: *They wanted to play
outdoors.*

warm (wôrm) *adj.* **warmer**, **warmest**
Somewhat hot: *I took a bath in warm
water.*

was (wŏz) *or* (wŭz) *v.* First and third
person singular past tense of **be**: *He
was late.*

watch (wŏch) *v.* **watched**, **watching**
1. To look at with care: *People stopped
to watch the parade.* **2.** To be alert
and looking: *Watch for the street sign.*

Pronunciation Key

ă	pat	ŏ	pot	ûr	fur	
ā	pay	ō	go	*th*	the	
âr	care	ô	paw	th	thin	
ä	father	ôr	for	hw	whoop	
är	farm	oi	oil	zh	usual	
ĕ	pet	ŏŏ	book	ə	ago, item,	
ē	be	ōō	boot		pencil,	
ĭ	pit	yōō	cute		atom,	
ī	ice	ou	out		circus	
îr	near	ŭ	cut	ər	butter	

watch·dog (wŏch′ dôg′) *n., pl.*
watchdogs A dog that is trained to
protect people or property.

watch·er (wŏch′ ər) *n., pl.* **watchers**
Someone who watches people or
events; observer.

watch·ful (wŏch′ fəl) *adj.* Carefully
watching; alert.

watch·tow·er (wŏch′ tou ər) *n., pl.*
watchtowers A tower from which
people can observe or watch over a
large area.

watchtower

Spelling Dictionary

way (wā) *n., pl.* **ways** **1.** A manner or fashion: *I answered in a polite way.* **2.** A method, means, or technique: *Do you know a better way to solve the problem?* **3.** A road or route from one place to another: *We found a way through the woods.*
♦ *These sound alike* **way**, **weigh**.

weak·ly (wēk′ lē) *adv.* In a way that lacks strength or power.

wear (wâr) *v.* **wore**, **worn**, **wearing** To have on the body: *I wear mittens on cold days.*

weigh (wā) *v.* **weighed**, **weighing** **1.** To find out how heavy something is: *He weighed himself on a scale.* **2.** To have a certain heaviness: *A grown elephant weighs four tons or more.*
♦ *These sound alike* **weigh**, **way**.

well (wĕl) *adv.* **better**, **best** In a way that is good, proper, skillful, or successful: *Tammy skis well.*

we're (wîr) Contraction of "we are": *Do they know that we're coming?*

were (wûr) *v.* **1.** Second person singular past tense of **be**: *You were in school yesterday.* **2.** First, second, and third person plural past tense of **be**: *We were there, too.*

weren't (wûrnt) Contraction of "were not": *Sam and I weren't sick yesterday.*

wet (wĕt) *adj.* **wetter**, **wettest** **1.** Being covered, moistened, or soaked in a liquid, especially water; damp. **2.** Not yet dry or hardened: *Don't touch that wet paint.*

what's (wŏts) *or* (wŭts) Contraction of "what is": *What's your middle name?*

where (wâr) *adv.* At, in, or to what or which place: *Where is the telephone?*

whis·tle (wĭs′ əl) *v.* **whistled**, **whistling** To make a clear, high sound by forcing air out between the teeth or lips: *I whistled a tune.* *n., pl.* **whistles** A device that makes a clear, high sound when air is blown through it: *The coach blew her whistle.*

whole (hōl) *adj.* Having no part missing; complete: *She read the whole book.*
♦ *These sound alike* **whole**, **hole**.

will (wĭl) *helping v.* **would** Something that is going to take place in the future: *They will arrive tonight.*

wind[1] (wĭnd) *n., pl.* **winds** Air that is in motion.

wind[2] (wīnd) *v.* **wound**, **winding** To wrap or be wrapped around something: *The vines wind around the posts.*

win·dow (wĭn′ dō) *n., pl.* **windows** An opening in a wall with a frame and panes of glass to let in light.

win·ter (wĭn′ tər) *n., pl.* **winters** The coldest season of the year, between fall and spring.

winter

338

wis·dom (wĭz′ dəm) *n.* Good judgment in knowing what to do and being able to tell the difference between right and wrong; knowledge.

with·out (wĭth **out′**) *prep.* Not having; lacking: *We built the campfire without help.*

wolf (woŏlf) *n., pl.* **wolves** A wild animal that is related to the dog and lives mostly in northern regions. Wolves eat birds and mammals such as rabbits, deer, and some livestock but rarely bother people: *The wolf caught a rabbit.*

won't (wōnt) Contraction of "will not": *She won't forget to meet us.*

wood (woŏd) *n., pl.* **woods** The hard material beneath the bark of trees and shrubs that makes up the trunk and branches. Wood is used as fuel and for building.
♦ *These sound alike* **wood, would.**

word (wûrd) *n., pl.* **words** A sound or group of sounds that has meaning: *Do you know how to say that word?*

work (wûrk) *n., pl.* **works** The effort that is required to do something; labor: *Cleaning the house is hard work.* *v.* **worked, working** To have a job: *My parents work in a hospital.*

worm (wûrm) *n., pl.* **worms** Any of several kinds of animals that have soft bodies, no legs, and no backbone. Worms move by crawling: *The worm crawled through the dirt.*

wor·ry (wûr′ ē) *v.* **worried, worrying** To feel or cause to feel uneasy: *Your bad cough worries me.*

Pronunciation Key

ă	pat	ŏ	pot	ûr	fur
ā	pay	ō	go	*th*	**the**
âr	care	ô	paw	th	thin
ä	father	ôr	for	hw	whoop
är	farm	oi	oil	zh	usual
ĕ	pet	oŏ	book	ə	ago, item,
ē	be	oō	boot		pencil,
ĭ	pit	yoō	cute		atom,
ī	ice	ou	out		circus
îr	near	ŭ	cut	ər	butter

would (woŏd) *helping v.* Past tense of **will**: *They said that they would help.*
♦ *These sound alike* **would, wood.**

would·n't (woŏd′ nt) Contraction of "would not": *The sick cat wouldn't eat.*

wrap (răp) *v.* **wrapped, wrapping** To cover by winding or folding something: *Wrap the baby in a towel.* *n., pl.* **wraps** An outer garment, such as a coat, that is worn for warmth.

wrap

wreck (rĕk) *v.* **wrecked, wrecking** To damage badly or destroy, as by breaking up: *The accident wrecked both cars.*

Spelling Dictionary

wrink·le (rĭng´ kəl) *n., pl.* **wrinkles** A small fold or crease.

write (rīt) *v.* **wrote**, **writing** **1.** To make letters or words with a pen or pencil. **2.** To communicate by writing: *I wrote to tell my friend the good news.*

wrong (rông) *adj.* **1.** Not correct. **2.** Not working correctly. **3.** Not fitting or suitable: *You picked the wrong time to call.*

year (yîr) *n., pl.* **years** A period of 12 months: *We plan to return a year from now.*

yel·low (yĕl´ ō) *n., pl.* **yellows** **1.** The color of ripe lemons: *My favorite color is yellow.* *adj.* Having the color yellow: *He wore a yellow shirt.*

yes·ter·day (yĕs´ tər dā´) *n.* The day before today: *Yesterday was Tuesday.* *adv.* On the day before today: *I had to stay home from school yesterday.*

yo·gurt (yō´ gərt) *n., pl.* **yogurts** A thick, creamy food made by adding certain bacteria to milk. Yogurt is slightly sour and often sweetened or flavored.

Content Index

Numbers in **boldface** indicate pages on which a skill is introduced as well as references to the Capitalization and Punctuation Guide.

341

Content Index

Credits

Illustrations 3 Ethan Long 4 Aardvart 5 (l) Ethan Long (r) Aardvart 6 (l) Chris Lensch (r) Aardvart 7 Ethan Long 19 Shirley Beckes 20 Aardvart 21 Rich Colicchio 25 (t) Shirley Beckes (b) Jim Gordon 26 Ethan Long 27 Shirley Beckes 31 Jim Gordon 32 Aardvart 33 Chris Lensch 35 Linda Lee Studios 37 Jim Gordon 38 Aardvart 43 (t) Ethan Long (b) Shirley Beckes 44 Chris Lensch 45 Ethan Long 55 Chris Lensch 61 Ethan Long 67 (t) Shirley Beckes (b) Jim Gordon 68 Aardvart 69 Chris Lensch 73 Shirley Beckes 75 Ethan Long 79 Aardvart 80 Shirley Beckes 81 Linda Lee Studios 86 Linda Lee Studios 87 Linda Lee Studios 91 Ethan Long 92 Chris Lensch 93 Jim Gordon 97 Ethan Long 98 Linda Lee Studios 99 John Hovell 103 Ethan Long 104 Aardvart 105 Linda Lee Studios 109 Shirley Beckes 111 (scroll) John Hovell (boots) Linda Lee Studios 115 Chris Lensch 116 Shirley Beckes 117 Jim Gordon 119 Rich Colicchio 122 Chris Lensch 123 Ethan Long 127 Chris Lensch 128 Linda Lee Studios 129 Rich Colicchio 131 Linda Lee Studios 133 (t) Aardvart (b) Jim Gordon 134 Linda Lee Studios 135 Rich Colicchio 139 (t) Chris Lensch (b) Shirley Beckes 141 Ethan Long 143 Linda Lee Studios 145 Jim Gordon 146 Shirley Beckes 147 John Hovell 151 Chris Lensch 153 Aardvart 156 Shirley Beckes 163 Chris Lensch 164 Shirley Beckes 169 Ethan Long 171 Linda Lee Studios 175 Shirley Beckes 176 Ethan Long 177 Shirley Beckes 181 Aardvart 183 Chris Lensch 187 Ethan Long 188 Aardvart 189 Linda Lee Studios 200 Ethan Long 201 Linda Lee Studios 205 (t) Chris Lensch (b) Jim Gordon 207 Ethan Long 209 John Hovell 211 Shirley Beckes 212 Aardvart 217 Shirley Beckes 221 John Hovell 223 Ethan Long 229 Ethan Long 295 Argosy Publishing 296 (l) Argosy Publishing Recurring print media and TV backgrounds by John Hovell.

Assignment Photography 224 (br) HMCo/Sara Jean McIlvain 292 (r) HMCo/Sara Jean McIlvain

Photography 3 Photodisc 4 Royalty-Free/Corbis 7 Photodisc/Getty Images 8 (br) Photodisc 8 (cl) Photodisc 9 Mike Brinson/Getty Images 19 (cr) Artville (cl) Corel (c) Ingram Publishing 23 Photodisc 29 Photodisc 31 (cl) Photodisc (cr) Photodisc/Getty Images 37 Rubberball Productions/Getty Images 39 DK Images/Getty Images 41 (bg) Alan Schein Photography/Corbis (c) Gen Nishino/Getty Images 49 Tony Garcia/Superstock 50 Photodisc 51 Vision/Getty Images 55 Royalty-Free/Corbis 56 Digital Vision/Getty Images 57 Premium Stock/Corbis 59 Bob Krist/Corbis 61 Royalty-Free/Corbis 62 (tl) Ariel Skelley/Corbis (cl) Ed Bock/Corbis (bl) PhotoDisc (br) Photodisc (tr) Photodisc 63 Royalty-Free/Corbis 65 Jose Luis Pelaez, Inc./Corbis 67 Photodisc 71 (fg) Brand X Pictures/Getty Images (bg) Digital Vision/Getty Images 73 Kevin R. Morris/Corbis 74 (l) Digital Vision/Getty Images (r) Royalty-Free/Corbis 77 Comstock Images/Getty Images (cl) Corel 83 Charles Gupton/Corbis 84 (r) Corel (l) William Gottlieb/Corbis 85 Ghislain & Marie David de Lossy/Getty Images 86 Photodisc/Getty Images 87 William Gottlieb/Corbis 91 Thinkstock/Getty Images 95 Peter Gridley/Getty Images 97 Comstock/Getty Images 99 Photos.com 101 (bg) Photodisc (c) Rich Iwasaki/Getty Images 103 (cl) Adamsmith/Getty Images (r) Chris Carroll/Corbis (l) Photodisc/Getty Images (cr) Photos.com 107 Thinkstock/Getty Images 109 (tc) Ingram Publishing (tl) Photodisc/Getty Images 110 Photos.com 113 Royalty-Free/Corbis 117 Royalty-Free/Corbis 120 Robert Dowling/Corbis 121 Dallas Stribley/Getty Images 127 Yann Arthus-Bertrand/Corbis 137 (bg) Corel (c) Photodisc (t) Photodisc 143 VCL/Spencer Rowell/Getty Images 145 Corel 149 (bl) Corel (bg) Photodisc 149 (c) Royalty Free/Corbis 155 Ingram Publishing 157 Photos.com 158 Photodisc/Getty Images 159 Karen Moskowitz/Getty Images 165 Burke/Triolo/Getty Images 167 (bg) General Drafting Company (c) Photodisc 169 (c) Comstock Images/Getty Images (c) Comstock Images/Getty Images 170 (tr) James Cotier/Getty Images (tc) Photodisc (tc) Photodisc/Getty Images 173 Helen King/Corbis 175 Siede Preis/Getty Images 179 Corel 181 Photodisc 182 (cr) Corel (cr) Rubberball Productions 185 Photos.com 187 Steve Smith/Getty Images 191 (bc) Burger/Photo Researchers, Inc. (bg) Richard Hamilton Smith/Corbis 193 Britt Erlanson/Getty Images 194 Comstock Images 195 BP/Getty Images 199 Photodisc 203 (bc) Photodisc (bl) Photodisc (bc) Photodisc/Getty Images (bl) Ron Chapple/Getty Images 206 (cr) Corel (cr) Photodisc 211 (tl) Corel (tc) Ianin Crockart/Getty Images 213 SW Productions/Getty Images 215 (bg) Photodisc/Getty Images (c) Royalty-Free/Corbis 217 (c) Photodisc 218 Photodisc 219 Photodisc/Getty Images 221 (c) Corel (bg) Royalty-Free/Corbis 223 GK Hart/Vikki Hart/Getty Images 224 (bc) Corel (bc) David Young-Wolff/Photo Edit (c) Photodisc 225 Michael Melford/Getty Images 227 (c) NASA/JPL/University of Arizona (bg) Photodisc 228 Ariel Skelley/Corbis 230 Luis Veiga/Getty Images 231 Mike Brinson/Getty Images 235 (bc) Digital Vision/Getty Images (c) Photodisc 236 Christina Peters/Getty Images 237 Photodisc 239 Brand X Pictures/Punchstock 240 (br) Burke/Triolo Productions/Getty Images (tr) Tom & Dee Ann McCarthy/Corbis 241 (bc) Jeff Hunter/Getty Images 242 (br) David Trood Pictures/Getty Images (cr) Michelle D. Bridwell/Photo Edit 243 (c) Corel 244 Jim Cummins/Corbis 245 Photodisc 246 Bettmann/Corbis 247 Layne Kennedy/Corbis 248 Michael Newman/Photo Edit 249 Frank Cezus/Getty Images 250 Pixtal/Age Fotostock 251 (c) Ann Ackerman/Getty Images (bcr, bc) Corel (tbc) Photodisc 252 Corel 288 (cr) Roger Ressmeyer/Corbis (bl) Stewart Cohen/Getty Images 289 Daniel Bosier/Getty Images 290 Philip Marazzi; Papilio/Corbis 291 Artville 292 (l) Spencer Jones/Getty Images 293 Corel 295 Dennie Cody/Getty Images 297 (cl) Ingram Publishing (cr) Photodisc 298 Corel 299 Free Agents Limited/Corbis 300 Corbis 301 Eric Futran/Getty Images 302 Comstock 303 Photodisc/Getty Images 304 Royalty-Free/Corbis 305 Photodisc 306 (cr) Corel (r) Photodisc 307 Dynamic Graphics Group/Creatas/Alamy 308 Photodisc 309 Photos.com 310 Photos.com 311 Firecrest Pictures/Getty Images 312 Ingram Publishing 313 Paul Harris/Getty Images 314 Michael Keller/Corbis 315 Roger Ressmeyer/Corbis 316 Royalty-Free/Corbis 317 Fraser Hall/Robert Harding/Getty Images 318 Daniel Heuclin/NHPA 319 Photodisc 320 (cl) Karen Moskowitz/Getty Images (br) Photodisc 321 Sara Jean McIlvain 322 C Squared Studios/Getty Images 323 (br) Eric Simonsen/Getty Images (l) Tim Zurowski/Corbis 324 Bettmann/Corbis 325 (bl) Art Montes De Oca/Getty Images Photodisc 326 Adamsmith/Getty Images 327 Robert F. Sisson/Getty Images 328 (br) Photodisc/Getty Images (cl) Royalty-Free/Corbis 329 Ingram Publishing 330 (cl) ImageSource/Getty Images (cr) Photodisc 331 Comstock/Getty Images 332 (cr) David Papazian/Masterfile (tr) Royalty-Free/Corbis 333 Photodisc 334 (l) Photodisc (r) Royalty-Free/Corbis 335 Jules Frazier/Getty Images 336 Photodisc 337 (tl) Corbis (br) Richard Cummins/Corbis 338 Connie Coleman/Getty Images 339 Francisco Villaflor/Corbis

Handwriting Models

a b c d e f g h i
j k l m n o p q r
s t u v w x y z

A B C D E F G H I
J K L M N O P Q R
S T U V W X Y Z

a b c d e f g h i
j k l m n o p q r
s t u v w x y z

A B C D E F G H I
J K L M N O P Q R
S T U V W X Y Z

345

Words Often Misspelled

You use many of the words on this page in your writing. Check this list if you cannot think of the spelling for a word you need. The words are in ABC order.

A
again
a lot
also
always
another
anyone
anyway
around

B
beautiful
because
before
brought
buy

C
cannot
can't
caught
coming
could

D
didn't
different
don't
down

E
enough
every

F
family
favorite
for
found
friend
from

G
getting
girl
goes
going

H
have
haven't
here
his
how

I
I'd
I'll
I'm
into
it
its
it's

K
knew
know

L
letter
like
little

M
might
morning
mother
myself

N
now

O
o'clock
once
other
our

P
people
pretty

R
really
right

S
said
school
some
started
sure
swimming

T
than
that's
their
them
then
there
they
thought
through
to
today
tomorrow
too
tried
two

V
very

W
want
was
where
whole
would
write

Y
you
your
you're